DATE		

OCT 19 '89

ANTONIO STRADIVARI

His Life and Work (1644-1737)

*W. Henry Hill, Arthur F. Hill, F.S.A.,
and Alfred E. Hill*

With a new Introduction by
SYDNEY BECK
Head, Rare Book and Manuscript Collections
Music Division, the New York Public Library

and new Supplementary Indexes by
REMBERT WURLITZER

DOVER PUBLICATIONS, INC. NEW YORK

Published in Canada by General Publishing Com-
pany, Ltd., 30 Lesmill Road, Don Mills, Toronto,
Ontario.
Published in the United Kingdom by Constable
and Company, Ltd., 10 Orange Street, London
W. C. 2.

This new Dover edition, first published in 1963,
is an unabridged republication of the work first
published in 1902 by William E. Hill and Sons, to
which have been added new Supplementary Indexes
and a new Introduction especially written for this
edition by Sydney Beck.

All the illustrations from the 1902 edition are
reproduced in this Dover edition. However, in the
1902 edition the three views of seven different
Stradivari instruments appeared in color, whereas
in this Dover edition eight views of four instruments are in color and the rest are in black and
white. Furthermore, it has been necessary to reduce
slightly the two Stradivari letters (following page
174), the title of appointment granted to Stradivari
by the Archbishop of Benevento (facing page 244),
and Count Cozio di Salabue's announcement offering his collection of instruments for sale (facing
page 276), all of which were facsimiles of the
originals in the 1902 edition.

This Dover edition is published by special arrangement with William E. Hill and Sons.

Standard Book Number: 486-20425-1
Library of Congress Catalog Card Number: 63-17904

Manufactured in the United States of America
Dover Publications, Inc.
180 Varick Street
New York, N.Y. 10014

THIS BOOK WE DEDICATE TO THE

MEMORY OF OUR FATHER

WILLIAM EBSWORTH HILL

TO WHOSE EXAMPLE

WE ARE INDEBTED

BEYOND ACKNOWLEDGMENT

Introduction to Dover Edition

FOR MORE than half a century the Hill book on Stradivari has meant the most authoritative word on the life and work of the Cremonese master. Subsequent investigations, particularly into his earlier career,* have served only to emphasize the basic nature of the monumental study made by the three illustrious sons of William Ebsworth Hill, founder of the present firm on New Bond Street. It still remains, as Lady Huggins expressed it in the final words of her Introductory Note to the first edition, "a work which can never be out of date." The unrivalled opportunities the brothers Hill and their forebears had to examine at first hand virtually all the great examples of Italian violinmaking will never occur again. Detailed records and photographs accumulated by the firm as a result of their active contact with collectors and performers throughout the world include over six hundred Stradivari instruments. But an intimate knowledge of these instruments alone would not have been enough to produce the classic the book has come to be. What makes it a notable achievement is that it represents a kind of composite perception of men whose combined talents and interests and common background enabled them to set down in clear language the innermost secrets of the violinmaker's art, and at the same time to reconstruct a plausible account of the working career of the supreme master of them all. There have been other connoisseurs of rare violins who could have written on the subject—

---

*The most recent of them is the monograph of Arnaldo Baruzzi, published in Brescia in 1959, which delves into the Cremona archives to locate the house in which Stradivari first set up his shop immediately after his marriage in 1667. It presents some interesting conjectures about his possible apprenticeship as a wood-carver. An English edition including a supplement by Mr. Desmond Hill, giving information on the known Stradivari instruments constructed in this house, is now available. The full title of the volume reads: *La Casa Nuziale: The Home of Antonio Stradivari, 1667-1680.* Translated by Desmond Hill. W. E. Hill & Sons, London, 1962.

unfortunately men like J.-B. Vuillaume carried their knowledge to the grave—but none so well equipped to carry through the difficult task as the Hills of London.

From the start the Hills were a family of instrument builders and restorers as well as practical musicians, a balance which seems to have been traditionally maintained. "I consulted with Mr. Hill about ye altering of my Lute and my Viall," writes Samuel Pepys in his famous *Diary,* entry 17th of February, 1660. Nothing more is known of this Hill than that he had a "Musick Shop" in the Minories. Records exist, however, of a later ancestor, Joseph Hill (1715–1784) who was a prolific maker of violins, violas and violoncellos after the best Italian models, the violoncellos particularly being still in demand. Joseph was apprenticed to the violinmaker Peter Walmsley at the "Sign of Ye Harp and Hautboy" in Piccadilly (1742), and later set up his own business alternately in Angel Court, Westminster, at the "Sign of Ye Violin," in the Haymarket (1760), and as "Joseph Hill & Sons" in Soho. Of his five sons, all violinmakers, three were active as performers and one, Lockey Hill (1756–1810) who worked in Islington, became one of the best known makers of the time. Lockey's son, Henry Lockey (1774-1845) also enjoyed a good reputation as a craftsman; and it was the son of the latter, also Henry (1808–1856), who became the outstanding violist in England in the middle of the nineteenth century, admired for both his musical and his scholarly attainments. Berlioz in his *Evenings in the Orchestra* speaks of a "Mr. Hill, . . . an Englishman, one of the first viola-players in Europe, owning an incomparable instrument." Undoubtedly the reference is to the same Henry Hill who some years before had played the solo part in the composer's *Harold in Italy* on the occasion of its first performance in London (1848).

William Ebsworth Hill, mentioned above, was the second son of Henry Lockey and the brother of the violist. Following the family tradition, he developed as a violinmaker of genuine gift, winning first prizes at the exposition in London (1851) and in Paris (1867). However, he will probably be better remembered as a distinguished connoisseur and appraiser of old instruments whose opinion was the most respected in the field. It was his high ideals and vision which brought the present firm bearing his name to the unique position it now holds.

Three of William's four sons, William Henry (1857–1929), Arthur Frederick (1860–1939), and Alfred Ebsworth (1862–1940), the authors

of the *Stradivari* volume, became active in the business. Alfred was perhaps the most brilliant of them from the point of view of an intimate
knowledge of the work of the masters combined with a fabulous memory
and keen powers of observation. He was trained in Mirecourt, the cen-
turies-old center for *luthiers* in France, where he also acquired an absorbing interest in the art of bowmaking. This was later a decided asset to
the firm, whose bows are now much sought after. By 1915 the Hills had
become the "Sole Violin and Bow-Makers to His Majesty the King."
William Henry, like his celebrated uncle, was a fine viola player. It was
later in life that he joined the Hill staff, becoming the senior member
after the death of the father in 1895. Arthur was a born collector, a
man with a strong historical sense and a literary bent. His broad interests
included portraits, prints and manuscripts as well as old instruments. One
suspects he may have initiated or at least have been the guiding spirit
in the searches for documentary evidence on the lives and works of the
early violinmakers directed for many years by the Hill firm in Brescia,
Cremona and elsewhere; though all the brothers must have collaborated
in these attempts to fill important gaps in their knowledge, for themselves
and for their patrons. It was probably the upsurge of interest in rare
stringed instruments in the 1890's, particularly among amateur chamber
music players, that provided the impetus the Hills needed to organize
their copious notes and to put them into print. Here was an appreciative
and ever-growing audience. Encouragement came from several quarters—
from their good friends and advisors Sir William and Lady Margaret
Huggins, from those who worked in the field, like "Signor Mandelli"
(Commendatore A. Mandelli, one-time Mayor of Cremona) and from
numerous others who aided them in their researches.

Within a decade the Hills issued several valuable publications: two
monographs on famous Strads, the "Salabue" ("Messiah") and the "Tuscan" (1891); a valuable full-length biography of Maggini written by Lady
Huggins, "compiled and edited from material collected and contributed
by William Ebsworth Hill and his sons William, Arthur and Alfred"
(1892); and a small volume on the houses in which some of the great
violinmakers lived and worked, the first of a projected but ill-fated
series of illustrated texts on the general subject of "Violins and Their
Makers" (1893).

The more substantial Stradivari book, originally planned to be the
third volume of a trilogy of similar works (the first was to be the mono-

graph "On Gasparo da Salò and his predecessors," announced but never published, and the second the Maggini work), did not reach the public until just after the turn of the century, seven years after the death of the elder Hill. It was published in a deluxe limited edition, lavishly printed on heavy coated paper, and included many beautiful color plates reproduced by chrome lithography as well as a number of fine drawings. Primarily meant for wealthier patrons, collectors and the larger libraries of the world, it met with surprising success. Five years later it appeared in a French translation by Maurice Reynold assisted by Louis Cézard, with an Introduction by the French ambassador to Italy, M. Camille Barrère, replacing that of Lady Huggins. This French edition. published in the same general style and format as the English edition but on fine rag paper, was apparently prepared with the cooperation of MM. Silvestre & Maucotel and the Librairie Fischbacher, both of Paris.

A second, "popular" English edition in reduced size and completely reprinted, followed in 1909. Interestingly enough, the appearance of the new edition coincided with the year an American market for rare bowed instruments opened up after the duty on such items was finally lifted. This resulted in a marked acceleration in the importation of valuable old specimens, an activity in which the Hill firm participated to a larger extent than any other European house. We quote in full from the Preface to the second English edition:

> The first edition was published in 1902. Its reception was even more gratifying than was expected. The one thousand copies of which the edition consisted, were sold within three years.
>
> As the first edition is now only rarely to be obtained—and even then at a cost much exceeding that at which it was published—and as the demand for the work still continues, it is felt that the time for its re-publication has arrived, particularly in a much cheaper form, which will bring it within the reach of a more extended circle of readers.
>
> In taking the step, the authors believe they will be gratifying a large number of violin lovers desirous of having within reach the fullest and most trustworthy information accessible concerning the life and work of Antonio Stradivari.

The text and illustrations of this edition, except only that halftone plates are substituted for lithographic plates, are practically the same as those of the original edition.

The last statement is somewhat misleading in respect to the illustrations. The number of those reproduced by color lithography in the first edition is actually reduced by the omission of several plates (some of them of importance to the text, e.g., the "Long Pattern" Strad, facsimiles of two original Stradivari letters, facsimiles of two documents, and the Genealogical Tree of the Stradivari Family) and by the limitation of the halftone plates to one view each of the instruments shown, instead of the original three views—front, side and back. The second edition, however, includes the "Salabue" Strad in color as a frontispiece, a plate which does not appear at all in the 1902 edition.

This edition sold out within a relatively short time and the situation described in its Preface again prevailed. The demand was even greater than before, so much so that the possibility of a third edition was seriously considered in the 1930's. The Hills had just completed another major effort—the equally attractive and important companion volume on the *Violin-Makers of the Guarneri Family* (1931). In spite of the enormous cost of this venture, Alfred Hill expressed his willingness to undertake the republication of the Stradivari volume, in a letter to the late J. C. Freeman, at the time Director of the Violin Department of the Rudolph Wurlitzer Company in New York. However, nothing came of it, and his death during the war years put an end to any such plans.

The present edition, long overdue, offers at a reasonable price most of the advantages of the first edition in format, in completeness and in the exact duplication of the printed matter. For the sake of economy, only eight of the original lithographs are reproduced in color. They are reproduced on two covers, front or back and side views being combined; all the remaining plates appear in black and white. Those chosen for color treatment represent the more beautiful or unusual examples, that is, from the point of view of color and construction: the "Betts" and the "Tuscan," certainly among the most famous specimens; the "Long Pattern," an experimental model Stradivari abandoned after eight or nine years; and the "Inlaid" viola, a fine example of the master's extraordinary skill in marquetry and design.

To add to the volume's usefulness as a reference book, a Supplementary Index has been provided. It has been divided into two sections, one devoted to subjects and names and the other to a chronological arrangement of Stradivari's production. These supplements were suggested and especially prepared for this edition by Rembert Wurlitzer from notes made in his own copy. It had long been felt by Mr. Wurlitzer, and no doubt by many other readers, that valuable bits of otherwise unobtainable information, which turn up in the most unexpected places in a richly documented text, should not be lost to researchers for lack of a ready reference to them. We are grateful to him for his advice in this and in a number of other matters, and for his cooperation in making the necessary contacts with the Hill family with whom he has maintained for many years a close personal and professional relationship.

The name Stradivari has become a household word: its magic is universal. Stories of the sudden discovery of long-lost "Strads" in an attic, handed down in the family for at least three generations, are legion. (The Music Divisions of The Library of Congress and The New York Public Library annually receive so much correspondence requesting evaluations of Stradivari-labelled instruments, that form letters have had to be devised for their reply.) Let it be said at once that the Hill book will not help these people. Though it deals in a general way with "The Number of Instruments Made by Stradivari," the volume makes no attempt to list (even if it were possible)* all the known ones and their values. It merely cites outstanding examples to illustrate points in the text, and devotes a fascinating chapter to the relative prices paid during a three-hundred-year period.

It should be kept in mind that Antonio Stradivari is possibly the most forged name in the world. There are literally thousands of cheap copies of the master's work which bear his label. The problem is that he left no record of his work. But the probable number of instruments that he could possibly have made has been carefully estimated and those which have survived are fairly well known. The Messrs. Hill have accounted for slightly over 600 of a total of 1116 instruments, and there are reasons to believe that about 100 more exist. The chances that the

---

*A systematic attempt to identify all known Strads and their present owners was published in 1945 by Ernest N. Doring in a book entitled *How Many Strads? Our Heritage From the Master*, William Lewis & Son, Chicago. Most of the information was drawn from the Hill book and from available American sources, chiefly from the extensive files of the Rudolph Wurlitzer Company in New York.

remaining 400 or so have survived and have not been identified and recorded in the past half century are indeed remote.

Be that as it may, the supreme art and incredible perfection achieved by the long-lived "prince of *luthiers*" (his working life covered almost eight decades) stagger the imagination. The many accounts concerning the changing hands through which the individual instruments passed make exciting reading. They reflect a whole segment of music and art history, affecting the careers of some of the greatest performers of all time. These and cognate matters are expertly discussed and documented by the brothers Hill. Their biography is the only source book of reliable information on the subject to date. Since its publication in 1902, only one minor correction in historical fact has had to be made; it concerns their statement that Carlo Bergonzi was a pupil of Stradivari. The authors have since revised their opinion, and in their book on the Guarneri family frankly admit that they "had a vague feeling that it might in the course of time prove incorrect . . . since it never had been supported by any evidence. And the more we have been given the opportunity to reconsider the point, the less we are disposed to allow it to continue unquestioned" (p. 61). The scholarliness and integrity with which these gentlemen worked are altogether admirable. Theirs was a labor of love, and the sincerity and artistic sense of the writers can be felt on every page. For these reasons alone, if for no other, *Antonio Stradivari, His Life and Work* will always remain one of the most important contributions to the literature on the art of the violin. It should be widely read.

In conclusion, the reader is reminded that the Hills (Arthur Frederick and Alfred Ebsworth) have left another lasting memorial to the glory of Stradivari in bequeathing the most perfect specimen of his art, the "Messiah" Strad, together with other fine instruments, to the British nation. The collection is now housed in the Ashmolean Museum at Oxford, for all to see.

New York, 1962

SYDNEY BECK
Head, Rare Book and Manuscript Collections
Music Division, The New York Public Library

Preface.

THE idea of writing this book is in some measure due to the intelligent initiative of Signor Mandelli, of Cremona, to whom, as well as to our friends and subscribers, we owe some words of explanation and apology. Full of the desire to obtain fresh information concerning Antonio Stradivari, Signor Mandelli determined to make further researches in the archives of his native city, and thus add to the world's knowledge; and, his material collected, he approached us in the year 1890 with a view to its publication in English and Italian. The subject of Stradivari was an alluring one, and in a moment of enthusiasm we undertook the task of incorporating these interesting researches in a work more fully embracing the results of the master's career. Reflection, however, showed us that we had undertaken a task the labour of which we had underestimated; and time sped on, year succeeded year, only to find us still adding to our notes, yet unable—nay, unwilling—to prematurely publish that which we felt to be still incomplete. If we have thus long delayed the publication of this work, owing to the daily cares of our business absorbing so much of our time and energy, we trust that our readers will obtain some slight compensation both from the more correct information given and the broader treatment of our subject.

We decided to divide our work into twelve distinct chapters, and we believe that by this division the whole will have gained in clearness. Our illustrations will prove, we hope, both interesting and instructive. The instruments shown are selected from amongst the finest existing works of Stradivari, and each example is characteristic of the type it portrays. We cannot too warmly express our sense of obligation to Mr. Shirley Slocombe for his admirable drawings of the instruments; and to Mr. Nister, of Nuremberg, for the time and patience he has expended on their reproduction by chromolithography. Time after time has he gone over these plates; and though we do not claim that perfection has been reached, we believe it will be admitted that Mr. Nister has surpassed all previous efforts in this direction.

We have to thank our friends and colleagues at home and abroad for aid and assistance in our researches. More especially we would wish to mention Mr. George Hart, the late M. Gand and M. Silvestre of Paris, and Signor Commendatore Lozzi of Rome. To the Marquis dalla Valle we are under an exceptional debt of gratitude for having freely accorded us access to his unique collection of Stradivari relics.

The encouragement and advice ungrudgingly given to us at all times by Sir William and Lady Huggins have been of inestimable value; nor can we sufficiently acknowledge in words the friendship Lady Huggins has honoured us with in reading and advising upon the manuscript of our book. In conclusion, we venture to hope that the sincerity of our work will bring us that support which stimulates fresh undertakings. Much of absorbing interest to violin lovers yet remains to be written.

Contents.

CONTENTS

CHAPTER VII.

STRADIVARI'S VARNISH.

CHAPTER VIII.

STRADIVARI'S CONSTRUCTION.

CHAPTER IX.

STRADIVARI'S LABELS.

CHAPTER X.

THE NUMBER OF INSTRUMENTS MADE BY STRADIVARI.

CHAPTER XI.

THE PRICES PAID FOR STRADIVARI INSTRUMENTS AND THE GROWTH OF THEIR REPUTATION

CHAPTER XII.

STRADIVARI'S SUPPOSED PORTRAIT.

List of Plates.

List of Illustrations in the Text.

ANTONIO STRADIVARI

HIS LIFE AND WORK (1644-1737)

BY

W. HENRY HILL
ARTHUR F. HILL, F.S.A.
&
ALFRED E. HILL

WITH AN INTRODUCTORY NOTE BY
LADY HUGGINS

LONDON
WILLIAM E. HILL & SONS
VIOLIN MAKERS
140, NEW BOND STREET, W.
1902

The title page of the original (1902) edition

Genealogical Table of the Family of Stradivari.

STRADIVARI, ALESSANDRO = MORONI, ANNA.
born Jan. 15, 1602.

STRADIVARI, GIUSEPPE J.,
born March 20, 1623.

Stradivari, Antonio, born 1644; died Dec. 18, 1737. = Married = FERRABOSCHI, FRANCESCA (1), born Oct. 7, 1640; died May 25, 1698.
July 4, 1667.

(1) GIULIO, born Dec. 23, 1667; married 1688; died Aug. 7, 1707.

(2) FRANCESCO, born Feb. 6, 1670; died Feb. 12, 1670.

(3) FRANCESCO, born Feb. 1, 1671; died May 11, 1743.

(4) CATTERINA, born March 25, 1674; died June 17, 1748.

(5) ALESSANDRO, born May 25, 1677; died Jan. 26, 1732.

(6) OMOBONO, born Nov. 14, 1679; died June 8, 1742.

Stradivari, Antonio, died Dec. 18, 1737. = Married second time, = ZAMBELLI, ANTONIA, born June 11, 1664; died March 3, 1737.
Aug. 24, 1699.

(7) FRANCESCA, born Sept. 19, 1700; died Feb. 11, 1720.

(8) G. B. GIUSEPPE, born Nov. 6, 1701; died July 8, 1702.

(6) G. B. MARTINO, born Nov. 11, 1703; died Nov. 1, 1727.

(10) GIUSEPPE, born Oct. 27, 1704 (Priest); died Dec. 2, 1781.

(11) PAOLO, born Jan. 26, 1708 (Cloth Merchant); died Oct. 14, 1776. = TEMPLARI, ELENA, born 1705; died 1776.

ANTONIO II., born 1739; died 1789. = DALLA NOCE, MARGARITA, born 1739; died 1787.

FRANCESCA, born 1740; died 1809 (Nun).

CARLO, born Dec. 4, 1741; died 1808.

FRANCESCO, born 1744; died 1746.

PAOLO, born 1746; died 1792.

FRANCESCA, born 1767.

GIUSEPPE, born 1763.

LUIGIA, born 1765.

CARLO = Married = GIACOMO, born 1769; died 1828.
1797.
CORNIERI, GIUSEPPA, died Jan. 25, 1803.

GIACOMO = Married = CRISTINI, MARIA, born 1807.
1836.
= Married second time, 1821. = BONAZZI, ROSALINDA, born 1792.

GIUSEPPE, born 1802.

PIETRO, born 1800; died 1869.

CESARE, born 1798 (Physician). = Married = MAINI, LAVINIA, born 1808; died 1862.
1838.
= Married = PODESTA, GIOVANNA, born 1848.
1867.

GIACOMO 2nd, born 1822 (of Milan); died Jan. 2, 1901. = Married = ROSSI, FANNY, born 1835.
1861.

ANTONIA, born 1771; died 1816.

ENRICO.

EUFEMIA.

FANNY.

ELENA, born 1862.

SILVIA, born 1864.

PIERINA, born 1866; died 1894.

FAUSTO, born 1870; died 1888.

BICE, born 1876; died 1893.

LIBERO, born Jan. 29, 1840 (Barrister).

CLELIA, born 1868.

ANITA, born 1871.

ITALO, born 1872.

MARIO, born 1883.

Introductory Note.

HE life of Gio. Paolo Maggini, published in 1892, though complete in itself, was but one of a projected series of lives of great violin makers. To make this series complete, many lives, those of the Amati especially, must be written ; the history and work of many schools must be examined.

But, in considering the subject, certain men stand out so strongly as marking periods, that it seemed it would be useful to begin with works setting forth, broadly speaking :

(1) The beginning of violins ;
(2) The early development of violins ;
(3) The perfecting of violins ;—

a kind of trilogy, in fact, in which the leading parts are played by Gasparo da Salò, Gio. Paolo Maggini, and Antonio Stradivari.

For various reasons the " Life of Maggini " was first completed ; but the " Life of Gasparo " is well advanced, and will be published before long. It has been judged wise to make the scope of this work wider than that of either of the other lives, and the necessary research and reading have involved much time and labour.

The name of Antonio Stradivari, whose life forms the third part of the trilogy, is so well known, not only to violin and music lovers, but to people generally, that there is no need to try to claim interest for it by much speaking. But, as I have had the pleasure of close and prolonged examination of the collections and notes of Mr. Alfred Hill and his brothers in connection with this life, I am glad to have the opportunity of saying a few words about the book they have written.

It is possible to overrate expert knowledge; it is equally possible to underrate it. " Everything of something, and something of everything," is almost a counsel of perfection.

This book is frankly the work of violin experts. Outside counsel has been sought, it is true, and has been generously acknowledged; but this does not alter the fact that this " Life of Stradivari " is essentially by men, all of them peculiarly fitted, by hereditary natural aptitude, by long expert training, and by deep love of music and of musical instruments, to deal with the problems of Stradivari's history and of his immortal services to music through musical instruments, in ways new and striking, suggestive and exhaustive.

The illustrations deserve a word of special notice. To their selection and reproduction much thought and care have been given, so that they form, in themselves, a valuable contribution to the history of musical instruments; while the strange beauty of violins, which has delighted so many, has never been so well represented.

The study of this work cannot fail, I think, to be valuable, not only to makers of violins, but to musicians; while to the happily ever-growing number of those who use stringed instruments, it will prove a trustworthy source of information and pleasure. It is a work which can never be out of date.

MARGARET L. HUGGINS.

CHAPTER I.

The Ancestry of Antonio Stradivari.

E propose to touch but lightly on the ancestry of Stradivari, as researches on this subject have been published by Fétis, Lombardini, Hart, and others, and have now been supplemented by Signor Mandelli. All these writers agree that the family name, spelt in different ways, was borne by more or less notable citizens of Cremona as far back as the twelfth and thirteenth centuries. Signor Mandelli gives various documents in proof of this, the earliest one being dated May 13th, 1188, from which we learn that "the Priest Alberto, Canon and Chief Warden of the Cathedral of Cremona, lets to Giovanni Stradivarto and heirs two pieces of allodial land," etc., etc.

With regard to the derivation of the name, Mr. E. J. Payne says, " It is the plural form of Stradivare, a Lombard variety of Stradiere, a toll-man or douanier, a feudal official who was posted on the strada or high road for the purpose of exacting dues from passengers." *

---

* Art. 'Stradivari,' Grove's "Dictionary of Music."

Mandelli, on the authority of Professor Astegiano,* writes, "The form of the name 'de Stradaverta' as used in 1298 is derived from 'Strada averta' of the Cremonese dialect, in Italian 'Strada aperta.'" The earliest documentary evidence forthcoming concerning the direct ancestry of the violin-maker is furnished by Signor Mandelli, who quotes an extract from the Marriage Register of the Cathedral of Cremona, under date April 10th, 1600, recording the marriage of Signor Giulio Cesare Stradivari, of the parish of S. Michele Vecchio, to the Signora Doralice Milani, a widow, of the parish of the cathedral (Parrocchia del Duomo). To them was born in 1602 a son, christened Alessandro on January 15th at the Church of S. Michele Vecchio.

From the Register of Marriages of the Parish of S. Prospero, Signor Mandelli obtained the record, under date August 30th, 1622, of the marriage of Signor Alessandro, son of Giulio Cesare Stradivari, to Signora Anna, daughter of Leonardo Moroni.

From this union were born, as recorded in the baptismal register of the above-named parish, Giuseppe Giulio Cesare, March, 1623; Carlo Felice, September, 1626; Giovanni Battista, October, 1628. Then comes a complete blank in the records, and we are left to speculate as to whether any other children were born between 1628 and the year 1644, the date of the birth of Antonio, the subject of our enquiries. Repeated researches, made at different periods in the registers throughout the thirty-seven parishes of Cremona, have failed to yield further information. Signor Mandelli says:—

---

* A Piedmontese, who compiled the catalogue of the ancient rolls of the community of Cremona up to the year 1300, printed in two volumes at Turin in 1899.

"Supposing that Antonio was christened—which seems fairly certain, seeing that we have proof of the fact in the case of his elder brothers—I felt hopeful of finding some mention of the fact in the registers and documents of one or other of the parish churches of Cremona; and as no further entry of either birth or death of any member of the family of Alessandro Stradivari is to be found in the records of S. Michele Vecchio, I concluded that they had removed elsewhere. Aware of the fact of Antonio Stradivari's marriage in 1667, I turned my attention to the record of the same in the Marriage Register—the extract from which I transcribe later on—and I enquired for the marriage documents, to which the birth certificates of the married couple ought necessarily to have been added ; but the papers ' *Stradivari Feraboschi* ' have disappeared. I then went to the cathedral, where the registers and documents of the suppressed parish of S. Donato, which was the parish from which Stradivari married his second wife in 1699, are kept; and here again, strange to relate, I found the registration of the marriage, but neither documents nor birth certificates of man or wife."

Signor Mandelli is decidedly of opinion that these papers have, for some unaccountable reason, been either purloined or carelessly destroyed. He adds : " Bearing in mind the first marriage certificate, in which Stradivari is described as residing in the parish of S. Cecilia, I went to the Bishop's Palace, where the registers are kept, and perused them from beginning to end without finding mention of the name of Stradivari. I then examined the Census Book of that epoch, but with the same result.

" I now turned my attention to the registers of all the other parishes, and availed myself of every known channel likely to furnish any information, but with the same negative result attained by those who had previously searched them."

In the years 1628 and 1629 Cremona was visited by a terrible famine, which was followed in 1630 by the scourge of plague, the ravages of which caused many of the inhabitants to flee, even the bishops and magistrates, so that the population, in consequence of the deaths and exodus which ensued, was reduced to a third of its number.*

In the Census Book of the Parish of S. Vincenzo the parish priest confirms the deplorable state of the city, and under date 1628 he adds the following remark : " Many citizens have left Cremona to live quietly in other towns, and many have quite recently gone to the war."

Again in the Census Book, under date January, 1630, he records that the inhabitants of his parish have decreased in forty-four years from over one thousand to less than five hundred ; some have gone to the war, others have died, and many have gone in search of a country where they can live by the fruits of their labour and not die from starvation.

In April of the same year he once more reverts to the subject, and states that " rich people have by this time been reduced to such a state of poverty, caused partly by the quartering of soldiers in their houses and partly by the heavy taxes imposed, etc., that were it not for the shame of it they would go about begging." He also says that all the inhabitants, rich and poor, who were able to leave the city were doing so.

Additional testimony as to the sufferings of the people is supplied by the parish priest of S. Michele Vecchio, in entries made by him in the Marriage Registers. After mentioning the war and famine which preceded the plague,

---

* Robolotti, " History of Cremona."

he says : "This year, 1630, God our Lord has sent the scourge of plague all over Lombardy ; at Cremona it made its appearance in the early days of January, began to spread at the commencement of April, and raged to such an extent during the months of June, July, and August that the town was deserted and had the appearance of a wilderness." Here, then, is evidence which justifies us in assuming that Alessandro Stradivari was amongst those who fled from the city—most probably accompanied by his wife and children— apparently never again to return, otherwise their names would have been met with at some later date in the registers of births, deaths, or marriages, or in the census returns.

Signor Mandelli thus explains the non-existence of any record of the birth of Antonio in the city of Cremona. His parents had left their home under stress of calamity ; some of those dear to them may even have fallen victims to the plague * previous to their departure, and for one reason or another they determined to stay where they had found a haven of refuge.

Nothing daunted by failure, Signor Mandelli now turned his attention to the villages and other places in the province of Cremona, for it seemed quite rational to suppose that Antonio's parents may have settled down but a few miles from the city. He accordingly begged and prevailed upon the Bishop of Cremona to issue a circular, addressed to all the parish priests of the diocese, asking that research be made in the registers and census returns of every parish, including those suppressed since 1788, from the year 1628 until 1670, concerning the family of Stradivari.

The result was again disappointing : some of the parishes

---

* Hieronymus Amati, his wife and two daughters, were amongst the victims who died from the plague during 1630. Maggini also fell a victim at Brescia in 1632.

had no old registers to consult; others had been searched, but without success.

In conclusion, we think the above evidence points to the fact of Antonio Stradivari not having been born in Cremona; he may have come into the world in some neighbouring village, but in all probability his parents had gone some distance away. Be this so or not, the fact remains that henceforth Alessandro, his wife and children, with the sole exception of Antonio, occupy no place in the family history.

Nothing whatever is known concerning the early career of Antonio. Did his parents bring him back to Cremona in order to apprentice him to Nicolò Amati? What were the reasons that induced them to make him a violin-maker? As far as we can learn, no earlier member or connection of his family had adopted this calling. These questions, we fear, can never be answered. The first documentary intimation even of Antonio's existence in Cremona, as yet met with, is furnished by the label inserted in one of his violins, and dated 1666.* Then comes the announcement of his marriage in the next year. He married Francesca, the daughter of Francesco Feraboschi, and widow of Giovanni Giacomo Capra, who committed suicide with an arquebus on the Piazza S. Agata (now Piazza Garibaldi), in April, 1664. The following is the extract from the Marriage Register of the Parish of S. Agata: "On the 4th of July, 1667, having three times published the banns on feast days, the first on June 26th [wrongly written July in the register], which was a Sunday, the second on the 29th, the feast day of St. Peter, the third on Sunday, the 3rd of July, announcing the marriage which Signor Antonio Stradivari, of the Parish of S. Cecilia,

---

* See Chapter II.

intended to contract with Signora Francesca Ferabosca,* of my parish ; I hereby beg to declare that, no impediment of any kind having arisen, I, the Reverend Pietro Guallo,

Fig. 1.—THE HOUSE OF STRADIVARI.

Parish Priest of the Collegiate and renowned Church of S. Agata in Cremona, have united them to-day, here, in my church, in the holy bond of matrimony, in the presence of the

---

* We have retained the different spellings of this name as found in the original documents.

two hereafter-mentioned witnesses, namely, Signor Francesco
Feraboscho, of the Parish of S. Agata, and of Signor ——''
[remains unfilled].

On his marriage Stradivari appears to have left the
parish of S. Cecilia, and taken a house known as the Casa
del Pescatore in the parish of his bride.   The census returns
for the year 1668 describe it as being occupied by Signor
Stradivari, aged 28, Signora Francesca (his wife), aged 26,
and Giulia Maria (his daughter), aged 3 months.   The year
previously the house was occupied by a certain Francesco
Mazzini, his wife and two sons.   Here Stradivari seems to
have lived until 1680, in which year he purchased the house
now known as No. 1, Piazza Roma, formerly No. 2, Piazza San
Domenico (fig. 1).   His family had, in the meantime, increased
to five, one infant son having died.*   The house was bought
from the Cremonese family of Picenardi for 7,000 imperial
lire † (approximately equivalent to £840); the contract of
sale, first made known by Signor Lombardini,‡ is preserved
in the Notarial Archives.   From this deed, which is in Latin,
we learn that Stradivari paid 2,000 lire of the purchase
money in cash, and agreed to pay the remaining 4,990 lire

---

* See Appendix.   We give the later census returns taken from the
books of the parish of S. Agata, in which reference is made to Stradivari,
as collated by Signor Mandelli, in an appendix.   We may, however, here say
that the contradictory statements therein found as to the master's age are
so conflicting that we deem them to be of no value.   We understand from
Signor Mandelli that these census papers were filled up by the priest of the
parish, and not by the occupant of the house.   The evidence on which we
rely for the acceptance of the year 1644 as that of the master's birth is given
in Chapter II.

† The "Lira Imperiale" was, at the period of the above transaction, of
the approximate value of tenpence; its purchasing value would be about
three times that of to-day.   (See footnote, Chap. XI., p. 248.)

‡ Lombardini's "Antonio Stradivari e la celebre Scuola Cremonese"
(Cremona, Dalla Noce, 1872, 8vo).

within four years : the other ten lire were commuted by the
vendors in consideration of Stradivari paying the yearly
tithe of six imperial sols to the canons of the Cathedral.
We find, too, that the master's name is entered " Antonio
Stradivari, of the *late* Alessandro " ; thus showing that the

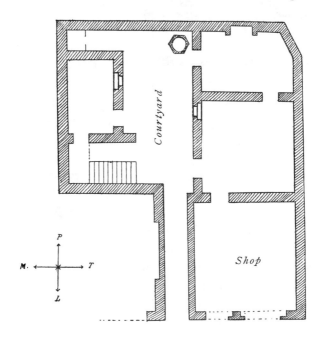

Piazza S. Domenico
(*now Piazza Roma*)
Fig. 2.—GROUND PLAN OF THE HOUSE OF STRADIVARI.

latter—who, as we have seen, was born in 1602—was then
dead, and that he was really the father of Antonio. Signor
Mandelli, who has spared no pains to glean details, however
small, concerning Stradivari, tells us that the house, as
purchased in 1680, consisted of a somewhat narrow structure
of three floors—that is, the ground floor, two storeys above

and a kind of loft and attic, also large cellars underground
(fig. 2). The rooms were distributed as follows : four on the
ground floor — viz. the
shop (which is specially
mentioned in the deed
of purchase), parlour,
kitchen, and a store-
room at the other end
of the court-yard ; on
the first floor four rooms
also, three on the second,
and the loft and attic
above (figs. 3, 4) ; while

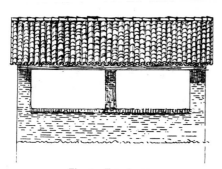

Fig. 3.—The Attic.

on the roof was formed a flat terrace, called in the Cremonese dialect *seccadour*, to indicate that part of the house
which is used for drying linen or fruits. Tradition says
that the master worked here — in the loft and attic —
during the favourable season, and also hung out his newly
varnished instruments to dry. This tradition was corro-
borated to some extent by finding, fixed to the wooden
beams of the loft, strips
of parchment, nailed
down and so arranged
as to form a kind of
tool-rack to hold the
worker's small tools; and
also by the discovery
some years ago of a
trap-door (cupboard, we
presume) containing
shreds and bits of maple and pine. It was in this house
that Stradivari remained until his death. It was here during
upwards of fifty years that the passer-by may have seen him

Fig. 4.—The Loft.

silently shaping those works which are now so eagerly sought throughout the world. Noble, musician, priest, and friend came to this modest dwelling either to admire his skill or to ask him to make an instrument as he alone could do. From the time that the mortal remains of the man, who lent such interest to the spot, were carried across the piazza to their resting-place in the Church of S. Domenico, the house remained practically unchanged until 1888,* when it was acquired by the proprietor of the neighbouring café, who, in the course of the next year, had carried out considerable structural alterations (fig. 5). The ground floor is now a billiard-room. One day during this partial demolition of the house Signor Soresini, the son-in-law of the owner, happened to be looking at what was going on, when he observed that several of

Fig. 5.—STRADIVARI'S HOUSE AS AT PRESENT.

the masons had broken up some boards for the purpose of making a fire to warm their frugal meal. At first he paid no attention to the circumstance, but presently asked to

---

* One of the writers visited Cremona in 1884, and very naturally evinced considerable interest on inspecting Stradivari's house ; he was not a little amused by the servant, who showed him over the different rooms, gravely taking a heavy tile from the roof and offering it as a souvenir.

see one of the pieces of wood thus being dealt with. On examination it turned out to be a portion of an old chest made of pine and then painted over, whereon the carved remains of the master's name, and parts of a painted coat-of-arms were still plainly visible (fig. 6); the chest had evidently, at some time, been broken up, and the pieces utilised for patching the wooden ceiling of the house.* This relic, as

Fig. 6.

well as a small piece of hæmatite in the shape of a human canine tooth, found at the same time, and which Stradivari possibly used as a burnisher, together with the stone breastwork of the well (fig. 7), as shown in the corner of the court-yard on the ground-plan of house, are now preserved in the Civic Museum of Cremona.

Let us now return to the subject of Stradivari's home

---

* Further notes concerning the house will be found in Appendix II

life.   In the year 1698 he had to mourn the loss of his wife,
Francesca Ferabosca, who died on May 20th ; the record in
the Register of the Parish of S. Matteo reads as follows :
" Francesca Feraboscha, wife of Sig. Antonio Stradivari,
recommended to God, and fortified by the Sacraments of
Penance, Holy Eucharist, and Extreme Unction, died at the
age of about sixty years.   Her body was carried into the
Church of S. Domenico."

A later entry, under date May 25th, says :   " Given

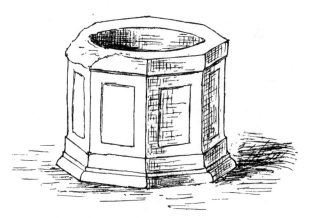

Fig. 7.—THE STONE BREASTWORK OF THE WELL.

burial to Francesca Stradivari Ferabosca in the tomb in
the choir."

In addition to the above extracts Signor Mandelli
was fortunate enough to find in the " Records of Funerals
ordered by the Ecclesiastical and Civil Magistrates,"
preserved in the Town Archives, the bill of the expenses incurred at the funeral of Signora Feraboschi
Stradivari.   This very interesting document we give
herewith :—

May the 25th, 1698.

Funeral of Signora Francesca Ferabosca Stradivari, of the Parish of S. Matteo, buried in S. Domenico, at 23 o'clock [11 a.m.].

	Lire	Soldi
Fourth part of the fee to Revd. Parish Priest .	12	10
Mass	3	0
Fourteen Priests and one Choir-boy . . .	7	0
Thirty-six Dominican Fathers	18	0
Sixteen Franciscan Fathers	8	0
Thirty-one Fathers of S. Angelo	15	10
Twenty-seven Fathers of S. Luca	13	10
Twenty-one Fathers of S. Salvatore . . .	10	10
Nineteen Fathers of S. Francesco	9	10
Orphans with Hat	12	0
Beggars with Hat	12	0
Twelve Torch-bearers	3	0
Four Torch-bearers of the Confraternity of the Rosary	2	0
Velvet and Gold Pall of the Cathedral . .	8	10
Bier in Church	1	0
Big Bell	9	0
Bell of S. Matteo	1	10
Bell of S. Domenico	2	0
Little Bells of the Cathedral	1	10
Four Black Draperies in the Church . . .	1	12
Sixteen Black Draperies at the House . . .	6	8
Grave-diggers with Capes	12	0
Fee to the Ecclesiastical Magistrate . . .	8	0
Fee to the Town Magistrate	8	0
Total . .	182	0*

Stradivari writes at the foot of the bill (fig. 8):—

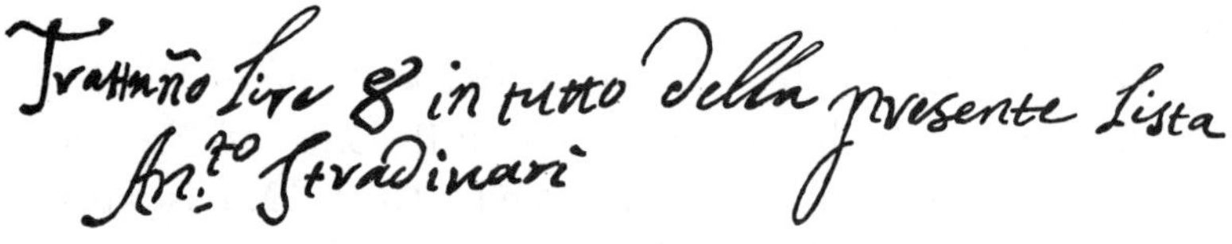

Fig. 8.†

---

* Approximately equivalent to £22 10s.
† "Deducted altogether 8 lire from the present bill.—"ANTº STRADIVARI."

The discovery of this document in the files of the year 1698 naturally caused Signor Mandelli to turn to the year 1737; but, alas! the file is missing. This is the more to be regretted inasmuch as we lose not only the record of the funeral expenses of the master, but that of his second wife also. Signor Mandelli adds, that, judging by the above bill of expenses, the funeral of Antonio's wife was probably among the most conspicuous of the time.

Stradivari did not long remain a widower; in August of the next year he married Signora Zambelli. The following is the extract from the Register of the Parish of S. Donato, August 24th, 1699: "Signor Antonio Stradivari, a widower by the death of his wife, the late Signora Francesca Feraboschi, of the Parish of S. Matteo, of Cremona, having previously obtained the mutual consent, as per form exhibited, has been united to-day in marriage, as hereby certified, with Signora Antonia Maria Zambelli, daughter of the late Signor Antonio Maria, of this Parish of S. Donato, the customary three banns having been published both in the Church of S. Matteo, as in this of S. Donato, on the 25th and 26th days of July and the 2nd of August, as by the regular declaration preserved in file, the ceremony taking place in the presence of the Very Revd. Don Francesco Bisoni, Parish Priest of S. Erasmo, invited by me, Don Cesare Rigotti, and in the presence of the witnesses Francesco Passano, son of the late Gio. Batta, of Casal Maggiore, and of Antonio Cervini, son of the late Domenico, of the Parish of S. Lucia."

This second marriage was blessed by five children, one daughter and four sons, making in all eleven (see Appendix). As will be noticed, several of the children died young, and of the others two only, Omobono and Francesco, embraced the career of their father, but neither of them can be said to have distinguished himself; they were, in fact, completely eclipsed by their brilliant and long-lived father. From the date of the second marriage onwards little is known concerning

Fig. 9.—THE CHAPEL OF THE ROSARY AND THE TOMB OF STRADIVARI.

Stradivari's private life; we can only assume, judging by the assiduity with which he kept to his work, that it was a fairly smooth one. We see that he lost a son, aged 24, in 1727, and another in 1732; but his wife remained to comfort him in his extreme old age, and died only a few months before her husband.

Stradivari had decided upon his burial-place in 1729, in which year he purchased from the heirs of Francesco Villani—the descendant of a noble Cremonese family—the tomb hitherto belonging to them, and which was situated in a small chapel, named after the Blessed Virgin of the Rosary, in the Church of S. Domenico (fig. 9). The tomb-stone which marked the spot bore the name and inscription of the Villani family around the sides, and in the centre their coat-of-arms, all of which Stradivari had effaced—an operation but imperfectly carried out, as traces are still clearly perceptible — and his own name and an inscription substituted (figs. 10, 11).

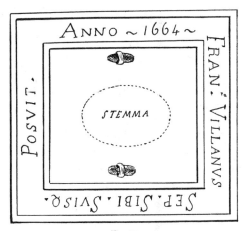

Fig. 10.

On the 4th day of March, 1737, the first member of Stradivari's family was laid to rest here. Under that date the Register of S. Matteo says: " Signora Antonia Zambelli, daughter of the late Antonio (Zambelli), who was the wife of Signor Antonio Stradivari, died, aged about seventy-three years, fortified by the Sacraments of Penance, Holy Eucharist, and Extreme Unction, and comforted with prayers for her soul, and her body was conveyed on the fourth day of this month by me, Antonio Maria Spada, Coadjutor Priest of the Church of S. Matteo, to the Church of S. Domenico, in which she was buried."

The Register of S. Domenico tells us that Signora Stradivari was interred in the Chapel of the Rosary in the tomb of Francesco Villani.

Antonio survived his wife until the following December, on the 18th of which month he passed away, and was buried on the following day. The record, taken from the register of S. Matteo, reads as follows : " In the year of our Lord one thousand seven hundred and thirty-seven, on the nineteenth day of the month of December, Signor Antonio Stradivari, a widower, aged about ninety-five years, having died yesterday, fortified by the Holy Sacraments and comforted by prayers for his soul until the moment he expired, I, Domenico Antonio Stancari, Parish Priest of this Church of S. Matteo, have escorted to-day his corpse with funeral pomp to the Church of the very Reverend Fathers of S. Domenico in Cremona, where he was buried." *

Fig. 11.

The Register of S. Domenico confirms that the burial of the late Signor Antonio Stradivari, whose body was interred in the tomb of Signor Villani, in the

"Long Pattern" Stradivari, dated 1693.

In possession of Mr. R. L. Harrison.

Chapel of the Rosary, took place on the 19th day of December, 1737.

Other members of the family were given burial in the tomb at later dates; the last was his son Giuseppe Antonio, who died in 1781.

There reposed the remains of Antonio Stradivari and certain of his descendants until the year 1869; but in that year the powers that be willed that they should be scattered to the winds. The Church of S. Domenico, like many another of Italy's noble monuments, had, during the course of long years, fallen into a state of decay, and its condition, going from bad to worse, had now reached a stage positively dangerous. To obtain the necessary sum for its restoration was out of the question. The town authorities therefore decided to take over the church, together with the adjoining deserted convent, pull them down, and on the site lay out a much-needed public garden. Signor Mandelli, an eye-witness of what was taking place, furnishes us with the following interesting description of the demolition of the sacred edifice. He writes: " In the summer of the year 1869 the work of demolition of the fine Church of S. Domenico was making progress; in fact, the great apses of the church, the tower, and the Chapel of Christ had already disappeared under the never-ceasing blows of the pickaxe, the dull sound of which was slowly re-echoing along the pillars and against the vaulted ceilings of the aisles of the chapels which still stood untouched. It was a sacrifice imposed by modern requirements, and the imperious exigences of civilisation and hygiene. When the work was once in full swing, the masons cared not which part was to be attacked; the pickaxe, incessantly in use, had already rained down its blows upon the Chapel of the Rosary, demolishing the cupola by Malosso and the ceiling by Cattapane. I still remember it, and vividly recall the remorseless destruction of this work of a past splendour. It seems to me but yesterday, as I never allowed a day to pass without going to view the progress made in razing the church to the ground. I well remember Aurelio Betri, the photographer, being present with his camera, taking

Fig. 12.—A Last Glimpse of the Church of S. Domenico.

views of the different parts of the building, one of which will, I think, prove of interest to the reader. It is taken from the spot whence a long vista of the row of arches on the left is obtained. On the right is seen the side wall of the Chapel of St. Peter the Martyr, which wall divided it from the Chapel of the Rosary (fig. 12). I was also present on a certain day when several distinguished people were assembled around the tomb of Stradivari. Amongst others, if my memory serves me well, were the Barrister Tavolotti; Mayor of Cremona; Dr. Robolotti; the Librarian, Professor Bissolati; and the Assistant Librarian, Professor Peter Fecit; and I recall, just as if I heard them now, the following words being pronounced by one of these gentlemen: 'There is such a confusion of bones, without any special mark whatever, that it seems useless indeed to make any further search.' On the same occasion I heard repeated several times the name of Stradivari; but I was young and ignorant of the significance of the name, and did not then grasp the importance of the search which these gentlemen were disposed to undertake. During the following days I saw men with baskets clear that tomb of all the human bones found within it—skulls, tibias, thigh-bones, and ribs; some of the bones were of an earthy tint, some of a blackish musty colour. I learnt afterwards that the men themselves interred the bones outside the city, with the exception of a few of the skulls, three of which were retained by Signor Ferdinando Rossi, the manager of the work, and by his partner, Francesco Ferrari. After retaining them some years the last named gave them to his brother-in-law, Dr. Vincenzo Ferrari, who kept them until he left his father's house, when his brothers, as a mark of respect to these human remains, sent them to be buried in the town cemetery; by this time they are most probably mixed up among the heap of departmental disinterments which periodically take place."

Thus disappeared the tomb of Stradivari. The *name*-stone alone remains, and is now preserved in the Municipal Museum. As Signor Mandelli suggests, "the matter of the desecration of the grave was perhaps too lightly decided on; in fact, the reverence now felt for everything appertaining to Stradivari had *then* penetrated but little in Cremona." The town council, however, shortly afterwards decided to dedicate one of the principal streets to his memory, and on several occasions since that period Signor Mandelli and others have striven to induce that body to raise a monument worthy of Cremona's most famed citizen, but unfortunately financial inability bars the way.

As already stated, the site of the church is now a fine public garden. On the pedestal of one of the ornamental vases which adorn the grounds is engraved an inscription, which we translate as follows :—

HERE WHERE FORMERLY STOOD

THE CONVENT AND CHURCH OF

THE DOMINICAN INQUISITORS

THE TOWN COUNCIL

HAVE PROVIDED

A PLEASANT PROSPECT

OF TREES AND FLOWERS

1878.

It is gratifying to be able to add that a commemorative tablet has also been placed on the wall of the house in the Piazza Roma in which Stradivari lived and died. It bears an inscription to the following effect :—

HERE STOOD THE HOUSE

IN WHICH

ANTONIO STRADIVARI

BROUGHT THE VIOLIN TO ITS HIGHEST PERFECTION

AND LEFT TO CREMONA

AN IMPERISHABLE NAME AS MASTER OF HIS CRAFT.

CHAPTER II.

Stradivari's Violins.

HE tradition that Stradivari was a pupil of Nicolò Amati has been handed down to us by successive generations; and there has been a general disposition to believe it to be correct. Still, doubts have not unreasonably been raised, as it has been hitherto impossible to point to the existence of any documentary evidence to confirm the tradition.

Stradivari, unlike several of Nicolò Amati's other pupils, did not make his master's name generally known by mentioning the fact that he was his apprentice on the various labels he inserted in his instruments during so many years. Andrea Guarneri, for instance, from time to time uses the words "Alumnus Nicolai Amati"; so also did Francesco Ruger*; whilst we believe this to have been the invariable practice of G. B. Rogeri, who worked at

---

* The several members of this family appear to have spelt their name Rogeri, Ruger, and Rugerius, though the name more frequently met with on the labels is *Ruger*. It is usual, however, to speak of them as "Rugeri." This family of makers must not be confounded with the two named Rogeri who worked at Brescia and who were of Bolognese origin.

Brescia. Lancetti, the Cremonese biographer, who about the year 1823 compiled a work on the different celebrated violin-makers (but it was never published, owing to its non-completion), in writing of Stradivari, states that he used a label about 1666 bearing the words "Alumnus Nicolai Amati"; and M. Chanot-Chardon, the well-known Parisian luthier, tells us that he recalls having seen in the possession of his father an autograph label bearing the following statement by Stradivari: "Made at the age of thirteen, in the workshop of Nicolò Amati." Unfortunately this interesting document is not now to be found.

Piccolellis, in his genealogy * of the Amati family, throws no light upon the connection of Stradivari with his master, although in certain of the archival documents which he publishes Andrea Guarneri and others are mentioned as inmates of Nicolò Amati's house. The absence of the names of Ruger, Rogeri, and Stradivari is possibly to be accounted for by these not having been indoor apprentices— *i.e.* they did not live and board with their master, and therefore did not figure in the return of the members of the household.

Now, we have searched long for the label mentioned by Lancetti, and have also consulted many of our colleagues, but always with the same negative result: no one had ever heard of its existence. We had at length given up hope of any success, when during a visit abroad we were fortunate enough to have a violin submitted to us which we recognised as an early work of Stradivari, and great indeed was our pleasure and surprise when, on deciphering its original label, we found the words: "Alumnus Nicolai Amati, faciebat anno 1666." Here, then, was the long-

---

* "Liutai Antichi e Moderni," Firenze, 1886.

sought-for confirmation of Lancetti's statement, proving by unquestionable documentary evidence (see reproduction of label, Chapter IX.) the fact that Stradivari was the pupil of Nicolò Amati. It is curious to note that in the very next year, 1667 (see label), Stradivari makes no mention of his master; nor apparently did he again do so throughout his life.

As we have already seen, Stradivari was born in 1644; and we may safely assume that his parents apprenticed him not later than his fourteenth year, possibly two years earlier, for even at the present day fourteen years is the average age of apprenticeship in both the French and German violin-making centres. Stradivari would, therefore, have commenced working in 1656-58.*

To whom could the parents have addressed themselves, if not to Nicolò Amati? No other name suggests itself to us. And when we recollect that Amati was the sole representative of the only old family of violin-makers we know of in Cremona, and that his fame far excelled that of all other makers throughout Italy, no other choice practically existed. That Nicolò Amati received apprentices was doubt-less well known locally. We may believe, then, that the boy Antonio Stradivari entered the workshop of Amati some time between his twelfth and fourteenth year, and, taking his allotted place at the bench, began, tools in hand, laying the foundation of that career which was to prove so fruitful and remarkable.

At Mirecourt, in the department of the Vosges, the centre of the violin-making industry in France, an apprentice

---

* In the Census return of Nicolò Amati's household for the year 1641 Andrea Guarneri, aged fifteen, is included. This shows that he was already an apprentice" (Piccolellis, "Liutai Antichi e Moderni").

of average intelligence learns to make a very fair instrument
in three years ; so we may conclude that Stradivari at the
age of sixteen—in 1660—would be equally competent. We
know that about 1660–1665 he printed his first labels, and
this fact points to his having reached a standard of excellence
sufficiently high to justify him offering his work direct to
his patrons. It does not follow, however, that Stradivari
had quitted the workshop of his master, for having labels
of his own simply shows that he was both competent and
free to make instruments on his own account if commissions
were forthcoming. That he did not do so to any extent is
certain, for singularly few of these early productions are to
be met with. Various reasons might be given to account
for this, but we are of opinion that by far the most
probable explanation is that Amati practically retained the
services of his gifted pupil until within a short time of
his death, which took place, at the age of eighty-eight,
in the year 1684. Such an assumption is the more
reasonable when we bear in mind the resources of an
establishment of reputation so high and merited as that of
Nicolò Amati, a reputation acquired during the course of a
whole century. Such a house, therefore, would be favoured
with most of the orders for fine instruments sent to
Cremona in preference to that of a new maker whose name
was possibly still unknown outside the walls of his native
city. Thus in all ways it probably suited Stradivari to
remain as a paid workman under the roof of Nicolò Amati
until about 1684.

Careful observation, carried on during many years, has
conclusively convinced us that very few of the later-dated
instruments of Nicolò Amati—i.e. after 1665–70—are the
work of an old man, and it must be remembered that he
was seventy-four in the last-named year. Clearly, then, he

was assisted by others; and without doubt these assistants were his pupils, amongst whom we may mention Andrea Guarneri, Giovanni Battista Rogeri, Francesco Ruger, Amati's own son Hieronymus, and, lastly, Stradivari.

Here, then, was the school in which Cremona's greatest fiddle-making son passed the first three decades of his working life, profiting by the guidance and mature counsels of the master who had maintained, and added to, the reputation gained by successive members of his family. During these years Stradivari must have vied with his fellow-workers in striving to improve : in fact, a healthy spirit of emulation no doubt existed amongst them ; and possibly the innovations that Stradivari was destined to carry out were then slowly and imperceptibly ripening in his mind, awaiting that moment when, in the natural course of events, the position held by his master would become vacant, leaving him a fair field for their development.

As to the exact position occupied by Stradivari while with Amati nothing is really known, nor does the most minute scrutiny of the workmanship of Nicolò Amati's later instruments enlighten us to any appreciable extent. We recognise in certain violins the unmistakable handiwork of Andrea Guarneri, of Giovanni Battista Rogeri, and of Francesco Ruger ; but we have hitherto failed to find a single specimen bearing the already strongly characteristic impress of Stradivari, or even agreeing with those instruments contemporaneously made by him and bearing his label, dated after 1665, but prior to 1680. In Hart's book we read that Lancetti says,* on the authority of Count Cozio, that the

---

* Hart, "The Violin, etc. : " London, 1887.   Lancetti obtained much of his information from Count Cozio, who doubtless had gleaned a good deal of correct information, though many of his statements have proved to be inaccurate.

instruments made by Stradivari in 1665, and others in 1666, bear the label of Nicolò Amati ; and he instances one, which was in the collection of the Count, to which Stradivari made a new belly in his best style many years later. Continuing, the writer adds : " It is certain that instruments as described by Lancetti have been recōgnised by intelligent connoisseurs as wholly the work of Stradivari, and, as may be imagined, they have no longer been allowed to sail under false colours, but have had their proper certificates of birth attached to them."

Now these statements are liable to be misunderstood, as they imply that a certain number of Stradivari's instruments of the earliest epoch exist, which were originally made for Amati, whose label they bore. Such, however, is not the case. If they existed, where are they ? We have certainly not met with them. The violin mentioned by Lancetti is known to us ; it is still in the possession of an Italian nobleman. If we may rely upon Lancetti's statement—viz. that the original ticket was one of Amati's (the one now in the violin is a false Stradivari label dated 1710)—then it does furnish an instance in point, for the work and style, with the exception of the belly, are undoubtedly those of Stradivari's early period, and, furthermore, are thoroughly characteristic. We may add that we are acquainted with only four other examples in which, similarly, the original label may have been one of Amati. In one instance only have we seen an Amati violin the head of which we can unhesitatingly affirm to have been made by Stradivari ; but of course it is easy to assume his co-operation in the construction of many others. Again, it may be that Stradivari was more especially employed in varnishing, in fitting up the instruments, and in generally supervising the work ; or perhaps he and Hieronymus, the son, worked conjointly, as was undoubtedly the case with Giovanni Battista and Pietro Giacomo Rogeri, of Brescia. Instruments thus made would necessarily lack the individual characteristics of both the one and the other, the whole being blended. However this may be, it is unquestionable that the later specimens of Nicolò Amati, of neat and perfect form and finish, which are dated as late as the year of his death, were either made by his son alone or jointly by his son and Stradivari. Further experience and research may perhaps enable us to determine this with more certainty than at present. In the meantime we may say that the scant credit accorded in various books to Hieronymus, the son of Nicolò, is most misleading : at times he made instruments worthy of the best traditions of his family.

We have not sufficient data to enable us positively to affirm in what year Stradivari definitely started working on his own account ; but the fact that he purchased a house in the Piazza Roma in 1680 tends to fix that year as the probable date, though we think it not unlikely that the separation from his veteran master was made gradually, and commenced a year or two previously. Mr. E. J. Payne, in a very interesting article contributed to Grove's " Dictionary of Music and Musicians," says that Amati appears to have retired in 1679, and that the workshop was broken up the following year. Such cannot have been the case, as we have both repeatedly seen and possessed instruments bearing Nicolò's original labels dated between 1680 and 1684. It is therefore apparent that the love of his art held him to his calling until the end ; and, judging by the extreme rareness of Stradivari's works at that time, we believe that he must have continued to give a helping hand to the last. Again, Hart,* on the authority of Lancetti, states that all the tools, models,

---

* Hart, Articles "Stradivari," p. 173, and "Amati," p. 87.

and patterns of Amati passed, at his death, into the possession
of Stradivari instead of remaining in the hands of his son,
Hieronymus. This may possibly have been the case, but we
are much inclined to doubt it ; for, as far as we can ascertain,
they have never belonged to the Dalla Valle Collection.*
Lancetti appears to have formed his conclusions from the
fact that a wooden rule or straight-edge and a model of the
" *f* " holes of the Amati form were found among the Stradivari
relics purchased by Count Cozio from the great maker's
descendants in 1775. The reasoning of Hart that this fact,
if true, would account for Hieronymus not always working
to the same forms as those which would be derived from
his father's instruments is unconvincing. We repeat that
the abilities of Hieronymus have been underrated. His
capacities were quite equal to striking out modifications of
form or outline if circumstances called for them.

The earliest dated instruments of Stradivari seen by ourselves are of the years 1666, 1667, and 1669. Hart mentions
a violin of the year 1666, and M. Silvestre, of Paris, tells
us that his uncles, Pierre and Hippolyte Silvestre, of Lyons,
also possessed one of that date. But Count Cozio says
that Stradivari worked from 1656 to 1736 ; and, as we have
already remarked, it is quite possible for him to have made
instruments and inserted his own label as early as 1660, his
sixteenth year—in fact, in a note-book in our possession,
compiled in the early part of last century, we find mention
of a violin of this early date ; though we cannot vouch for
the correctness of the statement, it being so very easy to
misread old and obscured figures.

Before proceeding to note the successive changes in
Stradivari's work as we approach 1700, we will pause and

---

* " The Contents of the Dalla Valle Collection," Chapter VIII., p. 205.

review those instruments made by him during Amati's lifetime—*i.e.* prior to 1684—and seek to find the point where
Stradivari's originality asserted itself. We cannot with
justice say that he commenced where his master left off,
nor do his earliest works foreshadow a man of such
exceptional and versatile abilities as he proved himself to
be. He did not, as we are often told, suddenly flash forth
as a brilliant genius endowed with the gifts and experience
of all his elders. On the contrary, he was slow to develop,
though from the first he showed industry, earnestness, and
persistency in carrying out his own ideas, whether good
or bad. The dimensions he adopted for his instruments
were those of the smaller form of violin more frequently
used by Nicolò Amati in 1660–70 ; and, with but slight
modifications effected here and there after 1660, he continued
to make instruments of these proportions until 1684. We
have, however, met with exceptions, one of them being the
" Hellier " violin, dated 1679, of which we shall speak later.

That Stradivari did not at once take the " grand "
Amati pattern as his standard of size is instructive ; for
it shows that he was still in doubt as to whether or
not these proportions would give a superior tone. It is
probable that the majority of players still favoured the
bright and responsive, though lighter tone, obtained from
the smaller form. Both the previously mentioned violins
of 1667 and 1669 are marked by the same character, and
reveal throughout considerable Amati influence—more so,
indeed, than any later specimens seen by us ; though at
the same time they distinctly and undeniably bear the
stamp of Stradivari. We observe already the beginnings
of that originality of style which we see more boldly and
distinctly asserted later on in the 'seventies and 'eighties.
Now, all pre-1684 Stradivari instruments contrast with Nicolò

Amati's contemporary works by their more masculine and solid build, accentuated in some specimens to a greater degree than in others. They lack that characteristic neatness of work shown in the small and light substance of the edges, the slender corners, delicately cut head, and "f" holes of Nicolò's violins, in which, in fact, every part is light of build and elegant in design. With Stradivari the curves are stiffer and less rounded, and especially noticeable is his treatment of the corners and the bouts; the two edges are broader in aspect and heavier in actual substance, all rendered the more apparent by an

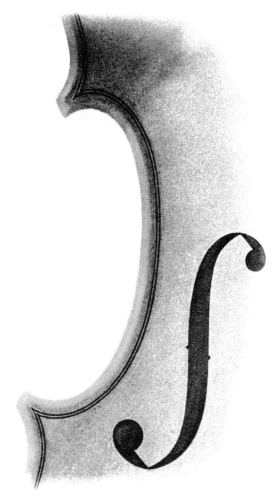

Fig. 13.—Edge, Purfling, and Sound-hole of an Example made in 1680.

increase of margin round the sides, and the purfling being set a shade farther in. The corners are short and blunt ; and the sound-holes, more angular in their curves, and placed more often closer together, are as a whole more substantial-looking. The model is that of his master, though perhaps less full round the edges than in the majority of Amati's violins of this period.

In the choice of material it cannot be said that Stradivari was particularly happy ; and this fact leads us to conclude that the remuneration he obtained for these early works, with possibly an exception here and there, was not sufficient to permit of his employing handsomely figured wood, though as regards its resonance there is but little fault to be found. The maple is either rather plain, cut the slab way of the grain, showing but little cross figure, and with veins running in a downward direction or in curves ; or it is of another tree, wood marked by a small and weak curl, this time cut the right way of the grain. Both these types of wood were evidently obtained from trees grown in the province. The pine is invariably of good quality. After 1670 we meet with bellies of a good width of grain, but on approaching 1680 it is generally very close—more so than one could wish. The most typical and interesting examples known to us—apart from the " Hellier," made, we believe, between 1666 and 1680—are the " Sellière," the violin owned by M. Desaint, and that in the possession of Capt. Saville. The latter instrument is perhaps as remarkable for its vigorous build as the " Hellier." All three, unfortunately, have had their original dates tampered with. Other examples also of this period are those owned by Mr. Nairn, 166–, Mr. Younger, 1667, and M. Bovet, 1677.

By 1680 we may safely assume that Stradivari had acquired a certain reputation, though possibly as yet only local. Nevertheless, as we shall see, it was spreading. We

Figs. 14 and 15.—HEAD OF A VIOLIN OF THE PERIOD 1680.

learn from the Arisi MSS.* that in 1682 the Venetian banker
Michele Monzi ordered from Stradivari a complete set
of instruments, which were destined to be presented to

---

* There were two brothers named Arisi, contemporaries of Stradivari, and
they both appear to have acquired some literary distinction in their native

James II. of England.* What better evidence of his growing prestige could we have? The death of his veteran master Nicolò Amati, which took place two years later, must have powerfully contributed to his advancement; for the increase in Stradivari's productions dated after 1684 is most noticeable. Thus stimulated, he was fast proving that he, and he alone of Cremona's sons, possessed an energetic grasp of his craft and a fertility of idea which were not only sufficient to maintain the glorious traditions of the past, but even to raise the art and renown of his native city to a still higher pinnacle. The years 1684 and 1685 mark a decided development both in form and construction, more pronounced than hitherto. The character of Stradivari's work remains the same, although he had at length perceived that the instrument as a whole required broader treatment. His dimensions are in most cases increased,

---

town of Cremona. The first, to whose pen we are indebted for the few interesting records of the great master and his works which have come down to us from those days, was Don Desiderio Arisi, a priest of the order of St. Jerome, belonging to the church of S. Sigismondo, situated about a mile outside the city. He seems to have taken much interest in art, and left two works dealing with the sculpture, architecture, and collections of pictures to be found in Cremona. These works are now preserved in the public library of the town. Don Desiderio is believed to have died about the year 1720, to which date his manuscript notes on Stradivari are assigned. His brother, Dr. Francesco Arisi (born 1657, died 1743), was a prominent lawyer and prolific writer both in Italian and Latin. He was elected President of the Society of Advocates of Cremona, was a member of most of the learned bodies of his day, and corresponded with the chief literary and scientific men of the period in Italy, France, and Germany. His writings comprised poems, dramas, speeches, and historical and miscellaneous works. His chief claim to fame rests upon his "Cremona Literata," a biographical account of all the writers who flourished in Cremona from the earliest times to his own day. The work was published in Latin at Parma, in three volumes, folio, 1732–41.

* We have no knowledge as to what has become of these instruments; they are not now amongst the royal possessions.

and are more in accordance with those of the "grand"
Amati. The heavy edge and breadth of margin round the
sides of some of the instruments of this period forcibly
recall the style of certain Nicolò Amatis made in 1640–50—
Nicolò Amati's own characteristic work. Typical examples
of 1683 and the following years are the violins in the
possession of the following :—

> The Irish Academy of Music, *ex* Dr. Jay, 1683 ;
> M. Suk, of the Bohemian Quartett, 1683 ;
> Miss Lamplough, 1683 ;
> Mr. Croall, 1684 ;
> Mr. Soames, 1684 ;
> Mr. Rosenheim, 1686 ;
> Miss Goddard, of Providence, Rhode Island, U.S.A., 1686 ;
> Baron Erlanger, 1687 ;
> Mr. C. Oldham, 1687 ;
> Mr. L. Mackenzie, 1687 ;
> M. Jan Kubelik, 1687 ;
> Mr. Carl Derenberg, 1688 ;
> Miss Gidley, 1689.

Most writers on the subject have divided Stradivari's life
into periods, and then over-praised or depreciated this or that
epoch. Such a procedure is to a great extent misleading,
for no man of Stradivari's commanding genius could be tied
down to act on strict lines. Broadly speaking, he profited
by experience, and avoided as he advanced in age the
shortcomings noticeable in earlier productions ; but, notwithstanding, he made at all times throughout his long life
various specimens which stand out prominently above others
of the same date. It is perhaps correct to say that he
experimented more frequently before 1700, though the more
we study his works the more clearly do we perceive that
Stradivari was always experimenting even to his last days.
Hence it came about that he produced works of varying

merit, here very successful, there failing somewhat, though he never made positively poor instruments; even the inferior specimens invariably present good points.

We cannot better illustrate Stradivari's earlier experiments than by discussing the "Hellier" violin previously mentioned. Made in 1679, it is one of the few inlaid violins, of which we shall speak later on. As regards the dimensions, it differs from any other violin seen by us dated before 1684–85; these proportions were, in fact, never at any later period exceeded. Thus we see that Stradivari was already contemplating that change of proportions to which he was more generally to give effect after 1685. The perfect symmetry of the head, and the position and admirable design and cutting of the "f" holes, are also in advance of any of his contemporaneous work known to us. On the other hand, the model, heavy edge and small purfling are thoroughly characteristic of his early work, and the whole presents a heaviness and solidity of construction such as we may almost venture to say borders on clumsiness. We may here incidentally remark that this violin shows that Stradivari occasionally enjoyed rich patronage previous to 1680, for he received no ordinary remuneration for the making of such an instrument.

During the next five years—*i.e.* until 1690—Stradivari's work undergoes no decided change. While all specimens bear the charm of personal distinction, they vary both as regards dimensions and the minor details of construction. In some instruments the dimensions are of large proportions throughout, while others, though of full length, have diminished widths or lower sides. In some cases the model is made to compensate, so to speak; in others, not. In character the model still remains Amatisé; here and there flat, but in the majority of cases fairly high at centre, gracefully hollowing towards the edges, and more noticeably so at the bouts than at the flanks. We have seen some specimens the model of which rises somewhat pointedly to the centre, thus lacking that fulness of appearance which is more pleasing to the eye. The heads show considerable variation. In some examples they are disappointing; they are wanting in vigour, and contrast strangely with the solid edge and more masculine treatment of the body. The absence of a decided chamfer or bevel especially tends to impart a meagre appearance; and again at times the design is too small for that of the body, though we have seen heads which were too heavy. In short, what we wish to point out is, that in these instances the perfect balance of symmetry between head and body is to a certain extent absent.

The year 1688 marks a notable improvement, and for the first time we see Stradivari making a more decided bevel and carrying out his very original idea of picking out the curves of the outline of the head in black.* He also treated the centre-line running down the middle of the fluting in a similar manner. Few specimens are now to be found with heads in that sharpness of preservation which enables the observer to note this latter feature; besides, we think he did it in but few instances, and never, as far as we have observed, after 1700. The blackening of the bevel he continued—with a few exceptions, dating between 1698 and 1703, and several of his inlaid instruments—to the end of his life. The year 1690 is perhaps one of the most interesting epochs in Stradivari's career; it certainly marks

---

* Some of Stradivari's copyists have blacked the mitre-joints of the sides of their instruments. This feature was originated by Joseph Guarnerius: Stradivari never did it.

the most complete innovation as regards the form, construction, and proportions of the violin which took place in his work; it can only be equalled by the change in the form of his 'cellos which he adopted years later. We refer to the creation of the "long Strad."

Before proceeding, we will again pause and more fully review the progress of the last few years. Stradivari had now reached the plenitude of his powers as a craftsman, for it cannot be gainsaid that in point of sharpness, accuracy, and beauty of finish some of the examples of the years 1686, 1687, 1688, 1689, and 1690 stand unsurpassable. This is but natural, when we consider that he was now in the prime of life. The perfect skill with which he handled his knife is seen in the cutting of the "f" holes, the insertion of the purfling, and the carving of the heads. The finish throughout marks him as having been one of the most dexterous craftsmen the world has ever known, and we emphatically assert that no violin-maker has ever surpassed and few have equalled him. No more unique example of his unrivalled finish of work exists than the "Tuscan" violin, made in 1690. It stands alone. Others equally fine were made, but the vicissitudes of time have not spared them to us. All pre-1690 violins are termed Amatisé, the style as a whole bearing the more or less marked impress of Amati's influence. But this must be understood only in a broad sense: it does not imply that those instruments are to any appreciable extent reproductions of Amati.

We have endeavoured to show that, from the very outset, Stradivari's originality asserted itself, and as it developed the points of similarity with Amati became weaker and weaker. A certain number, indeed the greater proportion, of his earlier instruments were covered with a varnish of a yellow colour, which fact furnishes a strong point of resemblance with Amati ; though we may here mention that from his earliest days Stradivari used a varnish of deeper tint, which towards 1690 and onwards became more and more pronounced. Another feature in common with Amati is the wood. Both makers showed a preference for maple cut on the slab ; and Stradivari, in the great majority of his works made previous to 1690, used it cut thus, sometimes for back,

Fig. 16.—Edge, Purfling, and Sound-hole of the Example known as the "Tuscan," made in 1690.

sides, and head, at other times for the back only, the rest being cut the right way of the grain. In contrast to Amati, the curl of Stradivari's wood is generally bolder and more often rather plain, while Amati usually chose wood strongly marked and of smaller curl. Stradivari's slab backs are with rare exceptions in one piece; those of Amati more often in two. After 1685 we find backs, both in one piece and joined, cut the ordinary way of the grain; those in two pieces were of plain wood and medium width of curl, those in one piece of strongly marked though small curl, generally placed in a direction slanting from right to left. The "Hellier" and the instrument known as the Spanish Stradivari, dated 1679 and 1687 respectively, have backs of broad curl in one piece; the latter is exceptionally handsome, and both are of wood of foreign, *i.e.* non-Italian, growth.

In the work published by us, "Giovanni Paolo Maggini: his Life and Work," we record our belief that Stradivari was influenced in the conception of the long-pattern instrument by Maggini's violins; and the more carefully and critically we examine the violins of the 1690 decade, the more evidence do we find in support of our views. Among the various relics from Stradivari's workshop purchased by Count Cozio from Stradivari's son Paolo, and of which we treat fully in Chapter VIII., there are no fewer than nineteen forms or moulds used by the maker for the construction of the sides. Several of them were made for the long-pattern instruments, and one bears the inscription, "A. D. I. 9. Novembre, 1691," and the letters S. L., which, possibly, as suggested by Mr. E. J. Payne, may mean "Stretto lungo." * If so, this would show that the term "long form" comes to us from the master himself. A second mould of this form is dated 1692. Now, were it not for our own observations, we should assume that these

---

* Article *Stradivari*, Grove's "Dictionary of Music and Musicians."

dated moulds marked the exact date of the commencement of this interesting type of violin; but such cannot be the case, as we had in our possession some few years ago an example dated 1690 in Stradivari's original figures. None anterior to that date has ever been seen by us, so we may take it that the year in question is most probably that of their birth.

A slight study of the different dimensions which Stradivari worked out between 1690 and 1692 furnishes some interesting

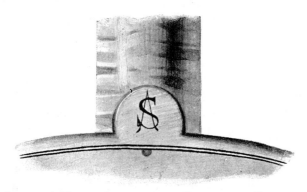

Fig. 17.—Stradivari's Monogram, carved on the Button of the Back of an Example dated 1689.

comparisons (see Appendix). It will be noted that in 1691-92 he made several violins of which the proportions are the largest we have ever met with. Not only have we the increased length, but combined with it the extreme width, and in one example the full height of sides. Specimens of these proportions are rare; we have only seen six. The examples in possession of Mr. Charles Fletcher, and that of Mrs. Ginn, of Boston, U.S.A., are typical instruments,—both are dated from the year 1691. The violin of M. Leopold Auer (of the same type as the two just mentioned) was also made about the same time.

It will be remarked that these dimensions are nearly identical with those of the smaller pattern made by Maggini. It is instructive to find that in 1692-93 Stradivari returned to his first idea, retaining the extra length, but narrowing the width, apparently convinced of the futility of attempting to attain the characteristic brightness of tone combined with the solemn depth of power of the Magginis. Until 1698, with but rare exceptions, he continued to make violins of the long pattern only. In that year we see a change, for, curiously enough, he returns, with a few modifications, to the pre-1690 type; 1699 gives us the orthodox long pattern again; but in 1700, as far as our observations go, he has dismissed it for good. We do not, of course, positively affirm that no long-pattern instruments were made in 1698, but only record that hitherto we have not met with any. The existence of fresh designs in 1698 undoubtedly shows that Stradivari was restless; and this, coupled with the fact of our having possessed another violin dated 1699, which, while preserving the "long Strad" width, is of the ordinary fourteen-inch length, tends to fore-shadow Stradivari's return to the pre-1690 proportions.

The varnish used by Stradivari after 1690 is, with notably few exceptions, of a deeper and richer colour than that of the previous years. We have hitherto been accustomed to see the traditional Amati yellow and its kindred tints, although, as already stated, Stradivari had from the earliest times occasionally employed varnish of deeper colour; but not until 1684 do we begin more frequently to meet with the warmer-tinted varnishes. Some of the long-pattern instruments are especially fine in this respect, and compare favourably with many of the productions of the next century.

Now, the outline, dimensions, and general construction

of the long-pattern violin admirably demonstrate Stradivari's

powers of originality; and that he should have succeeded in adding $\frac{5}{16}$ths of an inch to the total length, while retaining the relative harmony of top, bottom, and middle curves, is an additional proof of his keen sense of symmetry; and this is rendered the more noticeable when compared with the works of many of the other Italian makers, few of whom were wanting in originality, though some showed a lack of symmetry in their designs.

Fig. 18.—Edge, Purfling, and Sound-hole of a "Long-Pattern" Example made in 1694.

As we have just stated, every part of the outline is in proportion to the increase of length. The bouts are therefore longer and less curved, the corners a little shorter and less drooping (this latter feature being a marked characteristic), the edge is neater in aspect than hitherto, and the margin round the sides is lessened, as if to help to make up for the decreased widths. The purfling is of stout substance, and the mitres point straight up the corners in order to harmonise with their different curves. The model is, as a rule, flat, yet presenting a certain fulness which commences to swell imperceptibly from the purfling. It contrasts with the very graceful and more scooped modelling of Stradivari's earlier works. The " f " holes are more open, and generally set a little straighter; even the heads of these instruments—certain specimens of which we consider stand out pre-eminently by their marked beauty of curve and exquisite finish—are slightly lengthened in order to harmonise with the increased length of body; and then, so that the box of the head which carries the extra length should be in proportion with the scroll, the throat is cut farther up—*i.e.* more opened. Stradivari more frequently used backs in one piece for these violins; and we have seen several specimens of wood cut from the same tree—maple of native growth—marked with a small strong curl running nearly straight across. We now rarely meet with backs cut the slab way of the grain, though here and there he occasionally used one. His pine still continues, with but rare exceptions, of fine grain. The stop (*i.e.* length of string from the bridge-foot to top of the belly-edge) of these "long Strads" is $7\frac{3}{4}$ inches—that is, $\frac{1}{8}$ more than that of the great majority of Stradivari violins, and $\frac{1}{4}$ and even $\frac{3}{8}$ more than that of many instruments of other makers. In order to make this longer stop agree with the more general length in usage, some examples have been cut down at the top—an operation much to be deplored, as it must be remembered that the extra length compensates in some

measure for the narrower width.   Remove that extra length,
and you have an instrument of small dimensions, besides
destroying the symmetry of the whole.   Fine examples of
the "long Stradivari" are those in possession of—

> Mr. R. L. Harrison, dated 1693;
> Mr. Benecke, 1694;
> Miss Collins, of Boston, U.S.A., 1694;
> Mr. J. Cowan, 1694;
> Mr. K. S. Muir Mackenzie, 1694;
> Mr. Goetz, 1695;
> Mr. Muirhead, 1696;
> Mr. J. Mountford, 16—, ——.

The latter is a most charming specimen, though unfortunately
its original date has been altered to 1701.   The Paris
Conservatoire Museum also possesses an example dated 1699.

We have now arrived at the end of the century, and
before proceeding we will again pause to survey briefly the
result of more than forty years of Stradivari's working life—
a period which, in the case of many men, embraces their rise
and decline, but which finds him on the threshold of new
and greater efforts, still in full possession of an unerring
eye and steady hand.   That he had succeeded in surpassing
all competitors, and achieving something beyond the highest
efforts of the Amati, is unquestionable; but let not this
statement be misunderstood.   We must not suppose that
the beauty and exquisite finish of much of the work of
the Amati can be surpassed.   It is only when we consider
Stradivari's work as a whole that we find him to have
been possessed not only of their craftsmanship, but of a
greater and more expansive mind.   No purfling, no "f"
holes, no heads, have ever been more perfectly worked and
finished than those of certain Amati instruments; but with
Stradivari we find more often a greatness of general idea

which is closely accompanied by the admirable finish of the Amati. Thus, 1700 saw Stradivari occupying the position so long held by Nicolò Amati and his ancestors; he was, in fact, without a serious rival. Hieronymus, the last of the Amati family connected with our art, gave but little sign of life; possibly, enriched by the death of his father, he preferred to lead an easy existence.* Andrea Guarneri and Francesco Ruger, both pioneers in their work, had ceased their labours in favour of their sons, and all were apparently completely overshadowed by their fellow-townsman. Pietro Guarneri had migrated to Mantua; Giovanni Battista Rogeri had settled in Brescia.

"That which I have termed the Golden Period commences about 1700," says Hart. Fétis also speaks in the same eulogistic strain; and we, too, accept the statement, yet not without considerable reservation. We wish to point out clearly that the dawn of the century does not herald any eventful and brilliant transition or any sudden quickening in Stradivari's progress, but rather shows him silently plodding on with unflagging energy, producing yearly, nay monthly, fresh modifications in his works, which, though not always successful, attest on the whole the natural and fairly consistent development of the forms and models of past years.

Let us now return to 1698, the year in which, as we have previously stated, Stradivari reverted to his Amatisé forms. He leaves the flatter and less hollowed model of the characteristic "long Strad," and returns again to the teachings of Amati: outline of the bouts more curved, corners long, straighter and more splayed out, the absence

* H. Amati appears to have made comparatively few instruments after his father's death. He died in 1740.

of the more drooping curve allowing the elongated mitres of the purfling to point straight up the corners. The model, in full harmony with the general appearance, is hollowed on leaving the edge; in short, the whole bears a strong resemblance to that striking type of Nicolò Amati of the years 1640-50. What is more probable than that he was influenced by the sight of one of these violins, a considerable number of which were probably to be found in and around Cremona? The proportions remain those of the 1698 instrument. Thus Stradivari continued, with but few exceptions, until 1703-4; perhaps 1701 and 1702 are the years which offer the fewest exceptions, while they are also those in which we meet with this form at its best. The varnish is of a beautiful soft texture and fine orange-red tint of colour; the wood of the backs is invariably of broad markings, more generally in two pieces, and that of the bellies is still inclined to be close in the grain. Fine examples are those in the possession of—

> Lady Tennant, 1699;
> M. Blanchet, 1699;
> Mr. Young, 1700;
> M. Tivadar Nachez, 1701;
> Lord Newlands, 1702;
> Miss Lees, 1702;
> Mr. De Rougemont, 1703;
> The "Emiliani," 1703.

In 1703 we note Stradivari gradually leaving the Amati scoop, and developing a fuller and more strongly arched model, though not necessarily higher. We have seen some specimens with shortened corners, but they are quite exceptional.

The year 1704 brings us to one of the great productions of Stradivari's life: the instrument known as the "Betts." On looking at this violin, one cannot but

be struck by the beauty of the formation of the long and
relatively slender corners. It recalls to our minds some of
the happiest efforts of Antonius and Hieronymus Amati,
with the addition of a certain grandeur which they lack.
The corners are not really longer than those of some of
the violins of the preceding years, 1698–1703, but the fact
that the bouts are a little more curved, in addition to a
pronounced drooping of the corners, especially of the top
ones, which are also a little longer than the others, gives
that effect. In order that they should not have a too
protruding appearance, Stradivari pushed the mitres of the
purfling to the extreme limit—we have seen but few other
specimens treated in this way—and when he failed to get
the mitre right up the groove cut out for it, he filled
it in with a black mastic, which perfectly completes the
appearance he sought to obtain. The uniformity of the
outline presents the perfection of symmetry: the full,
rounded model swells away from the edge with but a
semblance of hollowing round the purfling; the "f" holes,
cut with masterly decision and placed in a comparatively
upright position, seem to fall naturally into complete
harmony with the surrounding features; the head, though
cut as Stradivari only knew how to cut it, lacks something,—there is a squareness in the design, the fluting is
wanting in breadth, the throat is hesitatingly cut; in a
word, it does not rise to the greatness of the occasion.
The beauty of the materials from which this instrument
is made leaves nothing to be desired. The back and
sides are of handsome maple, with well-pronounced broad
curl; the back in two pieces, with the figure slanting from
the joint in an upward direction—a feature but rarely met
with in instruments of earlier date. The pine of the belly
is more open in the grain than hitherto: fine at the joint,

but widening out to a full $\frac{1}{16}$th of an inch at the edges.

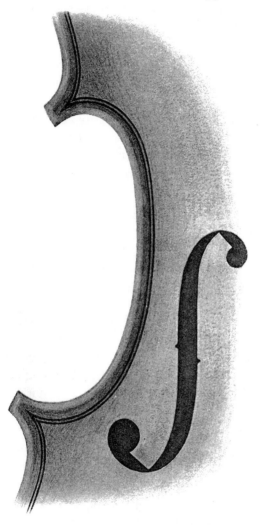

Another fine example of this date is the violin owned by Colonel Glennie.

The year 1704 marks, as far as our experience permits us to affirm, the last of those violins with pronounced long corners: we know of no specimen of later date. The years 1705 and 1706 are especially noticeable for the fewness of the violins produced. We are acquainted with only nine instruments: five of the earlier and four of the latter year.*

Fig. 19.—Edge, Purfling, and Sound-hole of the Example known as the "Betts," made in 1704.

* See footnotes, Chapter X., page 233.

One might suppose that, having attained such perfection of build as is represented by the main features and proportions of the " Betts," Stradivari would have rested for a time ; but fresh ideas, the result of his restless genius, continually crowded out the past, and, whether for better or for worse, he continued to put them into execution. Nevertheless, the violins of the years following 1704 show, by various parts of their construction, more especially the model, that Stradivari had settled upon certain points from which he henceforth but rarely deviated.

The greater number of the violins produced during the years under consideration (1705–10) are characterised by a certain conciseness of form and construction, every part being closely knit together ; and we are of opinion that they furnish us with examples which, in conjunction with fine proportions, represent the most compact type of violin made by Stradivari. The edges and corners are light, both in appearance and in actual substance ; the margin around the sides is equally neat ; the corners, shortened and more in accordance with those of his earlier instruments, are yet more elegant—*i.e.* less blunt : they recall, to a considerable extent, those of the long-pattern violins, with slightly increased curve or droop. The purfling, which is brought fairly close to the outer edge, helps to accentuate the light character ; and the mitres, instead of going straight up the corners, as in the " Betts " and the majority of the 1698–1704 instruments, are now pointed across them in a more noticeable way than hitherto. We believe the brothers Amati, in their earlier instruments, were the first to turn the mitres of the purfling from the centre of the corners ; but, owing principally to the latter being of different shape, they did not obtain such a good effect as did Stradivari. The archings of the model are worked in the same style as those of the "Betts," at times higher and even more rounded; but, on the whole, Stradivari's tendency was towards flattening the arch. The cutting of the sound-holes and the carving of the heads are broadly treated: the former, while retaining the same graceful curves and form characteristic of 1700, are perhaps more open in every respect; the top and bottom holes are, as a rule, less round, and shaped more in the form of a pear. The heads are of decidedly bold proportions and masculine appearance, which is, in some respect, due to the presence of a slightly heavier bevel.

During the years 1705, 1706, 1707, 1708, and 1709 Stradivari seems to have had a decided partiality for backs in one piece: we have seen several examples of the years 1707, 1708, and 1709 with backs cut from the same tree of maple wood, with a pronounced broad curl slanting across from left to right or *vice versa*; others, with identical backs, are of wood of a plainer character, the curl rather weak and undefined, and generally placed in a straighter direction. Typical specimens of this period are the violin of Mrs. Stothert, dated 1706; that of Sir William Huggins, P.R.S., dated 1708; the "Ernst" Stradivari, dated 1709, now the property of Lady Hallé; the violin of M. Soil, dated 1708; "La Pucelle," belonging to M. Glandez, dated 1709; the "Viotti," 1709, a grand example in every respect; the two dated 1709, owned respectively by Mr. Ludwig Mond and Mr. Simmonds; and those owned by the Vicomte de Greffuhle, dated 1709, and by M. Hammer, dated 1707. In the Museum attached to the Paris Conservatoire of Music there is also to be seen an example made in 1708—a most attractive specimen. The back is of wood cut on the slab (very unusual after 1700), handsomely figured, and coated with a warm orange-red-tinted varnish, which sparkles as though it were still in a liquid state.

Hitherto every ten or twelve years we have found Stradivari ripe for a change, and 1709–10 was to prove—though in a minor degree—no exception to the rule. We have shown that since 1698–1700 the general aspect has been continually transformed by different treatment of the curves and corners of the outline, model, etc. As regards dimensions, Stradivari kept to the 14-inch instrument; at least, he did not exceed that length except in such cases as that of the " Hellier " violin, dated 1679, and several examples of the years 1684, 1690, 1692; and never, as far as we know, did he exceed $14\frac{1}{16}$ inches in length, while retaining full proportions otherwise. These earlier tentative efforts were now to bear fruit, for about 1708–9 Stradivari struck out a new form, of the length of $14\frac{1}{8}$ inches, accompanied by the fullest widths. That he was in a very experimental frame of mind may be seen on referring to the Appendix, as during the years 1709–12 he varied and altered his proportions more than at any subsequent or previous time. We entirely fail to perceive any fixed idea or principle guiding Stradivari in determining the relative height of the sides in keeping with these changes of dimensions. He continually fluctuated: here $1\frac{3}{16}$ inch at the bottom and $1\frac{1}{8}$ at the top ; there $1\frac{1}{4}$ at the bottom and $1\frac{3}{16}$ at the top, the usual proportion ; in one case we have the extreme heights of $1\frac{3}{8}$ and $1\frac{1}{4}$; but any consistent plan, such as lowering or raising them in accordance with the model, or with either increased or diminished length and width, is in most cases absent. The consequence is that we meet with violins having sides of $1\frac{3}{16}$ to $1\frac{1}{8}$ inch, where, to judge by the general proportions, a still better tone-result would have been obtained had they been left at

$1\frac{1}{4}$ to $1\frac{3}{16}$. The actual curves of the $14\frac{1}{8}$-inch outline, with the exception of a broader sweep at the top and bottom, where the extra length is divided, differ but little from those of the 1706–9 instruments : the bouts remain of the same proportion. The edge, purfling, corners, model, and general character are also similarly neat. Stradivari does not seem to have made this type of violin a special feature during 1709 and the following years, but appears to have utilised this form and its proportions from time to time during the remainder of his life, the years 1711, 1712, and 1713 being those in which we more frequently meet with such specimens.

About 1709 good fortune evidently smiled upon Stradivari, and favoured him with a log of maple, from which he obtained some of the most handsome backs it is possible to see—of one piece and marked by a broad, strong curl of the most striking appearance ; they cannot be surpassed either in beauty or in acoustical properties. We meet with these backs up to the years 1715–16, but it is very rare that we find the wood of the sides and head to match. Stradivari probably considered that this was unnecessary, and, looking practically at the matter, he was well aware of the increased difficulties of bending the sides when made from extremely handsome wood. For the heads he no doubt used up all sorts of odd pieces—in the majority of cases selecting wood with but little figure, and thus economising and cutting his handsome wood to the best advantage. In 1710 Stradivari had attained his sixty-sixth year, and, notwithstanding advancing age, we still see him completing instruments of that concise, neat type of form and work which we have tried to portray ; but as we proceed we perceive that the whole character of the work assumes a broader and more substantial appearance.

That Stradivari may have sought to impart a still more

substantial appearance to his works than hitherto is to some extent possible ; at the same time we cannot ignore the fact that advancing years may have contributed, though insensibly, to this result. Rarely indeed do eye and hand at seventy still retain the cunning of earlier years; and Stradivari, though marvellously endowed with Nature's gifts—as we shall see later on—had to bow to the inevitable. Do not let this remark lead you to suppose that his productions now betray the hand of an old man. Such is not the case ; what we wish to imply is that his age is here and there betrayed by a certain breadth and solidity of style traceable throughout every detail. Edge and purfling have a broader aspect than hitherto, due principally to the former being less rounded and the latter generally of full thickness, and set a degree farther in. The edge, as a rule, is also stouter in substance, and at times of slightly irregular thickness ; the corners are decidedly broader, which causes them to appear shorter than is really the case, and their curves—especially those extending from the C's—are at times a trifle squarer-looking. The arching of the model continues on the lines of the 1704–10 instruments ; here, a shade flatter or higher ; there, a little more or less full at the flanks and around the edges. The sound-holes are well open, the sharp curves, as in the " Betts," being absent, and they are more heavily cut. The contour of the exterior curves of the heads is perhaps less bold than in 1709, though marked by a still increasing heaviness of bevel, broad centre-line to the fluting, throat well open, and a blunter termination of the volute.

The foregoing are the main characteristics of Stradivari's work until 1720–25. From year to year, nay, from month to month, we note continual deviation, but it is impossible for us to enter into these subtle distinctions. We think we have now made it clear that when Stradivari in 1708–9 originated the $14\frac{1}{8}$-inch outline, he did not give up the 14-inch form he had been using in the previous years: on the contrary, he continued working from both, and the violins made up to the year 1713 are generally of one or other of these forms. In this latter year, however, we find him reverting to dimensions similar to those of certain violins of the 1680-90 period, measuring $14\frac{1}{16}$ inches in length, with full width and depth of sides. He may have made a new mould, or very possibly it was the old one taken down from the wall and brought into use again after a lapse of twenty years. Henceforth we shall see instruments the curves of which may slightly differ one from the other, but the actual dimensions and the outline in its main features, with but very rare exceptions, will agree with one or other of those three forms. It is of course perfectly comprehensible that Stradivari should have here and there reverted to some of his early forms—possibly to supply special orders—and, as we have already stated, that of the "long" pattern is the only one that he appears to have definitely discarded with the dawn of the century.

Stradivari's powers of production seem to become more marked as his years roll on; his energy apparently inexhaustible, and his fertility equally unfailing. More instruments belonging to this decade than to any other period of his life are known to us, amongst them the majority of his most noble existing works. His sole aim in this world was his calling; and although we have but scanty knowledge concerning his daily life, we may safely assume that he was to be found day after day seated at his work-bench, with gouge, compass, or knife in hand, giving form to those instruments which were to prove models of perfection for future generations. Each succeeding year furnishes us with some exceptionally fine specimen of his work—all possessing

strong characteristics in common, though each is stamped
with an individual charm. The year 1710 gives us the
"Vieuxtemps" and the violin belonging to Mr. Louis Ries,
both specimens of high rank.

Of the year 1711 one of the most typical and finely
preserved examples is that known as the "Parke," until
recently in the possession of Mr. John Adam, formerly
owned by William Cramer, Fountaine, Plowden, and other
well-known amateurs. Its proportions, as will be noted
(see Appendix), are of full dimensions, and, combined
with a broad, robust aspect, it worthily portrays this very
manly type of Stradivari's work. Its varnish, of a rich
orange tint, is beyond criticism, the softness of its texture
being especially beautiful. Another example, dated 1712, in
possession of Miss Eldina Bligh, is also an equally characteristic, though a much less well-preserved example. In
addition to the violins, we are indebted to these years
for the "Mara," "Duport," "Romberg," and "Davidoff"
violoncellos, all instruments of the finest type. The year
1713 gives us an admirable violin, the "Boissier," now
owned by Señor Sarasate. Fétis mentions it as one of the
finest existing Stradivaris, and we can certainly confirm his
statement. Its outline is of the $14\frac{1}{16}$-inch form, the model
a little fuller, though closely following that of the "Parke"
instrument; the edge, corners, and purfling are perhaps a
trifle neater, and the sound-holes more lightly cut. The
varnish is also of great beauty, its tint being a shade redder
than that of the "Parke," and the whole instrument is in
very fine condition. The "Sancy" and the violin owned
by Mr. Alfred Gibson are fine examples of this same year.

Of the year 1714 we have a violin of wide repute—the
"Dolphin"—formerly in the Adam and Bennett collections,
now owned by Lieutenant Munro, R.N. The example in

7

the possession of M. Soil is also a specimen of the highest order. The "Batta" violoncello dates from this year.

The year 1715 is indeed a rich one; it contributes no fewer than six violins of the first rank : the "Gillott," three examples in the possession of Professor Joachim, another owned by Mr. F. L. Bevan, and lastly one which, in our opinion, ranks among the finest of the fine—the "Alard," the property of Baron Knoop. We may here remark that it

Fig. 20.

would be incorrect to single out any one of these violins as standing supreme in merit, for we cannot too strongly emphasize the fact *that amid all the finest Stradivaris still existing there is not one which can with justice claim absolute superiority over all others.* The neck of the "Alard" is original, and in the mortise of the head, still visible, are written the initials P. S. (see fig. 20). We conjecture that these initials are those of Paolo Stradivari, and they possibly indicate that the violin was one of those which

The "Alard" Stradivari, dated 1715.

In possession of BARON KNOOP.

The "Alard" Stradivari, dated 1715.

C   The "Alard" Stradivari, dated 1715.

came into his possession on the death of his brother
Francesco in 1742.* We have found these initials marked
in six other violins, all of which obviously retain their
original necks, otherwise the letters would have been cut
away when grafting on the new one: the most notable are
that owned by M. Soil, dated 1714; the "Blunt," dated
1721; and the "Sarasate," dated 1724. On the other hand,
we would point out that the "Messie" violin, which was
sold by Paolo Stradivari to Count Cozio, also has the original
neck, but does not appear to have been so marked.

The year 1716 furnishes three remarkable violins: the
one formerly owned by the Grand Duke of Tuscany, now at
the Musical Institute of Florence; the "Cessol," in possession
of Mr. Croall; and lastly, that unique example, the "Messie,"
of which we shall speak more fully.

The year 1717 claims that fine example known as the
"Sasserno," owned by Mr. Phipps; and an admirable
specimen left by the late Mr. Orchar, of Broughty Ferry,
to a local museum. This year also gives us the violoncello
in the possession of Mr. Holden.

The year 1718 also gives us two violins of high order:
the "Maurin," owned by Mr. John Rutson, and the one in
the possession of Mr. Avery Tyrell.

The year 1719 gives us the "Lauterbach" violin and
the "Becker" violoncello.

The fine violin of Mr. Kruse, and the famed violoncello
of the late Signor Piatti, belong to 1720

Let us pause here and try to sum up the characteristics
of these fine specimens of Stradivari's fully-matured genius.
Place side by side the "Boissier" and the "Dolphin"
violins, of the years 1713 and 1714 respectively. Both show

---

* See Chapter X., p. 222.

continuity of ideas, combined with individual freedom of treatment. We see a close similarity of form, model, sound-holes, and work in general, —the heads are twin brothers. True, the latter instrument is of 14-inch, the former of $14\frac{1}{16}$-inch form, which, added to a slightly decreased curve of the bouts, gives an increased sweep to top and bottom. Again, the model of the belly is a little fuller than that of the back; with the " Dolphin " it is the reverse. Look at the wood from which they

Fig. 21.—Edge, Purfling, and Sound-hole of the Example known as the " Dolphin," made in 1714.

are made : the backs of both are in two pieces, and cut from the same tree ; but, in order to diversify their character

Stradivari places the curl of the "Boissier" slanting down-
wards, and that of the "Dolphin" upwards. The wood of
the sides, in both cases, is plainer; that of the heads still
more so. For the bellies he selects pine of vigorous growth
and bold breadth of grain. In the earlier violin we see that
which is but rarely met with in Stradivari's instruments—
a belly in one piece, with the broader grain placed on the
treble side. Though unorthodox, this is immaterial from a
tone point of view, provided that the quality of the wood
is good.

The "Alard," which is unquestionably the *ne plus ultra* of
the following year (1715), approaches more to the "Boissier"
than to the "Dolphin" in outline. We see the same
shortened bouts and broader sweep of top and bottom curves,
though it is of 14-inch form, but it differs in its general
aspect, which is blunt and pre-eminently forcible in every
feature: in fact, the whole build of the violin, including the
more massively proportioned head, shows the strong and firm
touch of the old practised hand. It is perhaps second to
the "Dolphin" in elegance, but surpasses it in manliness.
With regard to material, though acoustically fine, the "Alard"
is not of such striking-looking wood as several other specimens of this year—such as, for instance, the "Gillott" and
the "de Barrau" (one of Joachim's violins), both of which
have backs in one piece, which cannot be surpassed. In
the matter of varnish all these violins are glorious—each
individually resplendent—the one favoured by its wood, the
other by a lovely tint of colour, by softness of texture, or
by the exquisite beauty attained through the varnish being
broken up in a most picturesque manner by time and usage.

The year 1716 will ever be a memorable year of Stradivari's life, for, as previously stated, we are indebted to it
for that remarkable violin known as the "Messie," which

stands alone for its unrivalled condition.

Fig. 22.—Edge, Purfling, and Sound-hole of the Example known as the "Messie," made in 1716.

Were it but eight days, instead of one hundred and eighty-six years old, it could not present a fresher appearance. Stradivari seems to have awakened to the fact that his work had assumed an air of breadth and solidity throughout, which, treated by less skilful hands, would have bordered on the clumsy. He therefore determined to retrace his steps, and immediately gives us, amongst others, an example which for lightness of build takes us back ten years. Once made, he never parted with it. Death came, and the violin passed successively to his sons

Francesco and Paolo; the latter retained it until 1775, in which year he sold it to Count Cozio di Salabue.* The character of the work of the "Messie" is as exceptional as its history. Sound-holes, edges, and corners are treated differently to anything we have hitherto seen or shall hereafter see; the model is flat, that of the belly most noticeably so; the sharp, unrounded edge, and slanting, youthful sound-holes, are admirably shown in our illustration (fig. 22). Critics may say these marked peculiarities of style are due to its freshness. That is true only inasmuch as it accentuates them. Other specimens exist sufficiently well preserved to indicate clearly the maker's intentions, and the most appropriate for present comparison is the Medici violin, preserved with the Tuscan tenor and violoncello at the Musical Institute in Florence. It is of the same year and in remarkable preservation, though not perfect; yet it differs in form, dimensions, model, sound-holes, edges, and varnish. To the casual observer it would be taken for the "Salabue's" brother, as it presents a close resemblance, whether as regards the back, which is in two pieces, the wood, which is similarly figured, or the varnish, which, though of thicker texture and somewhat deeper colour, has the same bright, unworn surface.

In the "Cessol," the third fine instrument of the year, we have a superb example in every respect, and quite of the character we should expect. Its structure is founded more on the lines of the "Dolphin" than of the "Alard": the wood is cut from the same tree, and the varnish is of an unsurpassable plum-red colour. In contemplating this specimen, we are reminded of what Charles Reade says in his third letter to the *Pall Mall Gazette*, published in 1874: "When a red Stradivari violin is made of soft velvety

---

* See "The Salabue Stradivari," London, 1891.

wood, and the varnish is just half worn off the back in a rough triangular form, that produces a certain beauty of light and shade which is, in my opinion, the *ne plus ultra*." Hart connects this expression of opinion with the " Dolphin " violin, but we venture to assert that it applies in a still more marked degree to the " Cessol."

Neither of the violins referred to of the years 1717-18 shows any further development of form or workmanship. The " Sasserno " is of the " Dolphin " outline and type, the " Maurin " of the " Alard " type ; both instruments, though, are of lighter construction in most of their details than those of pre-1716 years ; the sound-holes are especially neat, closely cut, and set well upright. These general remarks apply to most of the specimens of the preceding and following years. The example dated 1717, which was in the possession of the late Mr. Orchar, of Dundee, until his death in 1898, bears a closer resemblance to the " Parke " violin in form, and is of the 14$\frac{1}{8}$-inch outline ; while that of Mr. Tyrell forms quite an exception to this period, its proportion being both narrow and shortened. The maple of the back of the former instrument is in one piece, and cut on the slab—a feature, as we have already pointed out, not often met with between 1700 and 1720.

The year 1720 heralds in Stradivari's seventy-sixth birthday : four years more, and he will be an octogenarian.* One would think that, as in the case of his master Nicolò Amati, he would ere this have reached that moment when, in the natural order of things, he would have laid down his tools—if not entirely, at least in great measure—in favour

---

* The Cremonese monk Arisi compiled his notes regarding Stradivari in this year (1720). He writes as if Stradivari was still active : also he makes no mention of any assistant.

of younger men, and during his remaining years would have peacefully looked back with feelings of pride upon a fruitful and industrious past of over threescore years. He could still have superintended and given others the benefit of his unrivalled experience. Apparently, however, old age came lightly upon him. Hale in body and vigorous in mind, he still retained that marvellous power and facility in handling his tools which permitted of his continuing in the even tenor of his way. We cannot but believe that his two sons, Francesco and Omobono, born respectively in 1671 and 1679, and possibly Carlo Bergonzi, worked with him, each rendering assistance to the best of his ability; although the most minute scrutiny of the instruments of the period fails to reveal any signs of other hands than his own having contributed a share towards the building up of either violin, viola, or violoncello. Possibly—and this seems to us the only hypothesis—Stradivari permitted them to rough out the work, and went all over it after them, thus removing all traces of their co-operation. One of Stradivari's sons may possibly have made bows, patterns of which exist in the Dalla Valle Collection. Again, his assistants may have made the cases destined for the instruments, cases of considerable artistic merit; there were also the various fittings required, such as finger-boards, tail-pieces, bridges, pegs, etc. They may, as Lancetti suggests, have principally confined their efforts to repairing and adjusting instruments, aided in the varnishing and general management, so that the master might be free to devote himself unremittingly to the construction of his instruments.

The most characteristic features of the majority of the 1720-25 instruments are a certain squareness of the outline at the top and bottom curves, and the quickly rising models, which immediately swell away from the purfling. Stradivari seems to have preferred the 14-inch form, though we do

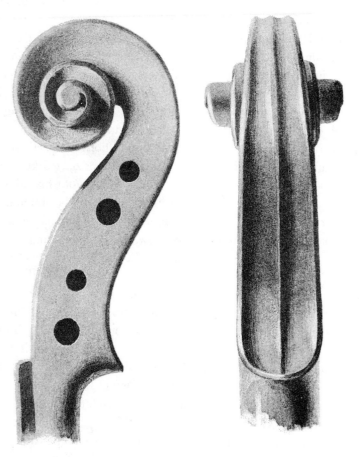

Figs. 23 and 24.—Head of an Example made in 1720.

occasionally come across that of $14\frac{1}{8}$-inch. No unmistakable indication of old age is apparent in the work, although the formation of the edge, the corners, purfling, cut and position of the sound-holes, and the more blunt carving of the head—points which are more or less pronounced—lack that firm precision to which Stradivari has so accustomed us, and betray the less controlled hand.   As regards the wood, his assortment of maple does not appear to have been equal in beauty to that of the preceding ten years, but it was as good acoustically.   We meet with a fair number of backs, both in one and two pieces, marked with a faint small curl, showing a nutmeg cross-grain; and we have seen several specimens dated 1722 with backs cut from the same part of the tree, stained by a sap-mark on either side of the joint.   We again find Stradivari returning to the use of this small-curl maple, of native growth, in violins dating from 1722 onwards.   His pine is, as a rule, of fairly open and very even grain.   The varnish of this period is characterised in the greater number of cases by a less rich appearance; it is of drier texture, and somewhat sparsely laid on.

There still remain to us some fine examples of 1721 and the following years, which, if not comparable with those of the preceding decade as regards beauty of wood and varnish, are in no way inferior to them in point of form and construction; indeed, some of the finest-toned instruments date from these years.   The violin invariably played upon in public by Señor Sarasate is of the year 1724.   Though unattractive in appearance, it captivates all hearers by its tone.   The solo violin of Wilhelmj dates from the following year, 1725.*   Of 1721 the example formerly in the possession of Lady Blunt is particularly remarkable for its fine state of preservation; that of M. Vormbaum is of equally high merit.   Of 1723 we have the example owned by Mr. D. J. Partello.   The year 1722 furnishes, amongst others, the fine specimen known

---

* Now owned by an American violinist, Mr. Kupferschmid

Fig. 25.

Fig. 26.

as the "De Chaponay," owned by Mr. G. W. Mackenzie; that formerly in the Goding, Janzé, and Camposelice Collections, later owned by Mr. T. W. Barnes, of New York; and that beautiful instrument known as the "Rode," which is, we believe, the last of the ornamented violins made by Stradivari.

We may here appropriately add a few words about these inlaid specimens.* The custom of elaborately ornamenting instruments was already dying out at the time of Gasparo da Salò and Maggini; in fact, its disappearance practically coincides with the disuse of the viol and the lute.

Fig. 27.

When we arrive at the epoch of the Amatis— *i.e.* during the seventeenth century—it had ceased, we may say almost entirely, although it survived in the ornamentation of the fittings,

---

* Stradivari's designs for the inlaying of the heads of his ornamented violins (figs. 25, 26, 27, 29, and 30).

such as the finger-boards, tail-pieces, pegs, and bridges. We
have seen two violins, the work of Nicolò Amati, which were
gracefully embellished with inlaid ornament : in one of them
the ornamentation consisted of double purfling, and a fleur-
de-lys inlaid in black at the corners of the back and belly,
interspersed with small precious stones, while a design of
similar character was let into the sides at the blocks.
Vuillaume, who purchased this violin at a sale held in
London in 1855, made several copies of it, one of which
was for some years in the hands of the late Mr. Pollitzer.
In addition to these two violins, there exist a few Amati
instruments ornamented with painted armorial bearings and
inscriptions, but we very much doubt whether these decora-
tions were carried out by the maker. Now, Stradivari, in
making his inlaid instruments, clearly sought to demonstrate
that, although the exquisite craftsmanship exhibited by the
old viol and lute makers in the often admirable decoration
of their productions with either carved or inlaid work, was
a thing of the past, he could vie with them if called
upon to do so. Certainly no decoration hitherto applied
to the violin appeals so much to the eye or charms us
so greatly by the lightness and simplicity of its design as
that introduced by Stradivari. We have often been asked
if he was the designer and did this inlaid work himself.
To this question we unhesitatingly answer, Yes.

Various drawings from his pen, some of which will
be found here reproduced (and, among them, those made
for the ornamented instruments in question), still exist in
the Dalla Valle Collection, and prove that Stradivari was
an excellent draftsman. A more than ordinary interest is
attached to the sketch of the arms of the Medici family
(fig. 28); and we here have in Stradivari's own handwriting
the statement: " Armi che ho fatto per li istrumenti per Il

Gran Principe di Toscana," which, we think, effectually proves
that he was his own designer. These arms, delicately cut out

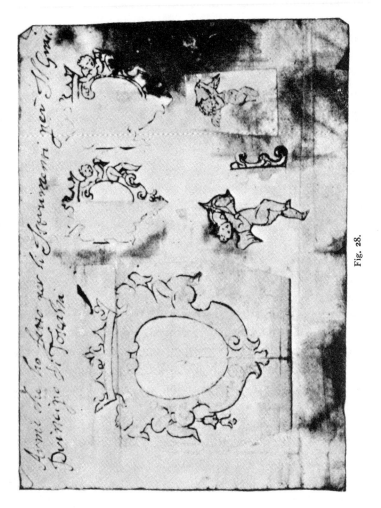

Fig. 28.

in mother-of-pearl, were inlaid in the finger-boards of the set
of instruments made for Cosimo de Medici in 1690; the
charming cupid design was for the tail-pieces. Of the set

the "tenore" alone remains in its original state as left by the maker, and can be seen at the Musical Institute in Florence.

We get further confirmatory evidence of Stradivari's having executed these embellishments himself from the valuable writings of the Cremonese monk Arisi, who was an intimate friend of the master, and who, as Hart remarks, gained his knowledge of the facts from Stradivari himself. Arisi * says : " His fame is unequalled as a maker of instruments of the finest qualities, and he has made many of extraordinary beauty, ornamented with small figures, flowers, fruits, arabesques, and gracefully inlaid fanciful ornaments, all in perfect drawing, which he sometimes paints in black or inlays with ebony and ivory, all of which are executed with the greatest skill, rendering them worthy of the exalted personages to whom they are intended to be presented."

How many of these inlaid instruments Stradivari made we know not. Probabilities point to there having been but few of them, and made only on exceptional occasions. They were destined for his most illustrious patrons, and the remuneration must have been in accordance with the time and pains bestowed upon such finished work. Stradivari states on the designs above mentioned that they served for the instruments made to the order of the Marquis Carbonelli of Mantua, but gives neither date nor information as to their number. Hart gives the year 1687 as that in which Stradivari made the beautiful set of inlaid instruments for the Spanish Court ; but, as we shall see hereafter, this statement is erroneous.

If we again refer to Arisi, we learn that Stradivari made a concerto of instruments which he intended to present to Philip V. of Spain on the occasion of the

---

* Hart, " The Violin : its Famous Makers," etc., p. 175.

passage of that King through Cremona in 1702, for which
event he had prepared a memorial ; but he was dissuaded,
"and," adds Arisi, "the instruments are still in his possession." Now, it must be remembered that this interesting
information was committed to paper by the worthy monk
in 1720, showing that Stradivari had already retained them

Fig. 29. Fig. 30.

some years. In the course of inquiries made both in Italy
and Spain, we have been fortunate enough to obtain the
subsequent history of the instruments which, we believe,
formed this interesting concerto. It consisted of two violins,
two violas (one a "tenore"), and a violoncello. They were
still in Stradivari's possession at his death in 1737, and then
passed to his son Francesco, who, dying in 1742, left them

to his brother Paolo, by whom they were sold in the year 1775 to a priest of the name of Padre Brambilla, for the sum of 125 giliati.* Padre Brambilla took them to Madrid, and there disposed of them to the Spanish Monarch, thus possibly fulfilling the maker's original intention with regard to their destination.† The purchase was most probably due to the musical taste of the Infante Don Carlos, who played the violin. This Prince ascended the throne in 1788 as Charles IV. We learn furthermore that in 1776 Antonio, the son of Paolo Stradivari, at the instigation of Count Cozio de Salabue, tried to repurchase the instruments, but without success. We have ascertained these facts from the correspondence exchanged between Count Cozio, Paolo Stradivari, and his son Antonio.

At the above-mentioned period there was living in Madrid a priest, Dom Vicenzo Ascensio, who, besides his spiritual calling, seems to have had a strong passion for the art of fiddle-making, in virtue of which he enjoyed the patronage of the principal musicians of the Court. We were fortunate enough to meet, at Madrid, the gentleman who owns the account-book so carefully and minutely kept by this priest, a perusal of which throws still further light on the history of the above-named instruments. The following entries are not without interest :—

"On March 5th, 1783, Don Cajetano Brunetti, custodian of the Royal instruments, brought me, by order of H.R.H. the Prince, a Stradivari violin of the year 1709, and requested me to improve the quality of the tone, which

---

* Two additional violins were included in this transaction. (See Chapter XI., p. 248.)

† We say "possibly" because we have no conclusive proof of the fact. We believe, however, that this concerto of instruments is the identical set that Stradivari wished to present to King Philip.

was bad" (*sic*). The worthy priest took the violin to
pieces, and, after enumerating various more or less injudicious
alterations, he adds, " If after this work the violin is not
improved, I think it hopeless unless I put a new back
and belly to it, but then one could not say it was by
Antonio Stradivari." Fortunately the necessity for such

Fig. 31.—Designs for the Ornamentation of the Sides.

drastic treatment was averted, as he tells us that the tone
was rendered excellent according to the opinion of Brunetti,
Christobel, and Andreasi (Court musicians)—so much so
that the first-named player entrusted him with the second
violin of the quintet, to be treated in similar manner.
The entry terminates as follows: " For this exact and
extensive restoration, taking all circumstances into account,

and seeing especially that the violins were intractable and unplayable, I consider the repairs to each worth 700 reals" (approximately £7 at that period).

Under the date July 17th we read: "Don Cajetano Brunetti gave me the key of the cases which contained the instruments of H.R.H., in order that I could see to anything they required." On August 6th: "I had the two large cases standing on feet brought to my house; one of them contained the Quintet of inlaid Stradivaris; the other, several violins, a tenor by Stainer, some bows and music, so that I could have them at hand and be able to arrange the instruments according to the desires of Señor Brunetti. The smaller viola belonging to the Quintet I took to pieces, and replaced the bar. I also removed the parchment, which oppressed (*sic*) the tone of the instrument, from the sides,* and thinned the neck. The viola of large size I treated likewise. The violoncello, which is of very large proportions—larger than those Stradivari usually adopted—I wished to reform (*sic*) [by which the writer means cut it down], so that it might be of the same size as the one belonging to Brunetti. I also proposed to do the same to the large viola; but before carrying out these changes I determined to consult the wishes of H.R.H. the Prince. He, however, would not agree to it, and simply wished to have the instruments put into good playing order. I obeyed, and arranged the viola as already stated, and did as follows to the violoncello: I pieced the centre, replaced the bar by one adjusted to mathematical proportions based on that of Stradivari. I corrected the thicknesses, pieced the four corner-blocks, took

---

* Stradivari fixed parchment to the sides in order that they should not give: they were rendered a shade weak by the cutting for inlaying the design. This explanation is a general one; it does not apply to this viola, as the design is painted on only, and is not inlaid.

the back off and inserted a piece in the centre, as it was
too thin. I had to replace the neck, which I did in the
most careful manner. I then adjusted the instrument, the
tone of which was rendered excellent by all these changes.
It took me three months to do, and I consider the repair
worth 1,000 reals (approximately £10). . . . I restored the
red velvet lining and repaired the case, which contained the
five inlaid instruments ; I arranged the niches and places for
the bows, also the hinges, and put a blue ribbon to support
the lid when open : 380 reals " (approximately £3 16s.).

Under date 1790 we find a further reference to the
violoncello as follows : "I took to pieces the violoncello
belonging to the Quintet, and mended a crack in the belly
on the post side."

The Prince's decision not to allow either the tenor or
the violoncello to be reduced in size was one for which he
deserved the thanks of posterity ; but alas! the fate of the
violoncello was only deferred, as Ortega, the pupil and
successor of Dom Vicenzo Ascensio, performed this ever-
delicate operation in the most drastic and barbarous manner
conceivable, and the instrument, ill-conditioned and uncared-for,
a ruin of its former self, is to-day to be seen reclining
against the wall of the organ-loft of the Chapel Royal at
Madrid. The head alone remains to speak of its original
grandeur.

As stated in our chapter on the number of existing
Stradivari instruments, the large-sized tenor vanished at the
dispersal of the Royal Collection. Whether it had been previously cut down or not we cannot say, but the probabilities
are that it did not escape. Curiously enough, Stradivari does
not appear to have made or finished this concerto of instruments at one and the same time, as the still-existing tenor
is dated 1696, and the two violins 1709. The violoncello

was certainly made at the same time as the tenor : its proportions and style are of pre-1700 date, and its original label
also : but some vandal, probably Ortega, deliberately cut out
Stradivari's figures, substituting 1709 in their place ; the
object of this being, apparently, to make the date agree
with that of the violins which alone remained of the set.
Possibly Stradivari did make a whole concerto in 1696, but
afterwards disposed of the two violins, replacing them at
a later date.   The fact, however, of the varnish of these
examples being yellow and their general character much
more in accordance with that of his pre-1700 work, adds
weight to our belief that they were made about the same
time as the other instruments of the set, though they were
not actually completed and labelled until 1709.*

The number of inlaid instruments known to us is
ten : eight violins, one viola, and one violoncello.   The
earliest specimen is of the year 1677 ; it is a violin of
characteristic Amatisé type, which for many years belonged
to the late M. Wilmotte, of Antwerp.   The next in
chronological order is dated 1679, the " Hellier " violin,
which, besides its ornamentation, is remarkable for its large
proportions and very heavy style of work ; then comes a
charming example of small size, dated 1683, formerly the
property of the late Cipriani Potter.   The year 1687 gives
us a violin which has hitherto been known as one of the
instruments of the Spanish set, mentioned as such by Hart
in his book ; but, as we have already seen, it could not

---

* We have observed that Stradivari did at times, though with rare
exception, label his violins years later than they were made. We may
instance (1) a violin owned by M. Blanchet, dated 1699, but made in
1690-92 ; (2) a violin in the possession of Baroness Wilma Boeselager, dated
1720, but which is clearly the work of 1702·3 ; (3) a violin owned by
M. Luce, dated 1727, also the work of some years earlier.

have formed part of that concerto. Ole Bull, from whom it was purchased by the late John Hart, who sold it to Mr. Plowden in 1861,* bought it in Budapest, and not in Madrid, as stated by Hart. Mention is made of this instrument in Ole Bull's Memoirs; and no doubt the legend that it came from the Spanish Court emanated from that violinist, the reliability of whose statements may be judged when we read his assertion that this is the only violin that the master made inlaid with ivory and ebony.† 1709 is the next date in order, and that year furnishes three inlaid violins : the two already mentioned, and still preserved in the Royal Palace at Madrid ; the third belonged for many years to a well-known amateur player, the late Rev. John Blow. It afterwards passed into the collection of Mr. J. Adam, on the dispersal of which it found its way abroad. Its present owner is the Vicomte de Greffuhle. The eighth violin is the " Rode," made in 1722.

We do not assert that this list embraces all the inlaid violins made by Stradivari ; in fact, we have in our possession melancholy evidence to the contrary. Some few years ago a very common old English violin, the belly of which, to our intense astonishment, proved to be that of an inlaid Stradivari, was brought to us by a curiosity-dealer of Norwich. How the belly came into such ill-assorted company, and what has become of the rest of the instrument, remains a matter for conjecture. It would be difficult to say which of four or five of these eight violins excels in merit : each has the characteristics of the period to which it belongs, and all have individual charm. Judged as a whole, the " Rode " would perhaps meet with the more general

---

* Mr. H. C. Plowden was a well-known amateur who died in 1867.
† The black inlaying is formed of composition, not ebony.

approbation. The designs on the sides and heads of these instruments are inlaid, with the exception of the last-mentioned violin, the viola, and violoncello, which are delicately painted. The depth of the inlaying is but slight, though sufficient to preserve the design from obliteration, even at those parts where the hand, coming constantly in contact with it, has worn the wood bare.

We will now return to the year 1725, and proceed to 1730, years in which we see Stradivari placidly plodding on: now producing specimens of an unquestionably high order, before which we stand amazed at the dexterity of the man; now failing to rise to his accustomed level, and so awakening us to a sense of his advanced age. His productions are less numerous; the craftsmanship throughout less sure, at times wanting in truth and squareness, the outline of back and belly disagreeing. Yet how admirable are they in comparison with the works of many of his younger contemporaries! What a struggle is going on! Though forced to resign to others a greater share of the construction of his instruments, we find him still clinging to his beloved calling and completing an instrument on the label of which he proudly inscribes, in his own handwriting, "fatto de Anni 83." *

Representative examples of these years are those in the possession of—

Mr. D. J. Partello, *ex* Duke of Edinburgh, dated 1725;
M. Plotenyi, *ex* Ernst, 1726;
Captain Harvey, 1726;
M. Halphen, 1727;
The violin known as the "Deurbroucq," 1727;
Mr. F. Smith, falsely dated 1714;
M. Levêque, 1727.

---

* The violin bearing Stradivari's label dated 1727 with this inscription is that in the possession of M. Levêque.

In dimensions the violins of these later years vary between the 14 and 14⅛-inch form, and are, as a rule, of broad appearance, though the edge and purfling, especially up to 1727, are not noticeably heavy. In some specimens Stradivari flattened his models to an extreme degree; in others, and more generally, he preserved the full swell of the majority of the 1720–25 instruments.

Fig. 32.—Edge, Purfling, and Sound-hole of an Example made in 1726.

Both in wood and lustre of varnish they are but rarely to be compared with those of earlier times. His maple continues either plain in figure or of native growth marked by a small curl; the backs generally in two pieces, sometimes in one, or, again, cut on the slab. It is difficult to account for the absence, with but rare exceptions, of the handsome foreign maple. Was there for the time being a dearth of it, or did Stradivari feel that his declining efforts no longer justified the use of this more expensive wood? Whatever the reason, we note the change taking place. Now, admitting that Stradivari was at last forced to allow his assistants to take a greater part in the making of the instruments dating between 1725 and the year of his death, the question naturally arises, Who were they that thus lessened the burden of the old man? We say lessened, for it is beyond any doubt that, to the last year of his life, he kept on constructing instruments with his own hands; and in order to elucidate this point we involuntarily turn for information to the various books that give the names of his alleged pupils.

Fétis, on the authority of Vuillaume, names Joseph Guarnerius del Gesù, Lorenzo Guadagnini, Carlo Bergonzi, Francesco Gobetti of Venice, Alessandro Gagliano, Michel-Angelo Bergonzi, and Stradivari's own sons, Omobono and Francesco. Hart mentions Lorenzo Guadagnini, Alessandro Gagliano, Montagnana, Carlo Bergonzi, and also the above-named sons; he also cites Balestrieri as a possible pupil. The suggestion that Joseph Guarnerius was a pupil of Stradivari can be dismissed in a few words, as not a shred of evidence exists connecting him with his great contemporary; and we may add that we fully agree with Hart in assigning him as pupil to his uncle, Joseph *filius* Andreæ Guarneri. If Gobetti and Alessandro Gagliano were pupils of Stradivari—which we very much doubt—then it must have been in the master's early days, as both were working, the one in Venice and the other in Naples, as early as 1700. Neither is there any documentary evidence of Montagnana

being connected with Stradivari, beyond the mere fact of
his calling his house by the sign of "Cremona"; nothing
can certainly be found in his work which would lead us
to believe that he was either a Cremonese or a pupil
of Stradivari. We should be inclined to suggest that he
was taught his trade by either Gofriller or Gobetti, and
was probably a Venetian by birth. Lorenzo Guadagnini
may have been a pupil of Stradivari, though this matter,
too, is shrouded in some doubt. Was he a Cremonese, or
are we to believe, as stated by Hart, on the authority of the
present members of the Guadagnini family, whose knowledge
of their ancestors we have found by personal intercourse to
be most hazy, that he was born in Piacenza? In certain of
his works there are traces of Stradivari's influence, and we
possess an original label, one of the only three ever seen
by us, on which he states, "Laurentius Guadagnini, fecit
Placentiæ, alumnus Antonius Straduarius, 1740." We obtained this label, with several others, from the executors
of the late Charles Reade, and on the paper to which it
is attached we read the following significant remark : " N.B.
At Piacenza it was easy to call himself a pupil of Stradivari
—he dare not have said so at Cremona." With this
characteristically terse statement by Reade we are rather
inclined to agree. Balestrieri was clearly a pupil of Pietro
Guarneri of Mantua. Michel-Angelo Bergonzi, doubtless,
was taught by his father.

Hence there remain but three names, about which
there can be but little doubt : the sons, Omobono and
Francesco, and Carlo Bergonzi. They alone, as far as we
can see by actual observation, have left traces of having
shared Stradivari's labours, and that only in the later years
of his life. Those specimens, which we believe to be the
joint productions of either Stradivari and one of his sons,

or of the master and Bergonzi, have often given rise to controversy as regards their authenticity. Stradivari himself seems to have sought to make a distinction by labelling them, "sotto la disciplina d'Antonio Stradivari," but in doing so he probably never thought that the time would soon come when the removal and substitution of these labels by more orthodox ones would prove profitable to the vandal who did it. Not only have the tickets "sotto la disciplina" been removed, but also those which were inserted in the instruments made entirely by Omobono and Francesco respectively, facsimiles of which are given in Chapter IX. Furthermore, to complete the confusion, there is still a third type of instrument which has been similarly treated.

At Stradivari's death he must have left, besides the finished stock of instruments referred to in Chapter X., a certain number, though probably small, of unfinished instruments and their component parts, such as backs, bellies, and heads—the rejected of earlier days; and nothing is more likely than that his successors worked up these parts, adding what was necessary to complete the instruments. Hence, it happens that while clearly recognising in a given specimen, say, the back and sides, or perhaps other parts, as the work of Antonio Stradivari, we find that the rest, though more or less closely related, is made by a strange hand. The varnish and agreement in the construction proves to us that the whole was put together at the same time; nevertheless, upon scrutinising the label, we invariably find that it is a forged Stradivari, thus proving that it was originally labelled otherwise, probably "sotto la disciplina," etc.

It is fortunate, then, that the impress of Stradivari's work is as marked in his old age as in his younger days, and, notwithstanding the confusion brought about by this nefarious exchanging of labels, the few connoisseurs who have had the opportunity of studying the instruments dated year after year throughout the master's life, are able to distinguish, in most cases clearly, Stradivari's work from that of his pupils or assistants.

We are now entering on the last period of Stradivari's life. In 1730 he attained his eighty-sixth year, but was still hale and able to continue his daily occupation. That he thought man's allotted time upon this earth had, in his own case, well-nigh expired is evidenced by his having in 1729 chosen and prepared a resting-place for his remains. No record exists of any other member of his calling having been able to use his tools at such an advanced age. The second Carlo Bergonzi, the grandson of Stradivari's pupil, who died in Cremona in 1838, is stated to have attained the age of eighty, but we know of no instrument of his dated later than 1833. Of Nicolò Amati, who died aged eighty-eight, we have already stated our belief that he ceased working several years previous to his death. In France, the elder Derazey and George Chanot, senior, both worked up to eighty years of age. Cuypers, the Dutch maker, seems also to have worked to an advanced age, which fact he frequently recorded on his labels. We have had a violin made by him, dated 1808, on the label of which he says, "ætatis suæ 84." As far as England is concerned, we know of no makers whose longevity equals that of Stradivari. The Kennedys and Craske were probably those whose lives approached nearest to it in length.

The instruments dating between 1730 and 1737 are of diverse type and character. It is impossible to suppose otherwise than that Stradivari's collaboration in the construction of instruments must have decreased from year to year as he drew nearer to his end; yet in the greater number of the specimens of this period we can invariably trace some part wrought by his hand. Others he apparently made entirely by himself, for we cannot admit that either of the sons or Bergonzi—who proved themselves, as witnessed by their signed works, to be, if not technically of the first rank, at least good average workmen—would have cut those palsied sound-holes, in which we discern not only the trembling hand, but also the failing sight—for instance, those of the " Habeneck" Stradivari, dated 1736, where the right-hand one is set quite $\frac{1}{16}$ of an inch higher than the other. Then there is the " Muntz" violin, on which sand-paper marks show plainly all over the sides (and the same is the case in some of the later-dated J. B. Guadagninis). The irregular purfling we meet with tells the same tale: the grand old man's hand trembled so much in cutting the grooves for its insertion that his knife played sad havoc in all directions,—so much so that to have filled up the trenches it would, in places, have been necessary to use purfling of violoncello thickness.

Our illustration (fig. 33) of the sound-hole and section of the edge and purfling of the " Muntz" violin, 1736, pathetically portrays the veteran's work. The formation of the corners and edges is ponderous, blunt, irregular, and of square appearance. This is but natural when we consider the difficulty experienced by the old and enfeebled, though practised, hand, of bending the sides of the centre bouts with well-rounded curves; and it must be remembered that the curves of the outline follow those of the sides. The modelling is heavy, full, and abrupt; we notice the absence of that graceful blending with the fluting around the edge. The heads, while distinctly exhibiting the work of less skilful hands, are not so much like the work of an old man as the bodies, and we cannot but believe that Stradivari made a certain number in former years which he now utilised; we are also of opinion that his sons materially assisted him in this direction, hence the superiority of the finish of the one part over that of the other. The varnish generally shows, though not without exception, considerable deterioration. More often it is heavily laid on, wanting in softness of texture, and in perfect transparency and richness of

Fig. 33.—Edge, Purfling, and Sound-hole of the Example known as the "Muntz," made in 1736.

colour. At times it is even of a muddy and streaky appearance, which but too plainly demonstrates that the old man's sight failed him both in the mixing of the ingredients composing the varnish and in the use of his brush when applying it to the instrument.

Some of the most representative specimens known to us of these last years are :—

The " Kiesewetter," dated	1731, owned by			Mr. Charles Fletcher.
The Violin	,,	1732	,, ,,	Mrs. Tom Taylor.
,, ,,	,,	1732	,, ,,	the late Mr. Wiener.
,, ,,	,,	1733	,, ,,	M. Roussy.
,, ,,	,,	1734	,, ,,	Lord Amherst of Hackney.
,, ,,	,,	1734	,, ,,	Mr. Phipps, *ex* Ames.
,, ,,	,,	1735	,, ,,	M. Lamoureux (the late).
,, ,,	,,	1735	,, ,,	Mr. Hartmann.
The " Muntz "	,,	1736	,, ,,	Mr. Higgins.
The Violin	,,	1736	,, ,,	Mrs. Sassoon.
,, ,,	,,	1736	,, ,,	M. Roussy.
,, ,,	,,	1737	,, ,,	M. White.

We are also acquainted with other equally characteristic examples of this period, but are unable to give their exact dates, as the labels have either been changed or their figures tampered with. The excellent instrument of that distinguished artiste, M. Heermann, of Frankfort-on-the-Main, is of one or other of these years—most probably 1731 ; also the " Habeneck" violin, that of Mr. Tangye, and the solo violin of M. Ysaÿe ; likewise the " Kreutzer," owned by M. Doyen—this latter an admirable example in every respect. But only when we take one of these 1730-36 examples, and place it side by side with another of the 1710-15 period, and a third of the 1720–25 epoch, do we fully realise the gradual change which has taken place. The veteran has in nothing forsaken his principles of form and construction ; he steadfastly adheres to them as long as life leaves him the use of hand and sight : in fact, model, form, curves, edges, sound-holes, purfling, and head lack nought but the power of execution and the firmness of hand of former years.

It is generally known that we rely for the date of the year of Stradivari's birth upon information gained through the master having recorded his age on several labels inserted in instruments made during the last ten years of his life. Fétis was the first to publish this information, and he based his proof upon Stradivari's statement " d'anni 92 " written on a label dated 1736, found in a violin only a short time before in the possession of Count Cozio di Salabue.* The Count, before his death, had sold this instrument to Tarisio, who took it to Paris, and disposed of it to the elder Gand in 1831. In the course of time it found its way to our shores, having been purchased in Paris from the firm of Gand and Bernardel, Frères, by the late Mr. H. M. Muntz, of Birmingham ; at that amateur's decease it came into our hands, and subsequently became the property of Mr. Higgins.

The year of Stradivari's birth, as thus recorded by Fétis, remained uncontested until a few years ago, when Mr. E. J. Payne, in the article on Stradivari contributed to Grove's Dictionary, cited a violin dated 1732, then in the possession of the late Mr. Wiener, upon the label of which was written, in Stradivari's handwriting, " d'anni 82." The label, the handwriting, and the figures are undoubtedly original, and equally so are those in the above-mentioned violin referred to by Fétis ; yet if the one version were correct the other could not be. Hence, at the time when Mr. Payne's article was written (1882), the matter was even

---

* Count Cozio makes mention in the notes left by him of the purchase of this violin, with others, in 1775 from Paolo Stradivari. (See " The Salabue Stradivari.")

to ourselves an unsolved conundrum, although one circumstance somewhat influenced us in favour of the statement
apparently recorded in the Wiener violin. The figures 92
of the " d'anni 92 " on the Cozio violin label are inscribed
on a small piece of paper separate from the ticket itself ;
and why this should be so was at the time inexplicable,
and very naturally gave rise in our minds to a suspicion
that they had been written by other hands than Stradivari's,
and probably covered the master's true figures. As time
passed on, and the instrument came into our possession,
we, in order to elucidate the matter, decided to detach this
piece of paper from the label, and, on doing so, found
underneath, to our astonishment, similar figures, only the
" 9 " was less distinctly made. We were therefore still
further perplexed as to the reason for covering them. The
explanation came a few years later, when we were fortunate
enough to purchase in Italy a small violin by Stradivari
made in 1736, and which also bore his inscription " d'anni
92," but this time entirely written on a separate piece of
paper glued along the bottom of the label. On taking it
to pieces for repairs we availed ourselves of the opportunity to remove the inscription, and the key to the
mystery was then found. The old man, proud of the fact
of making an instrument in his ninety-third year, strove
to record it in his handwriting at the bottom of the label,
but his eyes being dim and his hand lacking guidance,
the inscription ran downhill so much that he had to cut
it through in order not to leave an excessively wide
margin on the ticket. Unwilling to waste it, he again
wrote down his age, this time on a separate piece of paper,
cut it out, and glued it on the label over his first effort.
The same explanation applies to the inscription in the
Cozio violin : Stradivari, fearing his figure " 9 " of the " 92 "

was indistinct, re-wrote both, and placed them similarly on the label over the others.

Armed now with increased knowledge and strengthened convictions, we once more scrutinised the ticket of the Wiener violin, and the explanation of it dawned upon us. Both Mr. Payne and ourselves had wrongly deciphered Stradivari's faulty figure " 9 " as " 2." Read it " d'anni 89," and it tallies with all other inscriptions, as the master, though eighty-eight years of age in 1732, obviously celebrated his eighty-ninth birthday during the year, and this instrument was made after that event. The label dated 1737 is of quite pathetic interest. Apparently the master could no longer trust himself to add either figures or inscription, so this was done for him by his son Omobono (see the written label of Omobono for comparison). The facsimiles of these interesting tickets are given in our reproductions.* Several other instruments have been seen by us on the labels of which Stradivari recorded his age. These are : first, a violin dated 1732, "de anni 89"; second, a violin dated 1735, " d'anni 91"; third, a violoncello dated 1736, " d'anni 92 "; fourth, a violin dated 1737, " d'anni 93." This last is probably the instrument mentioned by Count Cozio as belonging in 1822 to Professor Bertuzzi, of Milan. Later the property of M. de St. Senoch, of Paris, it is now owned by a distinguished Brazilian violinist, M. White. The " Habeneck " violin, referred to by Hart, we do not cite, as, though unquestionably of the latest period, neither label nor inscription is original. We thus have eight records, all of which are in agreement, and we may therefore conclude that, with the clearing up of the one hitherto presumed contradictory statement,

---

* See Chapter IX.

the matter may be considered as finally placed beyond controversy.

A few words as to Stradivari's precise age at death. Paolo, the son, in correspondence with Count Cozio di Salabue, states that his father died at the age of ninety-four years, in 1738; but in this latter date he was in error, as will be seen on referring to the extracts from the Registers of the churches of S. Matteo and S. Domenico in Cremona, showing that Antonio Stradivari was interred in the vault of Signor Francesco Villani in the Chapel of the Rosary, on December 19th, 1737 (see Chapter I.). Hart apparently assumes from this that the age given was also incorrect. We, however, believe not, as it is very possible that Stradivari had actually passed his ninety-fourth birthday before death called him away—perhaps only by a few days: he would therefore be in his ninety-fifth and not in his ninety-fourth year.

The following is an extract from the registration of Stradivari's burial in the church of S. Domenico in Cremona. It will be noted that his age is there described as "about 95":—

"Anno Dñi mill^{mo} septing^{mo} trig^{mo} septimo, die decima nona mis xbris. Dñus Antonius Stradivari viduus, aetatis annorum nonaginta quinque circiter, heri mortuus, praemunitus SS. Sacramentis Ecclesiæ, ac adjutus commendatione animae usque ad ejus obitum, hodie ejus cadaver associatum fuit cum exequiis a me Dominico Antonio Stancari hujus Eccl^e S. Matthei Praeposito ad Ecclesiam M. R. R. P. P. S. Dominici Cremonæ in qua sepultum fuit."

CHAPTER III.

Stradivari's Violas.

TRADIVARI made few violas. We are acquainted with only ten examples. In an old note-book in our possession there is a reference to one, dated 1695, but we have failed to find its present owner. Arisi tells us that in September 1685 Bartolomeo Grandi, called " Il Fassini," ordered from Stradivari a whole set of instruments for the Court orchestra of the Duke of Savoy: this set would have included at least two violas. Again, in 1707 the Marquis Desiderio Cleri wrote from Barcelona to Stradivari by order of King Charles III. of Spain, ordering six violins, two violas, and one violoncello. Not one of these violas is now known to exist, whilst of the two made for the Grand Duke of Tuscany in 1690 only one remains ; and similarly, of the pair which formed part of the set of inlaid instruments that passed into the hands of the Spanish Court in 1772, one example only can be now accounted for.

At the commencement of the master's career the accepted design and dimensions for a viola were those defined and carried out by Gasparo da Salò and the Amati during upwards of a century (see Appendix), the general proportions of which varied but little. The attention of those accustomed to these dimensions, and occasionally to even larger ones, is at once arrested by the considerably smaller form of the earliest known Stradivari viola, made in 1672, and some explanation of this departure from the previously accepted design is naturally sought for.

We cannot accept Stradivari as the originator of the smaller type of viola, for, in addition to other evidence, we know of a fine A. and H. Amati made in 1615, a Stainer made in 1660, and several notable examples by Andrea Guarneri—contemporaneous productions—which are of similar size. The A. and H. Amati viola, being earlier and the work of famed craftsmen, served in all probability as a model for later makers. Stradivari in particular seems to have profited by the study of it, for we observe great similarity of form and dimensions in his viola of 1672, though the Amati, with a small and delicately proportioned head of violin pattern, is by far the more gracefully designed instrument of the two. Was the smaller form of viola initiated by the brothers Amati? We think it was; but can make no positive statement, owing to the ruthless manner in which many of their violas have been reduced in size—some of the old violas being even converted into violins.* We can only conjecture what were their original proportions.

The viola of 1672 shows in the arching, long corners, form of edge, sound-holes, design of head, and the pale golden varnish, just what we should expect from its date—

---

* See Chapter X., p. 235.

a following of the Amati tradition ; though the whole
instrument, with its unsymmetrical outline (too wide for the
length), ungainly head, and general stiff robustness, is without
the grace inherent in the productions of the Amati. The
wood of the back and sides is of poplar; that of the
belly in width and straightness of grain is admirable, the
whole selection being acoustically faultless. The dimensions
agree with those of Stradivari's later examples, with the
exception of the widths ; the sound-holes are also placed
higher up on the belly. The condition of this viola is
practically perfect ; the neck is the original one, and it is
interesting to remark that the label is signed "Antonins"*
—the "u" inverted.

The gradual introduction about this period, 1660–90,
of the smaller type of viola, which offers greater technical
facility to the performer, is difficult to account for. The
printed music of the time provides no clue, for the earliest
important viola part, that of Corelli's "XII Concerti
Grossi," published in 1712, could be quite easily played on
a Gasparo or Amati, and in a performance the balance of
sound would be incomparably better preserved by the tone
of the larger viola. Even later, in the time of Handel,†
the compass of viola parts seldom, if ever, necessitated the
shifting of the hand above the first position ; therefore
no difficulty was presented by the use of a large viola.
It is astonishing, too, to observe how small is the quantity
of chamber music, which included a part for the viola,
written from 1683, the date of Corelli's earliest composition
("XII Trios for Two Violins and Bass"), until nearly a

---

* See Chapter IX., p. 217.

† See interesting analysis of the orchestral parts of the "Messiah" used
by Handel, and now preserved at the Foundling Hospital, by Dr. E. Prout
(*Monthly Musical Record*, April 1894).

century later, when Boccherini and Haydn * were ensuring permanency for the string quartet.

Corelli's celebrated "Forty-eight Trios for Two Violins and Bass" met with such universal approval that this combination became the favourite one, and later composers of all degrees of merit adopted it, to the exclusion of nearly all other forms of chamber music. The finer form of string trio, that for violin, viola, and violoncello, seems only to have come into existence with the string quartet; and of Boccherini's † published collection of fifty-two string trios only twelve are for this combination of instruments.

Seeing, then, that the music of the epoch can scarcely have led to the introduction of the smaller viola, what other cause can be assigned for the change? It was an experimental age in instrument-making, and the small viola may have been an experiment at first, subsequently securing a permanent position because it proved more convenient to the ordinary viola player, who would in nine cases out of ten be a violinist, and therefore find playing on a large viola fatiguing and disturbing to his technique. The violin had been evolved from and superseded the smaller types of viols, and the violoncello of reduced proportions was on its trial; therefore makers may have reasoned that a smaller type of viola might equally supply a want.

The next viola known to us is dated 1690—eighteen years later—the year which gives the first of the "Long Strad" violins as well as the "Tuscan" set—and the creative capacity displayed in these instruments is equally

---

* Boccherini's "First Set of Quartets," Paris, 1768.   Haydn's first quartet was composed in 1755.

† Boccherini's "First Set of Six Trios for Violin, Viola, and Violoncello," Op. 14, Paris, 1768.

traceable in the viola. The distinctive features at once apparent between this and the former viola are the narrower outline, the lower and more slanting position of the sound-holes, flatter arching, broader edge, and shorter corners. The

diminution of the outline in width at top and bottom (see Appendix), and the lower position of the sound-holes, clearly improve the proportions. The wood of the back, sides, and head is of attractive appearance; and though the varnish is not sufficiently definite in colour, the fine style and preservation afford ample compensation. The principles and details of the work are those embodied in the violins of this period. We know not which to admire most — the determination Stradivari evinces to form a style of his own, or the in-

Fig. 34.—Bridge made by Stradivari for the "Tenore" of the "Tuscan" Quintet.

tuition which enables him at this stage to design the form which was to serve for all his subsequent violas, with the exception of the two large ones.

The "Tuscan" viola, preserved in the Musical Institute of Florence, is of extremely large dimensions, exceeding those of Gasparo and Amati. It is worthy in every respect of its surviving companions of the quintet—the violin and violoncello; wood and varnish are identical with those used for them, though the viola seems a shade lighter in colour than the violin.

Stradivari's very graceful monogram * is stamped in the mortise of the neck, which is original, as are also the finger-board, tail-piece, tail-pin, tail-nut, and even the bridge (fig. 34). Indeed, except for somewhat serious beetle ravages, set up probably through the instrument being locked up in a museum rather than remaining in the hands of a loving appreciator, it is as it left the maker, and is a truly grand example. We know of only one other similarly proportioned viola made by the master—namely, the corresponding instrument of the inlaid quintet. The moulds and other necessary patterns used in making the violas of the "Tuscan" set are preserved in the Dalla Valle Collection, and we note with interest that Stradivari calls the larger one "tenore," the smaller "contralto"; † the moulds are also lettered *T.V.* and *C.V.*‡ (fig. 35). The distinctive titles favour the supposition that these two distinct types of violas were then generally recognised and known respectively by the names cited. These pairs of violas by Stradivari were doubtless intended to be played in compositions of the character of the "Sonata a cinque," by G. Legrenzi § (1625–90), and the "Sonata Varie," by J. B. Vitali ‖ (1644–92).

A brief reference to the course which viola-making followed may prove instructive.

---

* See reproduction, Chapter II., p. 44.
† See reproduction of Stradivari's writing to this effect.
‡ Tenore viola and Contralto viola.
§ Wasielewski, "Die Violine im XVII. Jahrhundert."
‖ Grove's "Dictionary of Music," art. *Tenor Violin.*

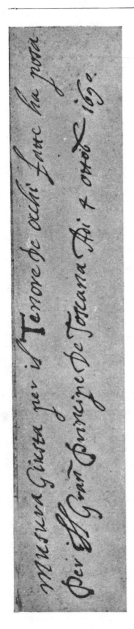

Fig. 35.—*Translation*—Exact Measurements for the Sound-holes of the Tenor made expressly for the Grand Prince of Tuscany, the 4th day of October, 1690.

Before 1660 we find the makers—Zanetto, Gasparo, Maggini, the Amati, and others—frequently constructing the large viola, but very rarely the small one. From 1660 to 1700 the small viola was superseding the large one, though fewer violas of any kind were then made. Between 1700 and 1750 there was almost a cessation of viola-making in all countries; this coincides with the dearth of chamber music composed at this period in which the viola was given a part.

We now pass on to 1696, which year gives us two remarkable violas—that of the quintet of inlaid instruments which for some years was owned by the Spanish King, Philip IV., and another known as the "Archinto," from having belonged to a Count of that name, who was also the owner of a Stradivari quartet. We presume he was the "Conte Giuseppe Archinto" to whom the well-known Alessandro Rolla dedicated some of his duets for violin and viola. The inlaid tenor, illustrations of which we give, exhibits a masterly combination of choice material, appropriate ornamentation, and refined style. The figure of the maple used for back, sides, and head is charming, and homogeneous throughout; the beauty of the slender and wavy curls being shown up by the delicate golden varnish of perfect transparency and lightness of texture. The freshness of this instrument's appearance and its state of preservation are extraordinary; the sound-holes and head convey the impression of their having been wrought but yesterday; even the black lines with which Stradivari outlined the curves of the head are unworn, and the original neck still remains.

The "Archinto" viola is equally beautiful, presenting a number of interesting variations on the previous example, though the maple used is very similar; the arching of the model is fuller, the corners longer. These, added to the neat edge and graceful purfling, again reflect Amati's teaching. The head and sound-holes remain distinctly Stradivarian, and the varnish is of a lustrous red, perhaps the most brilliant in appearance of any used on the violas.

We now come to probably the best-known example of the violas—that named the "Macdonald," dated 1701. It was brought to England at the end of the eighteenth century by the Marquis dalla Rosa, and was subsequently successively owned by Lord Macdonald, Mr. Goding, the Vicomte de Janzé, and the Duc de Camposelice. A record in our possession made a century ago gives the date as of the year 1701, but at some later time the last two figures were clumsily altered to read 1720. So things remained until recently, when a slight repair necessitated the instrument being taken to pieces, and enabled us to critically examine the label. Pleasurable indeed was our surprise, on removing it, to find that the original ink had passed through the paper and clearly showed the traces of its correct date.

The style of this viola in certain details—the flat model, the squarer outline and corners, broad edge, and very sturdy aspect as a whole — plainly heralds that of many of Stradivari's later productions ; but the rather small and slightly Amatisé sound-holes and clean finish of the work are typical of the earlier period. The wood of the back is of one piece, of broad and moderately handsome curl, the sides and head matching ; that of the belly shows a broad and well-marked grain ;

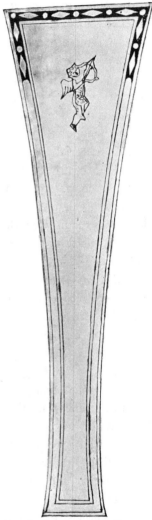

Fig. 36.—Design for a Tail-piece, probably intended for the inlaid Violas.

the instrument is well covered with the red varnish so favoured by the master (a red tinged with orange), and its state of preservation leaves no room for complaint.

We know of another viola which we should assign to the same period as the " Macdonald"; but again the original figures have been tampered with and, in this instance, rendered illegible. It is in all essentials closely related to the " Macdonald." The only distinctive features calling for notice are the joined back in lieu of the whole one and the slightly inferior state of preservation.

The construction of the violas is more uniform than that of the violins or violoncellos, and a comparison of the tone gives a corresponding result. Any difference of tone in the violas is so slight that their quality in this respect may properly be treated collectively. We have shown that Stradivari adopted other principles of viola construction than those of Gasparo and the Amati; and, in consequence, the deep expansive volume and timbre of the Gasparo viola are very different to those of the Stradivari instrument. In this we find a tone which reflects that of his violins in the clear and full woody quality, and in the easy and rapid articulation of the sounds, particularly on the G and C strings. There is, however, we consider, a deficiency in weight and reserve of tone in these two strings; and in listening to a Stradivari viola, associated with other fine instruments of the maker in the performance of a quartet, we have always felt, when a sonorous solo passage on the G and C strings was rendered, that the tone became tight and lost its resonance. In other words, the instrument was overtasked, and the player, with all possible skill and good-will, could not, owing to the more limited resources of the Stradivari viola, emulate or support his colleagues' efforts. The great similarity of the timbre in Stradivari's violins and violas deprives listeners, too, of variety in tone colour. The first and second violin parts of a string quartet naturally resemble each other in quality ; therefore the viola part should in its timbre be distinctive from that of the violins, and partake of the qualities of the contralto rather than of the soprano voice. The great composers, from Haydn onwards, have indicated by the nature of the solo passages allotted to the viola in their compositions how admirably they understood the true viola quality. One meets passage after passage which, for a perfect interpretation, requires the expressive plaintive quality—akin to that of the pure contralto voice—of the Gasparo, Maggini, or Amati viola. Nevertheless, the tone of the Stradivari viola must always command admiration for its beauty, purity, and easy enunciation, the demerits being such only as the expert would detect ; and, from the point of view of the violinist-viola player, it must be admitted that the instrument is completely satisfactory.

From 1701 we pass to 1727 before meeting with another viola ; other examples, the work of intervening years, may exist, but we have hitherto failed to discover them. In Gallay's curious and interesting book, " Un Inventaire sous la Terreur," a Stradivari viola dated 1710 was included in the list of instruments seized at the country house of Tavernier de Boulogne.* The instrument of this year (the last figure of the label has been touched, to make the inscription pass as 1721), though agreeing as a whole with its companion instruments, yet possesses some distinctive features, and may be said to be one of those examples in

---

* The instruments thus seized at the houses of the " Emigrés," by order of the Revolutionary Government, were classified by the distinguished composer and violinist Bruni. We question whether he possessed the requisite expert knowledge to name correctly the makers of the instruments.

which the master presents familiar ideas employed in a fresh way. Stradivari had now reached old age, and the stiffness of the curves, in short, the whole character of the work, betrays the fact. The original traits of this instrument, however—the model, pretty small curl of the wood of the back, ample covering of fine varnish, and fine preservation—go to the making of what must be admitted to be a production marked by strong individuality.

The next example was made in 1731; and here again we find the original inscription falsified, the date, as in the previous instance, being altered to 1721. The label is of 1730–37 type (see Chapter IX., p. 218), and the cunning falsifier, in order to hide this fact, cut out the lower half of the Roman *v* in "Stradivari"—one of the distinguishing features of the period of the label—so that it might pass as an accidentally mutilated letter of the previous type, as seen in pre-1730 labels.

Though showing noticeable signs of an old man's hand in the finish of the work, this viola exhibits a well-conceived and broadly-carried-out design, in agreement with that of the "Macdonald." In fine preservation, its appearance is rendered specially attractive by a whole back of broad curl, and varnish of Stradivari's favourite orange-red colour picturesquely worn. In the early years of the nineteenth century this instrument was in the collection of Mr. Stephenson, the banker,* and later passed into the hands of Corsby, the instrument-dealer, who in 1832–33 sold it to Paganini, the viola remaining with the great violinist until he died, when it was bought by Vuillaume. In 1833 Paganini's appreciation of the viola was the cause of his asking Berlioz to compose a solo for it, "Les

---

* See Chapter XI., p. 275.

Derniers Instants de Marie Stuart" being selected as a fitting theme (!) for the display of the virtuoso's extraordinary powers. Berlioz, happily, was soon afterwards inspired with a worthier subject—the symphony " Harold in Italy," which contains a fine solo part for the viola. Paganini, however, as was anticipated by Berlioz, neither approved of the part, nor would he play it; consequently, at the first performance of the symphony in Paris in 1834, it was played by C. Urhan, and by Henry Hill (uncle of the writers) on the corresponding occasion in London in 1848.*

The last Stradivari viola in chronological order known to us is also of this period, though its original label is unfortunately wanting : we refer to the viola which is the property of the distinguished player Mr. Alfred Gibson ; and those who have the pleasure of listening to his performances on it must admit that no artist could bring out its tonal qualities more effectively.

If we now review the violas as a whole, we find that their characteristics—*i.e* the wood, the colour of the varnish, and the principal features of the work and style—agree with those of the violins made during corresponding years, the " Macdonald " example being perhaps the chief exception. Excluding the two instruments of large size (tenori), and the viola made in 1672, we see that the example dated 1690 served as the model for all its successors. There is a difference in length occasionally of one-eighth of an inch, but this is to be accounted for by a broader edge ; and similar variations in the style led to other slight changes. Stradivari made all his viola heads of the same design as that of the Amati—a design originated, we believe, by Andrea Amati, and found on all their large-sized instruments. Both Gasparo

---

* " Hector Berlioz, sa Vie et ses Œuvres," Adolphe Jullien.

The Inlaid Viola made by Stradivari, dated 1696

and Maggini used the violin form of head. But the viola head of Stradivari is formed like those of the violoncello, and is distinguished from that of the violin by the cheeks protruding instead of being flush where the neck emerges from the head, and by an extension of the fluting at the back. Though, as designed and made by the Amati, this head possesses perfection of form and workmanship, and is in complete harmony with the body of the instrument, it is unsuitable for the viola because it inconveniences the player's left hand. With the introduction of the smaller-sized viola it was necessary to proportionately diminish the head ; and strangely in contrast with that fine sense of symmetry which Stradivari so frequently displayed, we here see a comparative failure—the scroll being too large for the box which it overhangs, and the whole being stunted and ill-proportioned. Still, in summing up the violas broadly, we must admit in them the same consummate mastery of Stradivari over his materials as is exhibited in his other productions. There is the same broad and æsthetic mode of treatment, and it is with the conception rather than with its working out that we find fault.

The violin having come to be recognised as the leading and most important of the stringed instruments, the viola occupied the attention of makers less and less. There was in existence at the commencement of Stradivari's career a considerable number of fine violas by Gasparo and the Amati, and in consequence the construction of violins and violoncellos afforded more scope for his exceptional powers. We may mention that neither Joseph Guarnerius *filius* Andreæ, Joseph Guarnerius del Gesù, nor Carlo Bergonzi appears to have made a single viola. David Tecchler of Rome, the maker of so many fine violoncellos, gives a little side information which is of interest here, when he records on the margin of his label, dated 1730, "*La terza viola.*" Thus in upwards of forty years of his working life he had made only three violas.

It is our loss, we believe, that the influences of the time were not in sympathy with the viola. With a greater incentive Stradivari would have risen to the occasion, and we can imagine the result—a viola constructed on Maggini lines, about $16\frac{3}{4}$ inches in length of body, a combination of Brescian principles and his own ideas, with a tone which, while retaining Gasparo quality and sufficient sonority, would have had in addition some of that woody brilliancy so characteristic of the instruments of Stradivari.

CHAPTER IV.

Stradivari's Violoncellos.

HE excellence of Stradivari's violoncellos is even more remarkable than that of his other productions; in fact, we can unhesitatingly say that his finest examples stand without rivals. His genius and versatility are never more clearly shown than by the several forms which he created and worked out, ever seeking to evolve an instrument which should successfully meet the changing conditions of the times. The process of evolution was perhaps slow, but a perfect form was at length attained. He fixed once and for all the standard proportions and dimensions of the violoncello. Posterity has not only admitted the correctness of his judgment, but re-echoes his triumph, as the further we experiment the more clearly do we perceive the futility of deviating from it in any respect.

It cannot be claimed for Stradivari that he created the more practical dimensions of the violoncello; on the contrary, he seems to have taken up the modified instrument where his fellow-workers left it. In the volume on Maggini * published by us we have recorded how remarkable was the judgment of that maker regarding instruments of the

---

* "Gio. Paolo Maggini—His Life and Work," by Lady Huggins. 1892.

violoncello form ; although now, armed with the additional information which we have acquired, we hesitate to re-affirm that such instruments as he made were not really intended for five-string viols.   Be this so or not, we are on absolutely safe ground in stating that true violoncellos were being made by Andrea Amati and his two sons, Antonius and Hieronymus, during the latter part of Maggini's life.   Of the time previous to this period we cannot speak with certainty, but towards the close of the sixteenth century, and even earlier, there were no doubt four-string viols.

The Amati family evidently differed widely from Maggini in their views regarding dimensions, making, we believe, their violoncellos, without exception, of large size ; and we account for this by the fact that the Church was the greatest patron of the makers   To facilitate their use during processions in the churches, a small hole was made in the centre of the back near the top to permit the insertion of a peg.   A cord or chain attached to this peg and passing round the shoulders of the performer allowed him to play upon the instrument thus suspended.   It is instructive to add that this peg-hole has been introduced in order to Italianise in appearance violoncellos—which are certainly not Italian.   Reference to the compositions of the period of Andrea Amati and his two sons (1540-1630) conclusively shows that no solo music was written for the violoncello ; in fact, at the latter date, this instrument was but in its infancy, and the viol-da-gamba still held considerable sway.   It was used exclusively as a fundamental bass in the concerted music of the Church, or as an accompaniment to recitative instead of the viol-da-gamba.*   No players

---

* " The instrumental music is much better than I expected.   The organ and violin they are masters of, but the bass-viol they have not at all in

used the register beyond the second or third positions; in all probability they confined themselves entirely to the first, hence the now all-important question of the length of string (*i.e.* the stop) was of little consequence. Matters remained thus until towards the close of the career of Nicolò Amati (son of Hieronymus), who died in 1684.

That this member of the Amati family advanced the progress of violoncello construction is unquestionable: we find that as early as 1640 he was experimenting with the interior thicknesses, and making in general an instrument of stronger build. The dimensions, however, remained similar to those in use by his ancestors—invariably large.

Wasielewski * states that among the earliest known Italian players who endeavoured to cultivate the violoncello as a solo instrument were Gabriel, born about 1640; Ariosti, 1690; Bononcini, 1672; and Francischello, 1692. Now this entirely coincides with our knowledge on the subject. A race of players was springing up which grasped the capabilities of the violoncello and sought to demonstrate its merits. The time was, then, ripe for the makers to aid them by devising an instrument which would facilitate this new development. The excessive length of the stop and the otherwise cumbrous proportions, as well as the slower emission of the tone of the hitherto accepted instrument, must have forcibly struck the players directly they attempted to execute rapid passages. They accordingly talked with the makers of the period, amongst

---

use, and to supply its place they have the bass violin with four strings, and use it as we do the bass viol."—Extract from a letter addressed by Thomas Hill to his brother Abraham, written from Lucca (Italy) and dated October 1st, 1657. See "Familiar Letters of Abraham Hill." London, 1767.

* Wasielewski, "Das Violoncell und seine Geschichte," Leipzig, 1889.

others with Andrea Guarneri, Francesco Ruger, and Giovanni Battista Rogeri, all pupils of Nicolò Amati, and each one devised and made violoncellos of smaller dimensions. Of those of Andrea Guarneri we can only speak with considerable reserve; he appears to have made but few, as we have met with only five or six authentic examples, one only of these having originally been of smaller proportions than hitherto customary, the others reduced in size since. His form reminds us somewhat of that of Maggini—breadth disproportionate to length.

Francesco Ruger, the first of this Cremonese family of makers, and whose violoncellos were evidently in repute, judging by the number he made, seems in the majority of cases to have followed the Amati principles and constructed instruments of large size ; still, here and there, we see one of smaller dimensions : that played by the well-known violoncellist, W. E. Whitehouse, is an excellent example. Giovanni Battista and Pietro Giacomo Rogeri, who both worked at Brescia, were evidently associated : the strong similarity in form, model, proportions, and general design of their instruments shows this. They seem to have at once hit upon an admirable form of violoncello of excellent dimensions, which, although lacking the perfect symmetry of Stradivari's, is of high merit. A fine and characteristic example of the first-named maker is that owned by Colonel Wright, and the same may be said of the instrument by Pietro Giacomo, for many years used by Signor Piatti as his solo 'cello.* Curiously enough, neither maker seems to have varied much from the one form ; at any rate, we have never seen a specimen by them of larger dimensions.

* Now in the possession of Miss Muriel Handley.

We thus find that the change from the earliest type of true violoncello as made about 1600 to that of smaller form, which originated between 1660 and 1700, took close upon a century to effect. The struggle for supremacy between viol and violoncello was both long and keen, and it was only when makers built a violoncello upon lines more nearly approaching those of the viol-da-gamba in proportions, that this latter instrument received the final blow, to the effects of which it slowly succumbed.

It must not be assumed that when violoncellos of diminished size were in the hands of players, the making of those of large form was immediately discontinued. Quite the contrary appears to have been the case. The Church, slow to move—and her influence in the matter was paramount—apparently still preferred the larger size, and thereby materially retarded the change. Not until towards the time of Stradivari's death—*i.e.*, in the thirties of the eighteenth century and later—do we find the makers finally abandoning the old traditions as regards dimensions.

That Stradivari was not idle during this period of transition in violoncello-making, we may take for granted ; he could not but have seen the innovations of his fellow-workers, heard the reasons for and against, and, probably, mentally summed up the subject. Still, he does not seem to have actively moved in the matter for many years : in fact, previous to 1680 we know of no violoncello made by him. We do not of course assert that none exists, but only place on record that we have not yet seen or heard of an example made at an earlier date.

We have already stated how closely we believe Stradivari's early working life was interwoven with that of his master, who died in 1684, and that it is consequently most probable that part of his time was taken up in other ways than in

instrument-making.*   The earliest dated Stradivari instrument
of the violoncello family known to us is one made in 1667,
the master's twenty-third year and the year of his marriage.
It is a most interesting example, although it has been considerably altered ; and we are able to recognise that the
master tried to combine the principal features of both viol
and violoncello, for whilst retaining the flat viol back canting
off at the top, he adopted the violoncello outline, form of
sound-holes, and dimensions.   We believe this instrument
was strung as a viol, but cannot speak with certainty, as
the original head has vanished.   We are also acquainted
with a viol-da-gamba, or, to speak correctly, with the
material which once formed one.   The often over-ingenious
hand of the modern maker has employed itself in adding
fresh wood in all directions, with a view to transforming
the instrument into a violoncello ; and armorial bearings
have even been painted on it in order to hide the joints
of the new wood.†   Brought to France from Italy by
Tarisio in its original state, it may possibly be the viol
made by Stradivari in 1684 for the Contessina Cristina
Visconti, the patterns of which are preserved in the Dalla
Valle Collection.   With what profound interest would we
not have gazed on these two intruments, which before falling
into the hands of vandals, were unique specimens of the
illustrious master's work—the former especially—forming a
link between viol and violoncello!   We have much evidence
to show that in the years following 1680 Stradivari turned
his attention more frequently to the construction of violoncellos.
His fame was fast growing, and we learn from the Arisi

---

* Chapter II.

† This instrument is now in the possession of an American lady, who
seriously assured us of her intention of going to Italy in order to trace the
origin of the coat-of-arms it bears.

manuscripts that he was receiving orders for sets of instruments and for single violoncellos destined for the highest in
the land: for Kings, Ducal Princes and other illustrious
patrons. We estimate that between 1680 and 1700 Stradivari
made at least thirty violoncellos: twenty-five are known to
us; and how instructive to note that all—without exception—
were made of large size! Was it that the instrument of
smaller proportions found as yet little favour with the
majority of players? or was it that, assuming they were only
to be used in churches and in the chapels attached to the
palaces of the nobles, the larger-sized 'cellos were preferred?
It may be Stradivari himself still clung to the Amati traditions
in this respect, although we cannot help believing that the
master would have constructed instruments of smaller
dimensions had he received orders for them.

The violoncellos of David Tecchler furnish us with an
instance of this long-prevailing preference for the larger-
sized instruments. He was without serious rival as a maker
in Rome during half a century (he worked from 1690 to
1747), and was no doubt the privileged maker to the churches
of the " Eternal City." Of his violoncellos we have seen
many—at least fifty—and of that number only four were of
small proportions.

The deplorable practice of altering the dates of the
labels inserted by Stradivari *—and the pre-1700 violoncellos
have been especially tampered with—renders it impossible
for us to point with certainty to the earliest example hitherto
met with. We can approximately fix the date of birth of
a given specimen, but are unable to do so with absolute
precision. 1684 is the first authentic date known to us:
it is that of the instrument in the possession of the well-

---

* See Chapter IX., p. 216.

known player, Leo Stern.   It was brought to England at
the beginning of last century by General Kyd, who entrusted
it to the hands of Dodd, one of the best makers of that period,
in order to have the size slightly reduced—which operation
was judiciously carried out.   Its proportions are still of the
largest ; and the presence of holes in the head for a fifth peg
clearly indicates the interesting fact that it was originally
strung with five strings.   In character the work is decidedly
heavy ; the edges, corners and head being particularly massive.
The wood of back and sides cut on the slab, and the varnish
of light yellow colour, are thoroughly characteristic of the
master at this period.   We do not propose to criticise this
instrument in detail as a representative pre-1700 example,
since, though built in every respect on the same lines as a
violoncello, it was clearly intended for a bass-viol of extra large
proportions, and, as far as we know, is unique of its kind.

   The firm grasp of their craft possessed by the great
Italian makers is more clearly brought home to us by the
study of their violoncellos, and nothing is more remarkable
than the fidelity with which they transferred to violoncello
form and proportions all the salient features seen in their
violins.   Each maker apparently sketched out his ideas in
the form of the smaller instrument, cultivating in nearly every
case a style peculiarly his own ; then reproduced the same on
a larger scale for his violoncellos, modifying in character
neither outline, model, sound-holes, nor head.   It was thus
the Amatis worked, and Stradivari continued on the same
lines.   In the chapter on violins we have shown how the
master, as time passed on, severed himself from the Amati
form and teaching, and asserted his own distinctive style; and
this severance is similarly illustrated by his pre-1700 violoncellos.   The most perfect and representative specimen of the
work of this epoch is the admirable instrument made in 1690

for Cosimo de Medici, now in the Musical Institute at Florence. The "Aylesford" bass, dated 1696, brought to England by Giardini about 1780 and sold to Lord Aylesford, is also a characteristic example. Both these instruments are of quite exceptional interest, for we see them as left by the maker as regards form and dimensions. We know of but one other in a similar state—the violoncello dated 1697 owned by the Marquis de Piccolellis, which was originally in the Castelbarco Collection. The remaining examples known to us have all been reduced in size—in some cases satisfactorily and judiciously, in others not so. The "Archinto" bass, dated 1689, now owned by the well-known Parisian 'cellist, M. Jules Delsart,* and the one dated 1691, for some years the solo instrument of M. Hollman, are both excellent examples ; the former being especially handsome in wood and in relatively fine preservation. In form and character Stradivari violon- cellos—e.g., the "Tuscan" and the "Aylesford"—differ from those of the Amatis, as do his violins. The general proportions were approximately the same, but in outline we find Stradivari's work more symmetrical, the elongated and less curved bout sharing more equally in the proportions of the whole. Edge, corners, purfling, sound-holes, and head all are of bolder treatment, and aid in imparting that masculine appearance which is so admirably in keeping with the large size. The modelling of both back and belly is full and well-arched, though not too high at centre, and is thus the better suited to the light interior thicknesses to which the instruments were worked by the master. Stradivari doubtless recognised, especially in the case of the belly, the weakness which would result had he, notwithstanding the light thickness, allowed

---

* We have to record with regret the death of M. Delsart since the above lines were written.

the model to scoop to any extent around the edge. The stronger curve of the arch obviously counteracted any such tendency. The cutting of the sound-holes, and the extreme accuracy with which the scrolls are carved at this period— not to mention the beauty of their lines—are beyond criticism : they stand unsurpassed, we may say unequalled, by any after effort of the master. The head of the " Aylesford " violoncello is especially remarkable.

We note that in the selection of his material for the violoncellos—as for the violins of these years—Stradivari was more partial to maple cut the slab way of the grain. That of the " Archinto " and " Tuscan " instruments is the exception, and in both cases very choice wood was used, cut the right way of the grain. He also in several instances used for the back, sides, and head, poplar-tree wood or a similar species, such as lime-tree wood—a feature much more frequently met with in the violoncellos of his contemporaries, notably in those of Francesco Ruger. The Amatis seldom used it, though Andrea Guarneri and his son Joseph did sometimes ; whereas Giovanni Grancino, the Testores, and their followers of the Milanese School rarely dispensed with it.

The pine used by Stradivari was with but rare exceptions of good quality, and generally of fine grain, though we have seen bellies of remarkably open and even grain made at this period. Like other makers, Stradivari at times (although less frequently) formed the bellies of several pieces of pine glued together—generally four. This was done in order to obtain the necessary size in pieces free from serious blemish. In the same way we see wings added at the bottom curves of the back, more especially in the large-sized basses. Stradivari continued thus without change until close upon 1700, constructing his violoncellos—we believe, without exception— upon the one form of large proportions. 1690 and the years immediately ensuing constituted a period of transition as regards his violins ; but in the case of his violoncellos the master remained passive, apparently awaiting the moment when he would be called upon to direct all his energy and fertility of invention to devising an instrument answering more fully to the requirements of the new school of players. The grandeur of Stradivari's violoncellos of this period is the more strongly brought home to us if we place an example such as the "Tuscan" bass beside those of similar proportions made by contemporary workers. We then see how he had outstripped all his fellow-craftsmen by the nobility of his conceptions ; we note with what freedom, tempered by care, he treated even the smallest detail, and the consummate, unerring dexterity with which he must have handled his tools. His brother-workers could not have failed to be impressed by such skill, and must have whispered among themselves that a giant had arisen to whom all must sooner or later bow !

We are disposed to question whether the tonal merits of the type of violoncello which we are here concerned with, be it the work of Stradivari, his predecessors or his contemporaries, receive fitting recognition from many players of to-day : we are bound to recognise the growing tendency to subordinate, or even sacrifice entirely, beauty of quality to power of tone—a tendency perhaps even more apparent in relation to the violoncello than to the violin.

The *A* or first string being the more easily rendered telling and effective, the habit has been acquired of treating the violoncello for solo purposes as an instrument of one, or at most two strings—the *C* or fourth string occasionally receiving some attention. Makers are therefore obliged, often against their better judgment, to seek to adjust fine violoncellos in such a manner that the tone of the *A* string shall be, above all, aggressive and trumpet-like, that of the

C string loud and metallic to the utmost degree. The two middle strings, the *D* and *G*, are neglected: as long as they speak freely, their quality and volume of tone are ignored.

Now, as the instruments of which we are speaking do not lend themselves readily enough to the development of such a tone, they are passed by as interesting, yet hardly useful survivals of the past. Such beauty and distinction of tone as is revealed to us in the middle strings of the violoncello by an adequate artistic interpretation of the subject given to the instrument by Beethoven in the opening of the first Rasoumowsky Quartet in F, and which depends for its true effect upon the peculiar richness and singing quality of the instrument, cannot be fully appreciated by those players who seek only to produce that kind of *timbre* of which we have been speaking. The broad appealing quality of the *A* string, the mellow weighty tone of the *D* and *G*, and the deep organ-like notes of the *C*, form a whole pre-eminently fitted for the interpretation of chamber music.

In 1699 we meet for the first time with a change of form, the earliest indication we have yet succeeded in tracing; and of the following year—1700—we have two representative examples made from the same design; these are, moreover, the only violoncellos known to us of that date. The 1699 bass has suffered severely; once it was a fine instrument; those of the year 1700 are both good examples;—the finer of the two, known as the "Cristiani," * formerly belonged to that gifted lady-player to whom Mendelssohn dedicated his "Romance sans paroles" (for violoncello). The other is the property of the Spanish Court, and is preserved in the Chapel of the Royal Palace

---

* Mdlle. Cristiani, born 1827, died 1853.

in Madrid, where it is played upon by Señor Victor de Mirecki, an excellent artiste, who, after repeated solicitations, prevailed upon the Court authorities to allow the instrument to be sent to Paris in 1889 for sorely needed restoration. We have been unsuccessful in obtaining any information concerning the early history of this violoncello; it does not figure among the Court instruments recorded by Ascensio in his account-book as having been entrusted to him for necessary repairs, as the others were, between the years 1770 and 1790 (approximately).* The dimensions of these two instruments, which are practically the same (see Appendix), are of special interest, as they enable us to trace Stradivari's steps in developing the smaller-size 'cello : we see that the whole has been diminished, the length of string (the stop) is shortened by about three-quarters of an inch. The consistency of the outline is admirably preserved, the curves of the middle bouts being shortened in the same proportion as those of the top and bottom. The model is flat and in great measure reminds one of that of the violins of the period. The beauty of the maple wood of both these specimens as well as that of the famous " Servais " bass of the following year (1701) is remarkable ; the back, sides, and head are marked by a strong and broad curl ; in fact, nothing could be finer, and we know of no previously or subsequently dated examples which can vie with them in this respect. The rich plum-red colour of the varnish covering the " Cristiani " is equally unique ; that of the Spanish and " Servais " basses, of a more orange-brown tint, though fine, is less remarkable.

At the death of Mdlle. Cristiani (which took place in 1853 at Tobolsk, in Siberia, during a professional tour in

---

* See Chapter II., p. 75.

Russia) her violoncello was brought back to Paris, and a few years later became the property of M. Benazet, an amateur of Baden-Baden. In 1884, through the medium of Gand and Bernardel, of Paris, it passed into the hands of Herr Hugo Becker, the well-known player, from whom we purchased it in 1894. It now belongs to Mr. Charles Oldham.

The "Servais" violoncello, as far as we know, stands alone. It is not only the sole example of the year 1701, but we believe it to be the only example which combines the grandeur of the pre-1700 instrument with the more masculine build which we could wish to have met with in the work of the master's earlier years. In wood, varnish, and general aspect it is the brother of the Spanish bass, but in form and dimensions it differs considerably from it— in fact, it takes us back to those of the "Tuscan" and "Aylesford" basses ; but although the measurements of its outline are practically identical with those of the two instruments just cited (see Appendix), in other respects it is essentially different, notably so in the model and in the height of the sides, which latter are deeper than those of any previously made 'cello, nor did Stradivari ever subsequently exceed this limit. This increased height of sides necessitated a less curved model, otherwise the tone would have been of a decidedly cavernous character—a fact which the maker doubtless recognised. The model rises in a very gradual curve from the edge to the highest point at centre, both back and belly being alike in this respect ; the edges, although of robust substance, are not too heavy ; the purfling is neat, and helps to impart a lighter appearance to the form. The sound-holes call for no special mention : that they are finely cut goes without saying. The outline of the head has a squarer aspect than those of earlier years; the bevel is more heavily treated, and this greatly influences its character. Looked at as a whole, its vigorous cut and proportions harmonise admirably with the body it adorns. The interior construction also shows that Stradivari sought to produce a different tone-result. He had hitherto considerably varied in that all-important point, the thickness —now making back and belly of stouter proportions, now thinner; but he appears to have at last decided that the increased substance was more favourable for producing a brighter and more strident tone. After careful examination, and comparison with instruments of later date, we find that the master never again varied his thicknesses to any important extent. The opportunity of thus minutely examining the "Servais" bass was afforded us in 1888, when it was in our hands for the purpose of restoration. The history of this violoncello prior to the early part of last century is unknown. It belonged to a well-known Parisian amateur, M. Raoul (whence he obtained it we know not), at whose death, about 1845, it passed into the hands of Vuillaume. Servais had only to see it to fall in love with it, as it was peculiarly suited to himself (he was a man of large frame and tall stature); but, alas! it was one thing to covet and quite another to possess, as at that time even the very moderate price fixed by Vuillaume (12,000 francs) was quite beyond the artist's reach. Thanks, however, to the generosity of a Russian admirer, the Princess Youssopow, the requisite sum was forthcoming, and Servais became owner of the bass. At his death, in 1866, the Stradivari passed to his son Joseph, also an eminent violoncellist, who died comparatively young in 1885. The family then sold it to M. Auguste Coûteaux, who presented it to his son Georges, then a student at the Brussels Conservatoire of Music. We understand that the price paid

for it by M. Coûteaux was 60,000 francs. Family troubles
brought the instrument once more into the market in 1893,
when it came into our hands ; and two years later we disposed
of it to the Prince Pierre de Caraman-Chimay, an excellent
amateur, and a friend and pupil of the late Joseph Servais.
We have already observed that this violoncello was
peculiarly suited to the elder Servais. Difficult to manage
on account of its size, it required a man of his build and
masterful power to bring out its admirable qualities. We
learn from M. Van der Heyden, an intimate friend of the
artiste, that Servais did not master it without a struggle.
He communicated his disappointment to Vuillaume, who
characteristically replied, "Qu'un artiste de sa trempe devait
s'identifier avec son instrument et le dompter ; en un mot,
le faire valoir," and it cannot be gainsaid that he did so.
Servais was an ideal bravura player, and the power of tone
which he produced from the third and fourth strings of
his famous bass was remarked by all who heard him. We
may add that Servais, after repeated experiments, found
that an exceptionally narrow bridge tended to add brightness
to the tone—a feature which is always, to some extent,
lacking in large-sized instruments.

The years between 1701 and 1707 are blank as far as
violoncellos are concerned, not a single specimen being known
to us. It may be that orders for violins more particularly
monopolised the master's attention during this period, or
possibly the price demanded for his violoncellos was considerably higher than that accepted by his contemporaries,
several of whom have left a greater proportionate number of
basses—notably Gofriller, Grancino, and Tecchler ; or again,
it may be that he saw fit to pause and reflect before entering
in the near future upon that new path of violoncello construction which was to prove of such importance. According

to our present knowledge, the " Servais " is the latest dated existing violoncello built upon the early lines ; if there be others of later date, they are still unknown to the world. We are certainly acquainted with several instruments of pre-1700 type having labels which bear a later date ; but, quite irrespective of the pronounced early character of these instruments, the labels themselves fail to bear our scrutiny : the figures either clearly show signs of having been tampered with, or the whole inscription proves to be a forgery. We are therefore disposed to assume that the day was at last at hand when the master was to break with past traditions and give to the world that incomparable form of violoncello which time has taught us to accept as the *ne plus ultra* of perfection. 1707 is the earliest date we have hitherto met with in an example of this form, and that notwithstanding our diligent research throughout Europe. Examination of Stradivari's forms and drawings throws no light upon this point. On a pattern which he drew for the sound-holes of one of these instruments he says : " Per far gli occhi della forma B. piccola dal Violoncello," but unfortunately gives no date. We do learn, however, from an inscription on the pattern of a violoncello head, that it was destined for the instrument made for the Contessa Cristina Visconti in 1707. A similar pattern is marked " Violoncello da Venezia," but bears no date. On comparison we find that both these outlines were of heads of large size—hence destined for bodies of similar proportions ; consequently the instrument made for the Contessa Visconti was not of the " forma B. piccola." We may mention that neither this violoncello nor that mentioned by Arisi under date 1702 as having been ordered by the Marquis Toralba and sent as a present to the Duke of Alba, has hitherto answered to the roll-call.

We are not justified in absolutely asserting that Stradivari

first gave to us his perfected violoncello in the year 1707 ;
but we believe this was the case, having examined all the
known specimens.   Possibly the master was only now carrying
out an early conception, strengthened by the fruit of ripened
experience, and was imbued with the belief that the right
moment had arrived for its production.   It is important to
bear in mind that the development of the violoncello as a
solo instrument had only just begun, consequently the demand
for that of smaller size was still a limited one, although
increasing year by year.   If we give credence to the following
statement of our ancestor, Lockey Hill, Stradivari as early
as 1690 made an instrument of the smaller pattern.   He
left on record that Frederick William, King of Prussia, who
played the violoncello and was a pupil of Duport *aîné*, consigned for sale to Betts, of the Royal Exchange, in the year
1806 a Stradivari violoncello.   That it was an instrument of
the first rank is evidenced by the fact that Betts requested
Lockey Hill to take the necessary patterns and make some
copies of it.   These patterns are still in our possession, and
the outline bears an inscription in Lockey Hill's writing :
" King of Prussia's Stradivarius, 1690." It seems that the
price asked—£500—was a prohibitive one, and Betts, failing
to find a customer, returned the instrument to its Royal
owner.   Whether or not Lockey Hill correctly recorded the
date is the pith of the whole matter.   Such an instrument,
so dated, is quite opposed to our experience.   We may add
that all efforts on our part to trace its present whereabouts
have hitherto proved unavailing.   We fear that it may have
been destroyed during the disastrous years Prussia was then
passing through.   The supreme merit of violoncellos of this
type, irrespective of their beauty of form, their purity of
style, and finished workmanship, consists in the exactitude
of proportions, which in their *ensemble* produce a tone

result but rarely—we may perhaps say never—found in any other instruments of the many and various Italian makers. They stand alone in representing the exact dimensions necessary for the production of a standard of tone which combines the maximum of power with the utmost refinement of quality, leaving nothing to be desired: bright, full and crisp, yet free from any suspicion of either nasal or metallic tendency. No authority can speak on the subject of their tone with more weighty knowledge than Piatti, who, during a long career, possessed many fine violoncellos—more, perhaps, than any other artiste. He says: "I have at times become enamoured at the sight of a fine instrument, have been impressed by its beauty, and when I have become its owner I have tried to believe that its tone equalled that of my Stradivari. Time, however, has invariably seen me return to my old friend with a feeling of satisfaction difficult to explain. True, the differences of tone between my Stradivari and other recognised fine instruments are subtle, but I can only say that I obtain from the former a depth and nobility of tone which ever affords me a sense of contentment; in fact, there is a something unattainable elsewhere."

The foremost players of the early part of the last century—amongst others, Brunetti, Boccherini, Baudiot, Crosdill, Duport, Mara, Romberg, and Vaslin—appear to have been convinced of this superiority, and they consequently sought to obtain, if possible, and to play upon Stradivari instruments of this form. Romberg writes in his "Method for the Violoncello," published in 1840: "The instrument upon which I play is an Antonio Stradivari, dated 1711, a small pattern. By the expression 'small pattern' is not meant that it is below the proper size, but it only signifies that Stradivari also made instruments of a larger size, which instruments are too large for the modern style of playing."

Whether or not Stradivari himself recognised the real superiority of these instruments over those of the past is highly problematical ; we think he did not. They were simply the outcome of altered conditions of playing, and were doubtless not intended to fulfil the same duties as the true "Church bass." On the other hand, the master must have perceived that he had struck out an eminently successful form ; he must have been warmly complimented by his patrons, otherwise it would be difficult to account for his so consistently keeping to this one form, and to it alone, until the closing years of his life ; in fact, we know of no violoncello of other type, bearing its original label, dated between the years 1707 and 1730. The exact number of these instruments which we can vouch for is twenty, but we cannot, of course, say that our total will never be increased—we hope the contrary ; still, as we have diligently sought far and wide, we fear but few remain unaccounted for. Examination and comparison of these violoncellos show that the size of the outline varies but slightly. The model Stradivari raised or lowered—often influenced, no doubt, by the thickness of the material of back and belly—as also the height of the sides ; but, as in the case of his violins, we fail to discover any fixed idea or rule which guided him in deciding the relative proportions. Hence, at times, we find the lower sides and flat model together, and *vice versâ*, whereas a different combination would have been preferable. One is impressed by the general closeness of build, and the absence throughout of any superfluous wood ; the interior blocks and linings are, for instance, of the smallest dimensions compatible with strength ; the wood of the sides is planed as thin as possible, then, as a precaution against breakage, or more probably against the tendency to buckle, which is so often the case with the sides of Italian violoncellos, he

reinforced them with small strips of canvas. Modern
wiseacres have, of course, seen fit to remove these from
certain of the instruments. The " Duport" bass (illustrations
of which we give) is thoroughly representative of the above
remarks : the edges and the margin around the sides neat,
purfling light, head and sound-holes closely knit ; but perhaps
the most striking feature of all is the model, which is
exceptionally flat. Vuillaume accepted this instrument as
his ideal, and the great majority of his violoncellos are copies
of it. We cannot say they are absolutely faithful reproductions, as most often they lack that grace and lightness of
build so very characteristic of the original.

Of the twenty known examples, the majority are notable
instruments. Among the foremost stand (1) the " Duport,"
dated 1711, (2) the " Batta," 1714, and (3) the " Piatti," 1720.
The others are those in the possession of—

4. M. Fau, *ex* Castelbarco, falsely dated
    1697, approximately . . . 1707-10
5. The Countess of Stanlein, *ex.*
    Paganini and Merighi . . dated 1707
6. M. Markovitch, *ex* Delphino . . ,, 1709
7. Baron Rothschild, *ex* Gore-Booth . ,, 1710
8. Signor Pezze, *ex* Whitmore Isaac,
    Crosdill, and Mara . . . ,, 1711
9. M. Küchler, *ex* Romberg. . . ,, 1711
10. M. Goupillat, *ex* Davidoff and Wielhorsky ,, 1712
11. Mr. Franklin Singer, *ex* Adam . ,, 1713
12. M. Loeb, *ex* Marquis de Corberon . ,, 1717
13. M. Küchler, *ex* Blair-Oliphant . . ,, 1717
14. Mr. Holden, *ex* Bonamy-Dobree . ,, 1717
15. M. Hugo Becker, *ex* Duke of
    Marlborough . . . . ,, 1719

16. M. Haussmann, *ex* Fountaine .   . dated 1724
17. M. Löys, *ex* Gallay and Vaslin   .   ,,   1725
18. Mr. Brandt, *ex* Baudiot .   .   .   ,,   1725
19. King of Portugal, *ex* Chevillard   .   ,,   1726
20. M. Mendelssohn, *ex* Ladenburg   .   ,,   1736

The history, as far as it is known, of several of these
violoncellos is not without interest ; and how much more
interesting would it have been if their eighteenth-century
owners had thought of recording all that was to be learned
concerning them ! We cannot do better than give the
history of the " Duport" in the words of the late M. Gallay,
a distinguished amateur violoncellist, who was always deeply
interested in the subject of old instruments, and who obtained
this information from M. Poigné, of Besançon, a pupil of
Duport. He says : " This fine violoncello, the perfection
of form and work, was made by Stradivari to the order of
a doctor of Lyons on the return of the latter from a visit
to Italy. The price quoted by Stradivari was his usual one,
but in deference to the wishes of the doctor, who desired
an instrument of the highest order—in fact, something finer
than usual—the figure was doubled. In due course the bass
reached Lyons, and was doubtless worthily appreciated by
the doctor. At his death it was sent to Paris to be sold,
but submitted without result to the principal luthiers of the
period, who apparently did not recognise the pearl that was
offered to them. The owners finally decided to sell it by
public auction, but, the reserve limit not being reached, it
was withdrawn. Duport was present in the auction-room,
accompanied by two of his pupils (the Prince de Soubisse
and Prince Guémenée), and, deeply impressed by the superiority of the Stradivari over his own Amati violoncello,
he was more than once on the point of bidding himself,

The "Duport" Stradivari Violoncello, dated 1711.

In possession of BARON KNOOP.

The "Duport" Stradivari, dated 1711.

The "Duport" Stradivari, dated 1711.

ashamed as he was at the want of enthusiasm displayed by the two noblemen ; but alas! he lacked the necessary funds. Withdrawn from auction, the instrument was left on sale with Cousineau, the luthier, better known as a harp-maker, Rue Mazarin, Paris ; and, no acceptable offer being forthcoming, there it remained for a considerable time. The owners at last communicated with Duport, who, after a good deal of bargaining, was fortunate enough to become its possessor at the price of 2400 francs." That this fine bass aided Duport in gaining and upholding the reputation he acquired for purity and breadth of tone none can doubt. He jealously guarded his treasure until his death, which took place in 1819.

Vidal, in his work, " Les Instruments de Musique, etc.," relates the following amusing anecdote *à propos* of Duport and his Stradivari : " One day, when Duport was playing a solo at a private party at the Tuileries, Napoleon suddenly appeared in the drawing-room, booted and spurred. He listened with pleasure, and as soon as the piece was over he approached Duport, complimented him, and, snatching the bass from him with his usual vivacity, he asked, ' How the devil do you hold this, Monsieur Duport ?' and, sitting down, he squeezed the poor violoncello between his spurred boots. The unfortunate artiste, whom mingled respect and surprise had stricken dumb for a moment, could not master his fright at seeing his precious bass treated like a war-horse, and made a hurried step forward, uttering the word ' Sire !' in such a very pathetic tone that the instrument was immediately returned to him, and he was thus able to give his demonstration without again letting it out of his hands."

At Duport's death the Stradivari passed to his son, also a violoncellist, who, after holding an appointment as principal 'cellist at Lyons for some years, decided to relinquish the profession of music and to return to Paris, where he established himself as a pianoforte maker. For years he refused all offers for his father's violoncello, and it was only after experiencing business reverses that he finally decided to part with it. Vuillaume, apprised of the state of affairs, called upon Franchomme and earnestly exhorted him to make an effort to secure the bass, saying to him, "You are Duport's successor, and you alone should have his instrument." The price demanded by Duport junior was a high one, and we are assured by Madame André, Franchomme's daughter, that the purchase-money was only raised by strenuous efforts on the part of her father. The price paid was 22,000 francs, = £880 (Fétis says 25,000 francs), at that time—1842 or 1843—an unprecedented one. At Franchomme's death the instrument was left to his daughter, from whom we purchased it in 1892 on behalf of the present owner.

The "Stanlein" bass is to-day only a moderate example, as it bears signs of considerable and injudicious restoration. The most interesting fact known to us concerning this instrument is the episode of its purchase early in the last century by Signor Merighi, a violoncellist of Milan, and Piatti's master. We have it on the authority both of Piatti and of Signor Pezze, also a pupil of Merighi, that in 1822, while the last-named was passing through the streets of Milan, he perceived a working man carrying, among other things, a violoncello on a truck or barrow. Merighi at once accosted him, and ended by becoming the owner of the instrument, which was in a dilapidated state, for a sum equivalent to 4s.! Eventually, about 1834-35, Merighi disposed of the 'cello to Paganini, who sold it to J. B. Vuillaume, who resold it in 1854 to the late Count Stanlein.

The "Mara" bass, made in the same year as the "Duport," strongly resembles it in character, work, and proportions, the model being a shade higher. Mara, husband of the celebrated singer of that name, appears to have been a man of dissolute habits and violent temper, and unfortunately his violoncello seems to have suffered somewhat from his viciousness. Traces of alcoholic liquor having been upset and allowed to drip from the top to the bottom sides, removing the beautiful varnish on its downward course, are still discernible. Whence Mara obtained this fine instrument is unknown. He brought it to England in 1784, and between that year and 1802, when he departed from our shores, sold it to Crosdill, the English violoncellist. In 1808 it was resold through Betts to a Mr. William Champion for £150, and two years later—in 1810—it was put up to auction at Messrs. Phillips', and there bought at the increased price of two hundred guineas by General Boswell, afterwards Lord Macdonald. It subsequently passed into the hands of Lucas, the player, who parted with it to Mr. Whitmore Isaac, a Worcester banker, about 1860. At this gentleman's death it came into our possession, and was sold by us to its present owner in 1888.

The "Romberg" bass is not without interest, and in one feature we believe it to be unique : it has only a single line of black purfling instead of the usual three branches (two black and one white). Stradivari probably did this experimentally, and not finding it successful—it has too meagre an appearance—returned to surer ground. In another respect also it is exceptional for its period : the back and sides being of plain wood,—poplar. We have pointed out elsewhere that in his earlier days Stradivari used this material more frequently than in later years. We have met with it in ten or twelve violoncellos made prior to 1700, whereas we have seen it in but three later examples : the "Romberg," the one dated 1717 in possession of M. Loeb, and that owned by M. Fau.

The "Davidoff" bass of the year 1712 was presented to that distinguished artiste in 1870 by Count Wielhorsky, an equally distinguished amateur. Of the latter it is related to us by one of his friends that, in order to have lessons from Romberg, he lodged him in his Palace at St. Petersburg for two years. The Count obtained this instrument from Count Apraxin under the following conditions, we are told. He gave for it his Guarneri 'cello, 40,000 francs (equal to £1600), and the handsomest horse in his stables. This violoncello bears the strongest affinity to the instruments of the preceding year. Its dimensions, form, character of work, and especially the model, are a reproduction of those of the "Duport." The curl of the wood of the back is small, strong, and runs nearly straight,—that of the "Duport" and "Mara" instruments being placed on the slant ; the sides are cut on the slab, and, curiously enough, five of them match and the sixth does not, which illustrates the fact that Stradivari could not afford to be so particular in this respect as modern makers. The varnish is rich in texture and is of a warm orange-red colour. This fine example suffered considerably during Davidoff's ownership, and it bears marks not only of wear but also of careless usage. It is now the property of a Parisian amateur, M. Goupillat.

The violoncello of the year 1713 was formerly in the collection of Mr. John Adam, later in that of the Duc de Camposelice, at whose death it passed into our hands, and was sold to the present owner. This instrument is the so-called "Bass of Spain,' the romance of the purchase of which by Tarisio is narrated by Charles Reade in his "Letters to the *Pall Mall Gazette*" published in 1872. The story will also be found in Hart's book. Reade confused this Stradivari with the one to which he refers as being then exhibited by M. Gallay at the Exhibition of

Ancient Instruments held at South Kensington. Brought from Madrid by Tarisio, who, we are assured, journeyed the whole way from Paris on foot, it was purchased by Vuillaume, who sold it to a Russian nobleman. At the death of the latter it was disposed of, with other instruments, to the late Mr. David Laurie, who brought it to England in 1876.

The "Batta" violoncello of the next year—1714—is a pre-eminently fine example, and bears the same impress as the type of violin of the same date—the "Dolphin," for instance. Increased substance and breadth of edge and purfling, slightly fuller swell of model, broader cut f's, and head of heavier design, combined with wood of a fine broad curl, tend to give it a masculine appearance in contrast to the unobtrusive neatness of the "Duport." Both this instrument (the "Batta") and that of the year 1726 (*ex* Chevillard), were sent from Madrid in 1836 to M. Thibout, one of the most capable of the Parisian luthiers of that time ; but, although we have tried to find out by whom they were consigned to him, we have failed to do so. We have on various occasions gleaned from M. Batta details as to how the instrument came into his possession. He says : "Meeting casually with Servais one day, I was both interested and amused to hear him say that he was spending all his time at Thibout's. Said he, 'Thibout has a Stradivari bass with a tone such as I have never before heard in my life. Do come and see it.' In consenting to do so I went purely as a matter of curiosity, and with no intention whatsoever of becoming its owner. Furthermore, I was perfectly happy with my own instrument, which I had only recently purchased, and was also well aware that the price asked for a Stradivari even then placed it far beyond the reach of both Servais and myself. I may add that, struck by the earnestness of Servais, I did feel a certain desire to compare the violoncello with my Amati, and thus form my own conclusions. I saw it, played upon it, and was completely captivated : never had I experienced such a passionate longing to possess an instrument. In my despair I called upon a dear friend, M. Place, to whom I shall ever owe an eternal debt of gratitude, and poured out my feelings to him. He immediately went with me to Thibout's, came to terms with him, and then and there presented the Stradivari to me. The price paid to Thibout was 7500 francs, = £300, which even at that time was extremely reasonable." We may add that this Stradivari has been Batta's lifelong companion, sharing in, and largely contributing to, his successful career. Tempting offers were made for it, but without avail. The most remarkable was perhaps that of a Russian nobleman, who tendered Batta his signed cheque on Rothschilds, begging him to fill in the figures ! The late Duc de Camposelice offered 70,000 francs, and expressed his willingness to increase the offer, but Batta declined to entertain any proposals whatsoever. In 1893 circumstances induced him to alter his decision, and we purchased the instrument on behalf of the present owner, Baron Knoop.

The three instruments of the year 1717 and that of 1719 are interesting examples ; in fact, as is the case with the violins, all possess that individuality which the hand of genius invariably imparts to its works. That of M. Loeb, a meritorious Parisian artiste, belonged formerly to the Marquis de Corberon, and, as already stated, it is similar in wood to the "Romberg."

That of M. Küchler bears the strongest resemblance in wood, varnish and character to the "Batta," but, unfortunately, neither the belly nor the head is original. The third example was for some years the property of Mr. Bonamy Dobree, and was frequently played in public by M. Lasserre. The wood of the back of this instrument is cut on the slab, and it is the only one so treated known to us of this pattern.

The 1719 example is also unfortunately not as left by the maker; its proportions, wood and varnish, are admirable. At the beginning of the last century it belonged to the Duke of Marlborough, and is now the solo instrument of that distinguished artiste, Herr Hugo Becker.

The "Piatti" bass, dated 1720, is indeed an admirable example, by itself a worthy monument of the maker. It was brought from Cadiz in 1818 by Mr. A. Dowell,* of Dublin. Mr. Dowell was evidently an admirer of Stradivari instruments, and apparently never missed an opportunity of purchasing them, as, to our knowledge, he brought into the country at different times six violins besides the above-mentioned violoncello; all came from Spain. In 1821 he sold the bass to the Rev. Mr. Booth, an amateur of County Carlow, on the recommendation of Alday,† a Dublin musician, for three hundred guineas; and ten years later we find it for sale in London at Messrs. Cramer & Beale's, when Pigott, a well-known Dublin 'cellist of the time, came over and succeeded in carrying it off again to the Emerald Isle. He was already well acquainted with the instrument, and probably eagerly availed himself of the opportunity of becoming its owner.‡ We do not know the exact price

---

* Mr. Allen Dowell was a wine merchant and army contractor during the Peninsular War, and lived for many years at Jerez, in Spain. An accomplished musician, on his retirement to Dublin he took considerable interest in all musical matters.

† Paul Alday bore the reputation of being a good violinist; he also kept a music warehouse in Dublin.

‡ We are indebted for some of the details of the history of this violoncello to Sir Francis Cruise, of Dublin.

paid by Pigott. In 1844 Signor Piatti came to England for the first time, and in the course of that year also visited Ireland, While in Dublin he casually heard of this Stradivari, and, keenly interested as he was in fine instruments, called on Pigott in order to see it. He says: "Great was my astonishment to see such a noble example, and I must confess I greatly envied its owner, who, I may add, seemed to thoroughly appreciate his treasure." Pigott died in 1853, and his widow entrusted the 'cello, with a view to its sale, to Sir Robert Gore-Booth, a friend of her late husband, who brought it to London once more. Sir Robert Gore-Booth was an amateur 'cellist, and himself possessed a Stradivari dated 1710, now owned by Baron Nathaniel Rothschild. He was acquainted with Piatti, and accordingly requested him to come and see the instrument, quite unaware that it was already an old love! Signor Piatti says on this subject: " I was agreeably surprised on immediately recognising my former acquaintance, and great was my chagrin at not being in a position to purchase it; I simply had not the means to do so. Happening to call upon Maucotel, the violin-maker, I talked about the instrument, and strongly urged him to see it and try to buy it. He followed my advice, and after some bargaining became its owner at the very modest figure of £300. It remained only a short time in his hands, as at my suggestion he offered it for £350 to Colonel Oliver, who accepted it; this took place in 1853. A short time afterwards J. B. Vuillaume came to London, and hearing through Maucotel of the cello, called upon its owner and there and then made an offer of £800 for it, but the Colonel refused to sell. I was a frequent visitor at the house, and often played upon the Stradivari. I used to restring it; in fact, looked upon it as if it had been my own child! One day—a day graven in my memory—in 1867, I was as usual at the Colonel's house, and was playing on and comparing the three violoncellos which he possessed—an Antonio and Hieronymus Amati, a Montagnana and the Stradivari. The Colonel suddenly said to me: 'Which ·do you prefer?' Laughingly I answered: 'One cannot have a doubt—the Stradivari.' 'Take it home,' was his rejoinder. I felt so embarrassed by what appeared to me a sudden resolve that I politely declined, and in due time took my leave and went home. To my astonishment, though—and I must say it was of a joyful nature—the Stradivari followed in my wake." *

In point of merit the Piatti violoncello is unquestionably of first rank; it is also in a high state of preservation, which speaks well for its different owners. Could it but tell us, we should doubtless learn that, as is the case with the majority of Stradivari's instruments, it has from the first day of its completion been confided to appreciating hands. It is a remarkable production, especially when we consider that it is the work of the master in his seventy-sixth year, and the most careful scrutiny fails to detect any unmistakable sign of its being the handiwork of an old man. True, in a few minute details—such as the mitres of the purfling, the form of the corners, and the position and design of the *f*s, there is not the perfect symmetry, the grandeur of a few years back; still, none but the most practised eye could possibly note these subtle differences. Its construction is magnificent: model rising at once, yet not abruptly, from the purfling, sides of the highest dimensions and set close to the outer edge—*i.e.* the margin around is but slight. The original strips of canvas on the interior of the sides

---

* On the death of Piatti, July 1901, his daughter Countess Lochis sold the violoncello to Herr Robert von Mendelssohn.

here remain untouched.   The purfling is of medium thickness,
and the substance of the edges light ; the head is sharp and
finely cut, and it is, we believe, the only one in existence
which still retains its original neck.   The maple of the back
and head is plain in appearance, although of fine sonorous
quality, and cut from a tree which Stradivari had evidently
acquired about the year 1720, as we meet with it in the
majority of the violins of these years ; the curl small and
faint.   The sides contrast by their handsome broad markings ;
and we observe that Stradivari employed this particular cut
of wood for the sides of several violoncellos, quite irrespective
of the fact that it did not match the backs.   The pine of
the belly leaves little to be desired, being of even grain,
neither too close nor too coarse.   One might perhaps wish
that the several twists and shades—caused through knots
being in close proximity to the piece from which the belly
is made—were not there.   The varnish is of a rich deep
red colour, the texture softer than is usually met with in
1720 ; it reminds one much of the varnish of the " Rode "
violin.   As a whole it is above reproach, and the more one
contemplates such an instrument, the more one is struck by
the complete harmony which reigns throughout.   As the late
Lord Leighton very truly remarked to its owner, " It appeals
even to the uninitiated."

Four years now elapse before we come to the next
example : the " Hausmann " violoncello, dated 1724.   The
early history of this instrument is uncertain, but we believe
that it also came from Spain, and passed into the hands
of that distinguished admirer of the fine arts, Andrew
Fountaine.   It was purchased from him in 1839 by George
Hausmann, a violoncellist of some reputation, who spent the
greater part of his life in this country.   On retiring from
his musical career, however, he went to Hanover, where

he died, and his Stradivari then passed to his nephew, Robert Hausmann, the well-known artiste of to-day.

The "Vaslin" violoncello of the following year, 1725, belonged to one of the foremost Parisian players of the present time, M. Loÿs.* It was purchased from Signor Fenzi, a Florentine banker, in 1827 by M. Girard (a violinist of some repute—pupil of Habeneck, whom he succeeded as professor, and as director of the Société des Concerts)—on behalf of his friend and colleague, Vaslin, a violoncellist of no mean order. The price paid was, we believe, £160. It remained the trusty companion of Vaslin during many years, and not until 1869 could he be tempted to part with it. Grown old and fidgety—he was over eighty years of age—M. Vaslin conceived the notion that something was amiss with the neck of his 'cello—in fact, that it was ill-shapen! In vain did the best luthiers of the day, such as Gand, Victor Rambaux and others replace it : nothing could satisfy him, and after having it changed times without number, he finally took to scraping it down himself, though still without satisfaction. The late M. Gallay, to whom we are indebted for these interesting details, adds : " I followed the wanderings of this admirable instrument to the different luthiers with a sad heart, and watched during many years for my opportunity to secure it. At last, in 1869, an offer of £600, *plus* my own Stradivari, which I valued at £400, obtained it for me. In 1880 I parted with it in favour of the present owner. Need I add that ' je m'en suis separé les larmes aux yeux.' "

The "Baudiot" bass was for many years in the possession of the artiste of that name, at whose death it was sold by

* We regret to record the death of M. Loÿs, which occurred in September 1901.

his widow (in 1850) for ten thousand francs, = £400. It subsequently passed into the hands of the Marquis de Pluvié, a most enthusiastic amateur violoncellist, who bequeathed it to his daughter, the Comtesse de Kerdrel, from whom we purchased it in 1894. As regards build and proportions, this example is very similar to the "Piatti," although in general characteristics the hand of the old man is becoming more perceptible to the observer ; nor can we wonder when we remember that the master was now eighty-one ! The varnish is also more heavily laid on. The sides, which are of quite plain wood, in contrast to the back, which is comparatively handsome, are curiously marked by a pronounced vein or sap-mark running round them all ; to the casual observer this conveys the impression that they have been heightened.

The "Chevillard" bass, dated 1726, is the last of this series of noble works that we can vouch for. As already stated, this instrument was in 1836 in the hands of Thibout, who sold it to M. Mulzer, an amateur, and it was subsequently purchased by the above-named artiste. In 1878 the latter parted with it through the medium of Vuillaume to the late King of Portugal, Dom Luis, who was an amateur violoncellist. The price paid by the King was 20,000 francs = £800. In form and dimensions this instrument does not differ from the preceding ones, but we detect points in the work and style which betray the fact that Stradivari was beginning to be assisted in his labours—no doubt by his sons. The head is of large size, and although, as regards varnish, it matches the body well, we are of opinion that it is of pre-1700 period. The next few years preceding 1730 are, as far as we know, blanks in violoncello construction, but in that year we come to a distinct type of Stradivari instrument. Form and dimensions have undergone a change, and the character of the work is no longer that which we have followed during the preceding twenty years. The master's advanced age may account for both changes. He doubtless realised, however reluctantly, that at fourscore years and more his physical strength no longer permitted him to undertake the task of violoncello construction ; consequently, while still assiduously applying himself to the making of violins, he in great measure resigned the violoncello work to his two sons, who were possibly assisted by Carlo Bergonzi. That his mind still to a certain extent guided them is apparent, but that his share in their construction was a minor one is, we think, conclusively demonstrated by a scrutiny of the instruments themselves. The principles of construction remain the same; but we miss the old man's trembling hand and failing sight, which make themselves so evident in certain of the violins of these years. The reason why the proportions should have been diminished is more difficult of explanation : it may be that the younger men asserted themselves and sought to carry out their own ideas : in fact, they had yet to learn the real greatness of the master's principles. On the other hand, we must remember that sufficient time had not yet elapsed for the absolute superiority of Stradivari's perfected instruments to be fully established and recognised. Even close upon half a century later we still find makers of repute, such as J. B. Guadagnini and C. F. Landolfi, constructing their violoncellos without exception of undersized form, which proves that the matter was still a debatable one. Of this late form of Stradivari we are acquainted with five examples; one, though, has been enlarged to make it accord with the earlier type of instrument, and another has been cut down still smaller, but the remaining three are excellent and characteristic specimens. That in possession

of Mr Murray—for many years owned by Mr. F. Pawle—
was dated 1730;* that owned by Braga, of "Serenata"
fame, 1731, and lastly the instrument of M. De Munck,
which, although dated 1710, really belongs to this period.
The last-named violoncello formerly belonged to M. de
Barrau, a Parisian amateur, who possessed several fine
Stradivaris, notably one of Joachim's violins.   It   was
subsequently lent to Franchomme, and destined for his only
son, who gave great promise as a player, but who died
young. Through the medium of the firm of MM. Gand
and Bernardel Frères, it then passed to the present owner.

The very interesting example owned by Herr Robert
von Mendelssohn, dated 1736 (?), calls for special remark.
It is the only example known to us made later than 1730
which brings us back to the pre-1730 type, its proportions
being of the best ; and it thus reasserts the fact that this
form, although apparently in abeyance, was not discarded.
The wood, varnish, and general characteristics are very
similar to those of the " Pawle" violoncello.   The back and
sides are cut from fairly handsome maple of native growth—
the wood cut slightly on the slab ; the belly of fine and
vigorous pine ; the varnish of warm orange-red brown
colour, the texture a little inclined to be chippy—in fact,
that which we expect in these years.   As already stated, it
bears a label dated, we believe, 1736 (the last figure is
unfortunately completely obscured); but as the master says on
the margin " D'Anni 92," the year must have been 1735
or '36.   Whether this label—which, although tampered with,
is undoubtedly original—really belongs to this violoncello we
hesitate either to affirm or deny ; that the instrument is
the work of the 1730 period is unquestionable, and further-

---

* Altered by the late Mr. Laurie, to 1720.

more the best of them.   It was purchased from Vuillaume in 1840 by a distinguished German amateur, M. Lemire, for, we believe, 6000 francs, and Vuillaume stated that it came from Paganini.   It subsequently passed into the hands of a violoncellist, Krumbholz by name, at the still moderate price of 8000 marks—approximately £400.   He died about 1876, when the violoncello was purchased from his heirs by Mr. C. G. Meier for 10,000 marks, and brought to London. It afterwards passed into the possession of M. Ladenburg of Frankfort, who sold it in 1895 to its present owner.

We have now shown clearly that the progress from the violoncello of large proportions and light build existing in Stradivari's youth to the modern form was a gradual one, the instrument being perfected step by step during a period of fifty years.   All the pupils of the Amatis contributed more or less to that progress, but to Stradivari must be awarded the credit of having created the most perfect form of violon-cello in existence : in fact, it was he and he alone who raised it to that state beyond which no further progress has been made.   We cannot, of course, foretell what may happen in the future, but we may emphatically say that no light task awaits the man who seeks to make a real improvement on the violoncello as left to us by Stradivari.   In the case of violins the difference is less marked, as the Amatis, Maggini and others all made instruments more approaching his in point of merit.

CHAPTER V.

Stradivari's Aims in Relation to Tone.

O understand properly the aims of Stradivari in relation to tone, and justly to appreciate the successful results he obtained, it is necessary to review briefly what had been accomplished in this direction by his great predecessors — Gasparo, Maggini, and the Amati.

Very few of Gasparo's instruments, with the exception of his violas, are known to exist; but the number of fine and well-preserved violas with which we are acquainted clearly show, by their uniformity of dimension and design, and by their simplicity of construction and material, that Gasparo produced a thoroughly satisfactory instrument, in which tone—probably for the first time—was treated as of paramount importance.

With greater attention to style and finish, Gasparo's celebrated pupil, Maggini, developed his master's principles in his more numerous violins so far as it seems possible to have done, and in their type of tone they are still unrivalled. They possess remarkable sonority, rich, full, and telling in quality, with a touch of pathos in it suggesting a fine soprano voice rendering some moving song. Maggini, in the smaller dimensions of a few of his violins and his slightly smaller violas, shows that he was taking part in a new tonal development, that which the Amati violins typify.

Springing from the Brescian school—contemporaneous with it for about seventy years, and outlasting it by half a century—the work of the Amati, represented by four generations, shows curiously little variation in its aims. These four generations of the Amati held to the same principles : to make a violin of smaller dimensions than the Brescian— therefore easier to play on—in which the tone was less weighty and full, but easier to produce and of lighter and brighter character. They developed finish of work and beauty of appearance to the highest degree, although somewhat at the expense of breadth and virility of style. Amati instruments met with immediate and lasting success ; and so well did they supply the needs of the period that for sixty years—from Maggini's death in 1632 until Stradivari commenced in 1690 to produce his long and flat patterned violin—they held absolute sway ; in fact, as the " Long Strad " hardly met with immediate recognition, the Amati violins really retained their position until Stradivari permanently challenged it by the definite and continued production of his later types commencing from 1704.

As celebrated players have either lacked proficiency with the pen or the inclination to use it, we must, in the almost total absence of any written record of the opinions of the many great performers who used Stradivaris and owed much of their fame to the superb tone of their instruments, attempt to supply this regrettable deficiency. Dittersdorf and Spohr have left us their autobiographies, but in neither of these well-known works is there any description or analysis of violin tone, or any word of praise given to the skilled craftsmen who have left for the use of posterity such

marvellous instruments.   And in spite of the much-vaunted
advance in education during the nineteenth century, and the
supposed greater tolerance, interest, and breadth of view of
our latter-day players, we as yet do not know of any instance
where a celebrated player has taken the trouble to soberly
put down on paper his views of an instrument, as Mozart
did, even in the midst of a busy life, when he made the
acquaintance of Stein's pianofortes.*

The training of Stradivari brought him in the early
part of his career almost entirely under the influence of
Amati traditions and characteristics, and the tone of the
violins he made previous to 1684 cannot be distinguished
from that of the average medium-sized Amati.   There is the
same bright soprano, woody quality of perfect purity, that
freedom of response which is so helpful to the average
player, and a sufficiency of volume for all purposes other
than that of the rendering of solos under modern conditions,
i.e. with a large accompanying orchestra in a great hall.

After 1684 the production of a violin of slightly larger
dimensions, a tendency previously foreshadowed only in a
few rare instances, which should equal in fulness and power
of tone the large—so-called "grand pattern"—Nicolò Amati
violins, occupied Stradivari's attention more or less continuously until 1690.   The construction by Stradivari of
violins superior in power of tone to the average Amati was
in all probability brought about by the existence then, as
now, broadly speaking, of two distinct classes of players :
the small but very important minority of soloists, to whom a
tone with a considerable reserve of power was essential for
performing in large buildings ; and the large majority, who
chiefly used their instruments for chamber music, etc., in

---

* " Life of Mozart " : Otto Jahn, vol. i., p. 360.

ordinary dwelling-rooms. And it is indisputable that the greater number of players were, on account of its brightness and freeness of speech, perfectly satisfied with the tone of the average Amati and the violins inspired by it—such as the Amatisé and smaller types of Stradivari, and the violins of Stainer and his imitators—until the end of the eighteenth century.

But by 1690 Stradivari evidently felt that it was time to throw off Amati influences, and put into practice the original ideas which had been maturing in his mind. He commenced the production of the "Long Strad," a type of violin remarkably individual in tone and design, though both are reminiscent of Brescian principles. There is the fuller, deeper quality, and greater reserve of power, less ease of production, and, owing to the longer stop, an increased difficulty for the performer. It must have been an attempt on Stradivari's part to combine in one violin the remarkable sonority and fulness of the Maggini with the brightness and easier speaking qualities of the Amati.

An additional proof of Brescian influences at this period is afforded by the few violins of still larger dimensions than the "Long Strad," made by the great maker in 1691 and 1692, and which really approximate in size to the full-sized Maggini. The discontinuance of their production after 1692 shows that this design was not appreciated so much as the "Long Strad." The continued construction of the latter type until 1698–99 speaks convincingly as to Stradivari's faith in his own creative capacity and the discernment of some at least of his patrons.

As if to signalise the year still more, and offer further proof of the mastery he had attained to, 1690 saw the production by Stradivari of one of his masterpieces—"The Tuscan." Of all the violins made in the period previous to

1704, the " Tuscan" represents most perfectly the greatness
of his ability.   The bold, original style, perfect technical
workmanship, and splendid all-round tone, completely con-
vince one for the first time of his great skill and originality.
The tonal characteristics of this fine and perfectly preserved
violin are a woody and intensely brilliant quality, clear
and resonant as a bell—but without a trace of metallic
shrillness—and a sonority made remarkably telling by the
brilliancy of the quality.   We remember Joachim's first
acquaintance with the " Tuscan "— how, after playing a
few passages on it, he stopped and exclaimed, " Listen !
how it rings!" then, after again preluding, " How pure
and brilliant !   I was led to believe that the tone was
unsatisfactory.   How is it possible for anybody to have
come to such a conclusion ?   Surely they could not have tried
it."   On similar private occasions it has been our privilege
to listen also to Lady Hallé, Piatti, Sarasate, and other
distinguished players trying Stradivaris and fine specimens of
the other great makers ; and although so individual in the
tone they produce, we have always noted one characteristic
which they possessed in common.   In testing the volume
of tone, they would strive to gauge the resonance, *i.e.* the
carrying or travelling power of the sounds ; and they knew
by experience that, for violin tone to carry in a concert-
hall, it must be produced in such a way that the strings
continue to vibrate after the bow has left them, which implies
that the strings must not be attacked with such force by the
bow that the vibrations are checked or damped.   We digress
to state this, as we find such a large number of players
leaning in the other direction, and evidently believing that
the greater the force with which they apply the bow to the
strings the more carrying must be their tone.   Many instruments can be most forcibly attacked and thoroughly satisfy

The "Tuscan" Stradivari, dated 1690.

the ear of the player; but to the experienced listener in a concert-room the result is lamentable—sonority, brilliancy, quality, and charm all being found lacking.

After 1699 no more "Long Strads" were made; and although during the years from 1690 to 1699 Stradivari made other violins more or less in accordance with this and his earlier designs—and, indeed, continued to use his earlier designs until 1704—there is nothing in their tonal characteristics to call for individual mention. Many violins of choice quality, with sympathetic responsiveness and sufficient volume of tone, can be found among those made between 1698 and 1704; but because Stradivari, in his desire to preserve some of the beauty and grace of the Amati form, made the arching somewhat Amatisé, they are not appreciated so much as they deserve to be.

The existing prejudice against violins apparently high in the arching is the result of the defectively constructed and exaggerated copies of Amati and Stainer, so lacking in power, distinction of quality, and fulness of tone, which were made in large numbers by workers of inferior capacity during the whole of the eighteenth century. As with most reactions, the pendulum has swung too far in the opposite direction; so that now violins of the highest merit, even by Stradivari, are apt to be condemned because the arching is not, as gauged by the eye of the average player or critic, of a "certain apparent flatness"; an impartial trial of the tone is out of the question—the eye has already decided!

In judging such questions as the arching or dimensions of a violin, the untrained eye is quite untrustworthy, and even the highly trained eye may be deceived. The form of the arching, springing at once and gradually from the edge, or dipping slightly before the rise commences; whether the edge is broad, narrow, ridged, or flat; whether the wood is handsome or plain, broad or narrow in the figure ; and, lastly, the colour of the varnish,—all these features, separately or in combination, tend to mislead the eye. Our experience teaches us that if the important factors in violin construction—*i.e.* graduation of the thicknesses, structural stability, height of sides, and general dimensions—are designed to be in proper relation with the form of arching chosen, the quality of the tone may be slightly varied, but the volume not appreciably so.

The " Betts " violin, another masterpiece, made in 1704, is a notable and wonderfully preserved instrument, standing out from the violins made in the adjoining years in a like degree to the " Tuscan," although any affinity with the latter in either tone or design is only indirect. The distinguishing features of the tone are the mellow brilliancy of the quality and the facile articulation. From the year of the " Betts " it is immediately evident that Stradivari had arrived at the principles of tonal or acoustical construction for his violins which were to serve him until the end of his career.

Although he is always varying in a slight degree the dimensions, outline, form and amount of arching, etc., the salient properties of the tone remain the same ; and there are no such remarkable innovations as the previous years have shown. Evidently Stradivari had solved his life's problem, viz. how to produce the character of tone that would meet with the approval of his progressive and increasing patrons and be likely to assure a future for his violins. To sum up, the tone had greater brilliancy, fulness, and power than that of the average Amati violin ; and although not quite equal in these qualities to the Maggini instrument, except in the brilliancy, the Stradivari violin offered less difficulty in playing to the performer, owing to its smaller dimensions.

Stradivari must have realised that the merit of his productions justified him in working for futurity ; he no doubt thought that as the instruments of his great predecessors were justly famous and sought for then, so would his own be in time to come.

We recall a violin of special tonal merit made in 1709— Lady Hallé's, formerly Ernst's. And who that has heard Lady Hallé play will not bear this statement out ? The ripe, woody, and yet sparkling quality, its perfect responsiveness and equality on all the strings, and the ever-swelling sonority, all contribute to delight the cultivated listener. Sir William Huggins possesses the fellow to this violin, made in 1708.* No direct traces of Amati influence are apparent either externally or in the tone ; the different arching, absence of hollowing, lightness of the edges, all denote a structure in which tone has become the paramount consideration.

The year 1712 provides us with a superb example— the violin used by Viotti until his death, when it was sent over to Paris, and sold with other effects by public auction. It is of the maker's largest and boldest form, extremely handsome in appearance, the tone being remarkable for luscious maturity of quality and sympathetic responsiveness to the lightest possible touch of bow and finger. The noble beauty of its tone seems to us to echo the elevated style of Viotti's compositions and his broad and impassioned playing. Viotti, we must recollect, was the first supremely great violinist and composer for the violin to introduce and prove to his audiences the merits of Stradivari violins ; and we find his followers and admirers—Baillot, Habeneck, Kreutzer, Lafont, Rode, and many others—all using Stradivaris, and

---

* It is figured in Grove's " Dictionary of Music," art. ' Stradivari.'

permanently establishing their position in the world of music. Several other Stradivari violins are associated with Viotti's name, and existing evidence points to his having been in the habit of obtaining violins for friends and admirers ; but the pedigree attached to this violin is undoubtedly authentic, and its superior merit cannot be questioned, although we fear that many of the rising generation of soloists would not appreciate its tonal qualities ;—they would find it lacking in assertiveness.

That the sense of beauty or distinction of tone is to-day cultivated to the same extent as formerly is, we venture to think, more than doubtful. The custom in modern orchestral scoring of sacrificing the individuality of the instruments in order to obtain effects of greater sonority or of technical dexterity, and the abuse of the full-sized concert grand pianoforte in chamber music, seem to be largely destructive of the feeling for beauty of tone.

We fear it would be monotonous and a trial to our readers' patience if we continued to analyse in detail the tone of the many renowned Stradivaris dating from the period 1704 to 1720 that we are treating of. The great pair used by Joachim ; the " Alard ;" the " Dolphin ;" the " Cessol ;" the " Messie," and many others, possess the same salient tonal characteristics that we have already described ; and it is only their owners and others intimately acquainted with them who can discern the subtle individual traits which distinguish the tone of one from that of another.

Listeners to Dr. Joachim's performances on one or the other of his fine Stradivaris—even those well acquainted with his playing—must often have marvelled at the multitudinous shades of tone which he could produce from them. The massive fulness, the mellow and entrancing woodiness, the intense and thrilling passionateness, and the brilliant vivacity—

all these varieties of tone, and many others too indefinite and subtle for our powers of description, would he draw forth from these unique instruments, as the spirit of the music he was interpreting prompted.

That famous example the "Alard" exhibits all the necessary qualities to constitute it one of Stradivari's most remarkable achievements. The searcher after the ideal in tone —and there are many such—will look for the combination in one violin of absolute beauty of quality, great volume, and perfect articulation. These perfections exist in a large number of the great master's instruments, but never in the proportions to suit the hypercritical. The quality of one Stradivari does not please him, another is wanting in power, and a third does not respond easily enough to the performer. However, the "Alard" possesses these attributes as happily blended together as is possible in a violin made by mortal hands.

During the years from 1704 to 1720 we find occasional divergences in pattern, in some cases intentional no doubt, as it is improbable that all Stradivari's patrons required the greater sonority of tone. Many of the dilettanti, the Roman Catholic ecclesiastic, and the elderly aristocrat, preferred the dulcet, easy-speaking tone of the smaller Amati; and this must account for the smaller-sized "Strads" which we find occasionally interspersed between the larger types. Sometimes, too, the nature of the wood in the back, though handsome, has caused a lack of sonority; at other times the belly wood is plainly responsible for the want of brilliancy; or occasionally the varnish or model is to blame. But with these reservations, what a marvellous result do these sixteen years give us! Instrument after instrument of wonderful tone; the notable points of his predecessors' instruments happily welded into a whole of surpassing merit—sufficient of the noble breadth and sonority of the Maggini, combined with the brightness and woodiness of the Amati, and at the same time a flexibility of tone as a whole ; thus placing in the hands of the player of average capabilities an instrument as efficient for him as for a great and inspired performer.

During 1720–22 Stradivari, still indefatigable, was most actively occupied in making yet another type of violin, one differing in tone from anything he had yet produced—a type, although of medium dimensions, presenting, owing to the square appearance of the outline and sound-holes, flatness of the arching, etc., an unusually sturdy and robust appearance, though somewhat inelegant.   Special features of the tone are a vigorous and incisive power, less flexible and less easy of production, and a quality slightly metallic, suggestive of that of a fine Joseph Guarnerius del Gesù or of a Carlo Bergonzi, which undoubtedly this type of violin foreshadows. The " Blunt " of 1721, the " Brandt " and " De Chaponay " of 1722, are perfect representatives of this type ; while the " Rode," although of this date (1722), and partaking of the same characteristics—except in regard to its ornamentation— is distinguished by a mature fulness and spontaneity of utterance somewhat wanting in the former.   In the greater number of the violins made by Stradivari personally from these years until the end of his career, the same distinctive tonal properties predominate.

The vigorous and incisive sonority and pungent quality formed a most effective tone for the use of a *virtuoso* ; and evidently this is the cause of a number of them having been used by such celebrated players as Baillot, Hermann, Kreutzer, Kiesewetter, Wilhelmj, and Ysaÿe ; and naturally the constant practice and great skill of these players would enable them to overcome the want of ease of articulation

which we have mentioned. Sarasate's Stradivari, made in
1724, stands apart by itself in both tone and style; and all
who have listened to this delightful master of the art of
coaxing forth pure and beautiful tone must have been struck
by the ethereal and sparkling quality of his " Strad "—
never sonorous, yet always clear and distinct, even when
passages of the most extreme rapidity and delicacy are being
rendered on it. The instrument and the performer seem to
be merged in one individuality.

The dawn of the nineteenth century saw the introduction
of Stradivari's instruments to the musical world at large: the
end of it finds the use of them as universal as their number
will allow of. Other reasons may have contributed to their
more and more extended use, such as their superior state of
preservation and robust build in comparison with the larger
number of the earlier makers' instruments; but the chief
reason, we believe, is the extraordinary capacity in the tone
of Stradivari instruments for meeting the needs of all descriptions of players. Any listener who has heard a sufficient
number of them in public and private, and who has reflected
thereon, must have noticed their perfect fitness for use by
the public performer of average attainments—how in such
hands they give forth a woody, round, and brilliant tone, full
of charm and singing quality. And in listening to various
Stradivaris used by different capable players one feels how
flexible is their tone—flexible in the sense that it so easily
adapts itself to various modes of production, the method
and temperament of the artist influencing the instrument so
that it represents his individuality as much as it does its
own. The bright, full woodiness is the most distinctive
quality in Stradivari tone; and it is precisely this character
which makes it so helpful to the average performer, as it
causes the tone to blend well with the majority of voices

and instruments, making the Stradivari above all the instrument for chamber music, while at the same time it is equally effective in the concert-hall.

It is interesting to remember, in passing that while Stradivari was exerting all his skill in perfecting the instruments which enable us to enjoy the highest and most ideal form of chamber music yet achieved—the string quartet—Corelli, his great contemporary and countryman, was composing the famous works that led to its development, and determined the lines on which a well-nigh inexhaustible store of lovely chamber music has since been written.

Those who have listened with discerning ears must have heard how different were the qualities of tone produced from their respective Stradivari instruments by Lady Hallé, Joachim, Sarasate, Piatti, and others. In the hands of such great artists Stradivari violins or violoncellos will entrance by their quality, astonish by their force and depth, and stir all the emotions by their varied capacity for expression. And these instruments, produced two centuries ago, are still for practical purposes superior to any which have since been made.

CHAPTER VI.

Stradivari's Material.

OST writers who have touched upon the subject of the wood from which Stradivari constructed his instruments would have us believe that he possessed a knowledge of acoustics, which, when brought to bear upon the selection of his material, helped him largely to achieve that wonderful excellence of tone possessed by his instruments; in fact, we are told that the marvellous acoustic qualities of this magic wood form the chief element in the success of Stradivari. Now, from such views we differ strongly. That the material from which an instrument is made is of great importance we would be the last to deny; but it is not more important than are suitable and consistent dimensions, model, general construction, and varnish—which last, as stated in our chapter on the subject, more or less completes and improves or injures the good qualities of the instrument. Even with faulty—we do not say absolutely bad—material, if construction and dimensions are right, and good varnish is successfully applied, a fairly good instrument will result ; but though the wood, and also construction and dimensions

be perfect, the result will be astonishingly bad if the instrument be badly varnished. Hence we are disposed to classify the relative importance of material, dimensions and construction, and varnish, as follows :—1st, varnish ; 2nd, construction and dimensions ; 3rd, material.

The early Brescians used in the majority of cases for the backs, sides, and heads of their instruments, poplar or wood of a kindred nature, such as lime, pear, and even cedar; for the bellies, pine—often of an exceptionally hard

Fig. 37.   Fig. 38.

SECTION OF A TREE SHOWING (1) THE WOOD CUT ON THE QUARTER, OR RIGHT WAY OF THE GRAIN, (2) CUT ON THE SLAB, *i.e.*, ACROSS THE GRAIN

variety, and cut the slab way of the grain (figs. 37, 38). As time passes on, and we arrive at the period of Maggini and of the early Amatis, we find that maple had all but supplanted the softer woods hitherto employed for the backs (figs. 39, 40), sides, and heads. This was because the makers had discovered that it gave a better all-round result; it permitted of the model back being worked out thinner, while retaining equal power of resistance to the sound-post; it tended to produce a brighter tone, and it was infinitely more pleasing to the eye—*i.e.* when handsomely figured All our information goes to prove that this wood used by the Brescians

and the Cremonese makers up to the time of Stradivari
was of local growth, and no difficulty could have been
experienced in obtaining it. The demands of a few cabinet
and fiddle makers could not absorb the produce of many
trees, and it must therefore have been both easily and
cheaply procurable. As for pine, then as now, it abounded
at no very great distance from Brescia ; and if we judge

 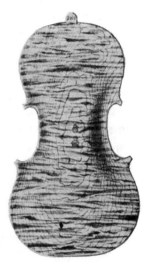

Fig. 39.—A Back in one Piece,
cut on the Quarter.

Fig. 40.—A Back in one Piece,
cut on the Slab.

by the free use the Milanese cheap-jacks * made of pine of
the finest quality, often for their commonest productions,
we are forced to conclude that it could also be had there
cheaply and plentifully. Only towards the end of Nicolò
Amati's career do we begin here and there to see other wood
than the ordinary native maple used ; it is easily distin-
guishable by the broader markings of the curl as contrasted

* See Chap. VIII., p. 191.

with that of the small, close figure to which we are so accustomed in the Amati instruments. All the members of this family showed a great preference for cutting their wood the slab way of the grain. It is quite conceivable that the growing importance of the fiddle-maker's art at Cremona should have created a demand for foreign maple—material of a finer kind and more boldly marked. Higher remuneration was possibly being received for the instruments, and, consequently, an increased price could be paid for the requisite materials. Fétis says * that the wood was brought from Croatia, from Dalmatia, and even from Turkey; and it would naturally come to the great emporium of the Adriatic, Venice—where, says tradition, it served to fashion the oars of the gondolas, possibly also their interior decoration; thence to Cremona was not a very long journey. Nevertheless the transport of heavy logs or trees—and probabilities point to the wood having been carried in bulk— must have somewhat enhanced the cost before it reached its destination, and its use, therefore, would be restricted.

In speaking of the construction of the violin by the Brescians and Cremonese, Hart says :—" There can be no doubt whatever that the Cremonese and Brescian artists were exceedingly careful in their choice of material, and their discrimination in this particular does not appear to have been exercised so much from a regard for the beauty as for the acoustic properties of the wood, to which latter point they very properly gave the first place in their consideration. We have evidence of much weight on this interesting subject in the frequent piecings found in the works of the old masters of the craft, who seem to have preferred to retain a piece of wood of known acoustic

---

* " Antonio Stradivari," by F. J. Fétis, p. 63.

properties rather than to work in a better preserved portion at the probable expense of tone."

We feel it a duty to say that we fail to perceive this remarkable discrimination, and we believe that the evidence of which Hart speaks is easily refuted. We cannot too much insist upon the fact that all these Brescian and Cremonese masters were purely and simply working artisans, guided by practical experience and the circumstances of the moment. When well remunerated, either in money or patronage, they did their best, and used the finest material then obtainable, and *vice versa*. Their powers of discrimination were in no way superior to those of the thoughtful craftsman of to-day— if, that is to say, we form our conclusions from examination, not of a small, but of a large number of the many existing specimens of their work. Various reasons may be given to account for the old practice of adding pieces to the wings of the back, and of inserting smaller pieces in different parts of both back and belly, or again, of making the belly of several pieces. In every case the solution of the problem is to be found by looking at the matter from the workman's, and not from the theorist's point of view. Stradivari frequently added a wing or wings to the bottom curves of the back in one piece, and in doing so he was guided by those same motives of economy which would prompt us to act in a similar way if handsome wood cost as much now as it did then. The same reasoning applies, with even still greater force, to the insertion of pieces. In the former case the necessity for adding a wing is recognised before starting, and the consequences weighed; in the latter some defect more often reveals itself when back or belly is well advanced. Then, rather than sacrifice both the material and the labour so far expended upon it, one elects to insert a piece or even pieces. No wood is more treacherous in this respect than pine, and for this reason all makers, including Stradivari, have generally made the bellies from two pieces; in other words, they found it much easier to obtain a perfect piece of pine, of upright, even grain, and free from resinous stains, of the width of four and a half inches than of nine inches; this is then split down the centre and joined.   It must not be supposed that Stradivari often inserted such pieces: he was far too particular about his work to do so; but so much cannot be said of many other less renowned Italian makers. That Stradivari brought to bear a certain amount of judgment in the selection of his materials is beyond discussion, but that he possessed any special knowledge other than that of an intelligent craftsman, well versed in the traditions of his craft, we are constrained to deny.   Take his pre-1684 instruments: all those known to us, with but few exceptions, are made (back, sides, and head) from home-grown maple of a decidedly plain appearance, acoustically good, it is true, yet not what either he—or we, let us say—would have chosen with choice unfettered. We are therefore forced to conclude either that he was poorly paid for these examples, or that the handsome and sonorous wood he used in later years was then unobtainable.   The truth probably lies between these two conclusions : his remuneration was relatively small, and handsome foreign maple fairly expensive, possibly not to be had at all during certain years. Nothing more ridiculous can be supposed than that the species both of maple and of pine which the Cremonese so ably utilised no longer exists ; and the height of absurdity is reached when we are gravely informed by Herr Schradieck,* a distinguished German professor of the violin now settled in

---

* The *Courier*, a musical paper published in Cincinnati, U.S.A. : Art. " A Lost Secret—The Violin."   No. 26, April 1884.

America, that the late Mr. Niederheitmann, an amateur enthusiast of Aix-la-Chapelle, discovered, after much research, that the secret of the unrivalled tone of Stradivari and of other fine instruments may be found in the fact that the bellies were made of " Balsam Pine," a wood which grew in Northern Italy at the period when those makers flourished, but has since gradually become extinct. We are still on the heights of absurdity when another German writes to assure us that the wood and varnish used by Stradivari have at length been discovered by him, after making about ten thousand experiments, and having recourse to the aid of the microscope.

We unhesitatingly assert that modern violin-makers have a choice of material equal in every respect to that which existed at the time of Stradivari, and of infinitely greater variety. The same forests whence came his timber are possibly still in existence, for what are two or three hundred years in the life of a not unduly disturbed forest? And we enjoy to-day all the advantages of a commercial age, when traders are willing to deliver at our doors wood from every part of the world, even sawn to given dimensions, and ready for use! We may here add a word as to the delusion that material taken from buildings, such as for instance Swiss châlets—in some cases centuries old—is preferable to that cut and seasoned during a lesser, but still a sufficient, number of years. We have tried both kinds—Vuillaume did so repeatedly—and we fail to find that the former possesses any real advantage over the latter; in fact, our opinion is rather in favour of the more youthful wood.

Our conclusions are, then, that Stradivari's choice of material depended upon two circumstances: 1st, the remuneration he was to receive for a given instrument; 2nd, the choice of wood he had at the time in stock. Some years offered an abundant selection, others only an indifferent one.

CHAPTER VII.

Stradivari's Varnish.

T is with considerable diffidence that we approach the much-discussed subject of the varnish used by Stradivari. It is a question which has absorbed, and continues to absorb, no inconsiderable amount of both our time and means. Consequently we are constrained to admit that we feel somewhat reluctant to give open and full expression to our views as to what were the constituents of that incomparable varnish so much admired by all—a varnish which we see not only on the instruments of Stradivari, but also on those of many other Italian makers. We hope, nevertheless, to place the matter before our readers in a truer light than that in which it has hitherto appeared, and thus to dispel much of the mystery in which the subject has been involved by the ever-ready pens and fluent tongues of the many self-constituted authorities. Monthly—nay, weekly—we receive communications on this subject. All think, and some are absolutely convinced, that they have attained to perfect knowledge about the varnish. They have

varnished pieces of cigar-boxes, bits of deal, strips of maple, or even a new German or French violin, invariably of the commonest kind, purchased for a few shillings in the white; and they are of opinion that the results reached justify the most sanguine expectations. We are referred to the remarkable tone given forth by one or other of these newly varnished crudities by persons whose knowledge of tone is, to say the least, rudimentary—nothing, in fact, being more difficult than to correctly gauge subtle differences of tone. Should one venture, however modestly, to dissent from the conclusions drawn from such experiments, or should one dare to suggest that the experimenter is endeavouring to grapple with a question of the A B C of which he is wholly ignorant, one is forthwith compared to Rip Van Winkle, or has addressed to him " a few plain words," such as these of a Scotch correspondent: "You will go on till the crack of doom, and even *then* you won't have made anything of it." Others, and by far the greater number, immediately discern " green-eyed jealousy " in any dissent from their views, and denounce you with withering scorn.

Now, it will come as good news to all lovers of our art to be told that the recipe of the varnish employed by Stradivari is still in existence. We cannot do better than give the following story, which is not without a touch of romance, in the words of the late Signor Giacomo Stradivari himself, who, in answer to the repeated requests of Signor Mandelli for information concerning his illustrious ancestor, wrote to him as follows :—

"Little is the information I am able to give you, because very few are the documents preserved at home relating to my family. Here, however, is all that I can transmit to you in answer to your queries : Firstly, I send you a facsimile of the testimonial, the original of which I gave to M. Vuillaume, of Paris, who, in a letter dated January 3rd, 1860, wrote to me thus: ' I have placed under glass the original of the testimonial given to your ancestor, which you have so generously presented me with.* I have exhibited it in my salon, where it remains an object of great interest to many admiring amateurs!' Secondly, the Bible, inside the cover of which was written, in the handwriting of Antonio Stradivari, the famous recipe for the varnish and the way to apply it, was destroyed. Previously, however, I made a faithful copy of the same, which I have jealously guarded, and which I have never been willing to part with, notwithstanding the repeated solicitations of M. Vuillaume and others. Thirdly, I have no datum to offer about the quarrel you allude to [Signor Mandelli had inquired whether he could throw any light upon the supposed ill-feeling said to have existed between Antonio Stradivari's sons and the town authorities of Cremona †]; but I recall the fact that one of my brothers gave to Signor Motta, Professor of Drawing, all the moulds and patterns which existed in the attic of our house, and which subsequently passed from Motta's possession to that of the violin-maker Enrico Ceruti. Fourthly, nothing else concerning my ancestor based on fact or tradition can I quote, because the family documents have undergone the inexorable ravages of time : I mean to say that by transmission from generation to genera-tion they have gradually diminished in number and got lost."

In answer to Signor Mandelli's further entreaties, made with a view to obtaining for publication some inkling of the

---

* The testimonial referred to is the title of appointment given by the Archbishop of Benevento.   (See reproduction.)

† See Hart, " The Violin : its Famous Makers, etc.," art. 'Stradivari.'

contents of this interesting recipe, Signor Stradivari again wrote to him thus :—

"You make an impossible request, one which I cannot grant you, as I have never confided the secret of the varnish even to my wife or my daughters. You may consider it an eccentricity on my part ; but nevertheless, until I arrive at a different opinion, I wish to be consistent with and remain faithful to the resolution of my youth never to reveal to anybody the contents of this precious recipe, holding steadfastly to the conclusions I arrived at when still a boy : that, if by chance other Stradivaris— my sons, nephews, grandsons, or grandnephews—should turn their attention to mechanics, more especially to the craft of our celebrated ancestor, they should then at least have the advantage of possessing the recipe of his varnish, the possession of which could not but be of material assistance to them. Let me prove to you the constancy with which I have kept to this fixed idea.

"In the year 1848, after going through the whole campaign * as a volunteer, I settled in Turin awaiting better political times ; and as the Austrian Government † did not permit her subjects to send by the post from their native towns any pecuniary assistance to the refugees, I was compelled to get my living by accepting a place as copyist at the Council of State, thankful for the chance of earning my bread. Well, a Frenchman, whose acquaintance I made at the house of the bookseller, Signor Pomba, and who was travelling in Italy in search of old instruments, offered me for the recipe at first twenty-five napoleons (500 francs), and then increased his offer to fifty (1,000 francs). Bear in

---

* Signor Stradivari was one of the followers of Garibaldi.

† Austria was in occupation of the Milanese provinces.

mind that, at that time, fifty napoleons would have been as many brothers to me ; still I had the courage to resist the temptation.   Again, in later years M. Vuillaume and Count Castelbarco made offers to me, but I still remained determined to stand by my resolution of earlier days.   Have I done wrong ?   Never mind ; I see no reason for repentance."

We have seen and conversed with the late Signor Stradivari on several occasions, and we have no reason to doubt the sincerity of his statements.   In answer to our inquiry as to the reason why he destroyed the original recipe in the handwriting of his ancestor, he gave the following explanation :—

"I was a boy when my father died, and a few years later it was decided that our family should remove to another house.   As a consequence, all our belongings were turned over.   In the course of looking through our old books, my eye was arrested by this Bible, and, opening it, I read the writing inside the cover.   I had heard repeated mention made of the skill of my famous ancestor, and of the fame of the varnish he used.   Here, then, was the prescription for the same.   I grasped the importance of my discovery, and determined to take possession of the book without mentioning the matter even to my mother.   But how to hide this bulky volume I knew not ; so I forthwith resolved, firstly to make a faithful copy of the prescription—it was dated 1704—and then to destroy the book, which I did."

Signor Stradivari very naturally perceived the foolishness of his act in destroying the only absolute proof of the veracity of his story ; but, as he truly remarked, " Young people cannot possess the wisdom of their elders."

We cannot claim for Stradivari the possession of a varnish superior to all others, but we do unhesitatingly say that his greater capacity gave him a power of manipulation which furnished results that, looked at as a whole, surpass those of all his competitors. It is one thing to have fine varnish, and quite another to apply it with the perfect success of Stradivari. Many of the Italian makers, departing occasionally from a mere system of routine, created and bequeathed to us some admirable instruments, which, especially in point of varnish, leave little to be desired—examples differing greatly from their every-day work. But with Stradivari we are accustomed to a more uniformly high standard of excellence, though even he at times somewhat failed in respect to the colour, the texture, or the transparency of his varnish. We are not disposed to agree with the generally accepted belief that the ingredients composing the varnish of the old masters and the process of making it were secrets jealously guarded and treasured by the few ; but we are of opinion that it is very probable that each maker had his own views as to the best proportions of gum, oil, and colouring-matter, as well as to the best method of mixing them and applying the resulting varnish. So far, then, we may admit that every man had his secret ; but that the ingredients of the varnish and the ordinary methods of applying it were processes open to all who sought to learn is clearly proved by the works left by the various Italian makers. Not only was " all about the varnish " known to the Cremonese and their immediate pupils, but also to their followers scattered throughout Italy : men, for instance, such as David Tecchler of Rome, originally from Augsburg ; and Matthias Albani, an Italian working at Botzen, in the Austrian Tyrol, neither of whom seems to have been taught his calling at Cremona, or even by the Cremonese. Even Jacob Stainer possessed the open secret of this varnish, and he certainly never—if we trust to facts, and not to fiction—worked or lived at Cremona.

Again, consider some of the Salzburg makers, some of the
early French and Dutch makers, and some makers among
our own countrymen : all these men had, and at times used,
a quite superior varnish, the constituents of which were
similar to those employed by the Italians. And it may well
be asked, How could such a matter have remained a secret
in a small city like Cremona, where fiddle-making, especially
in Stradivari's youth, was a flourishing industry ? The
ingredients, too, for composing varnish were in demand, and
apparently easily obtainable ; hence the improbability, nay,
impossibility, of any secrecy. It may be there was some
druggist in the town who supplied all the makers with the
requisite materials ; and he may even have mixed the varnish
and sold it ready-made ; for certainly some of the workers,
as their instruments show, were rare sluggards, and not fired
with Stradivari's zeal. No! Fine varnish was in the hands
of fiddle-makers long before Stradivari was born. The
Brescians had it, and it no doubt came to Cremona on the
introduction into that city of the fiddle-maker's art by
Andrea Amati, and we see its development keeping pace
with the improving principles of instrument-making. The
lute-makers of the fifteenth and sixteenth centuries had
already in use varnishes made from standard gums, oils,
and vegetable colours ; and we believe that these pioneer
workers were probably indebted for their knowledge of the
subject to the many great painters who had preceded them,
and had created a certain demand for the purest and best
materials.

We are indebted to the late Count Valdrighi for an
extremely interesting document found by him in the Archives
of Modena, and published in his work " Nomocheliurgografia,"
which throws some light on this question of secrecy. It
appears that the Duke of Ferrara desired to obtain a recipe

of the varnish then in use among the Venetian lute-makers,
and accordingly wrote to his correspondent in Venice—one
Jacopo de li Tibaldi, who, under date January 20th, 1526,
replied as follows: "The celebrated lute-maker Sigismond
Maler has promised to give me in writing by Monday
next the recipe of the varnish he uses, as well as the
manner of putting it on the lutes. This master also tells
me that he has two kinds of varnish, and that it is his
assistants, not he himself, who make it." * We learn in
this way that at that period the matter was not regarded as
a valuable secret, otherwise the master would hardly have
deputed the task of making it to his assistants or pupils;
and we see no reason to doubt that the practice which
then ruled also obtained in later years. Pique, the well-
known French maker (1758—1822), who employed Nicolas
Lupot, whilst at Orleans, to make violins in the white for
him, writes as follows to Lupot under date April 14th,
1792: "I would ask you to be good enough to let me
have some of your oil varnish, sufficient for several violins,
as I have run out of my own and have not the time at
present to make any." †

We may thus fairly assume that Stradivari was at an
early stage of his career initiated into the traditions and
methods practised by his master and predecessors. Once
freed from his connection with Amati, we see him seeking,
by changes effected in the colours of his varnish, to give a
different appearance to his instruments, as is evidenced by his
departure from the hitherto conventional Amati yellow. We
say "conventional," because, throughout the four generations

---

* "Nomocheliurgografia," p. 267.
† "Les Facteurs d'Instruments de Musique," Constant Pierre, 1893,
p. 128.

of that remarkable family, every member of it kept, with
rare exceptions, to the same tint of colour.

That Stradivari used solely a pure oil varnish, the
composition of which consisted of a gum soluble in oil, possessing good drying qualities, with the addition of colouring
ingredients, is, we think, beyond controversy. Charles Reade,
in his excellent articles on Cremona fiddles, written in 1873,*
at the time of the Loan Collection of Instruments exhibited
at South Kensington, contends plausibly enough that the
varnish was not wholly of oil—that, in fact, the colouring-
matter, contained in a solution of spirit, formed a distinct
body from the varnish used for the groundwork or for filling
up the pores of the wood. In support of his contention he
instances the chippy appearance of certain instruments of
Stradivari there exhibited. Had Reade put his theory to
the test, he would soon have discovered that it was unsound,
and that a spirit solution over a ground-varnish of oil is
infinitely less homogeneous than apparently is the varnish
of Stradivari. We say *apparently*, because we consider that
Reade was mistaken in stating that Stradivari's varnish was
wanting in homogeneity. Various reasons could be given to
account for the tendency to chip at times. It was due most
probably to the introduction of an extra quantity of colouring-
matter, or possibly to an increased proportion of gum. Either
cause would suffice to bring about the result in question,
and we recognise that the texture, as well as the colour, of
Stradivari's varnish varied considerably, though its essential
nature was always the same. Most gums suitable for fiddle-
makers' varnish are, in their pure state, of a chippy nature.
The tendency to chip must be overcome by the judicious
adjustment of the medium wherein they are dissolved, and

---

* Republished in " Readiana."

Molto Illustre e molto Reverendo mio Signor Padron colendissimo !

Compatirà la tardanza del violino perchè è stato la causa per la vernice per le gran crepate che il sole non le faccia aprire. Però V(ostra) S(ignoria) lo riceverà ben aggiustato dentro la sua cassetta, e mi spiace che non ho potuto far di piu per renderla servita. E per la mia fattura V(ostra) S(ignoria) mi manderà un filippo,* che merito di piu—ma per servire la di lei persona mi contento. Cosi qui resto con riverirla di tutto cuore ; e se valgo in altro la prego degli suoi cari commandi, e le bacio le mani.

Di V(ostra) S(ignoria) molto illustre e reverendo

Devotissimo Servitore

Antonio Stradivari.

Cremona 12 Agosto 1708.†

Most esteemed, very reverend, and illustrious Sir !

I beg you will forgive the delay with the violin, occasioned by the varnishing of the large cracks, that the sun may not re-open them. However, you will now receive the instrument, well repaired, in its case, and I regret that I could do no more to serve you. For my work, please send me a filippo ; it is worth more, but for the pleasure of serving you I am satisfied with that sum. If I can do anything else for you, I beg you will command me, and kissing your hand,

I remain, most illustrious and reverend Sir,

Your most faithful servant

Antonio Stradivari.

* Filippo : a silver coin then current in Lombardy, of the face value of five shillings ; its purchasing power now would be approximately fifteen shillings.

† As the facsimile gives the actual text with all the orthographic mistakes, the above transcription shows the letter in its simplicity, but free from such errors. In the original the principal mistakes are either the duplication of certain letters, or the use of one only instead of two, or *vice versa*, such as "statto" (instead of stato), "agiustato" (aggiustato), "facia" (instead of faccia) ; or the use of wrong vowels : "solo" (for sole), "mane" (for mani) ; or the introduction of a word taken from the Cremonese dialect, such as "vallio" (for valgo), or the omission of a syllable : "rivrila" (for riverirla).

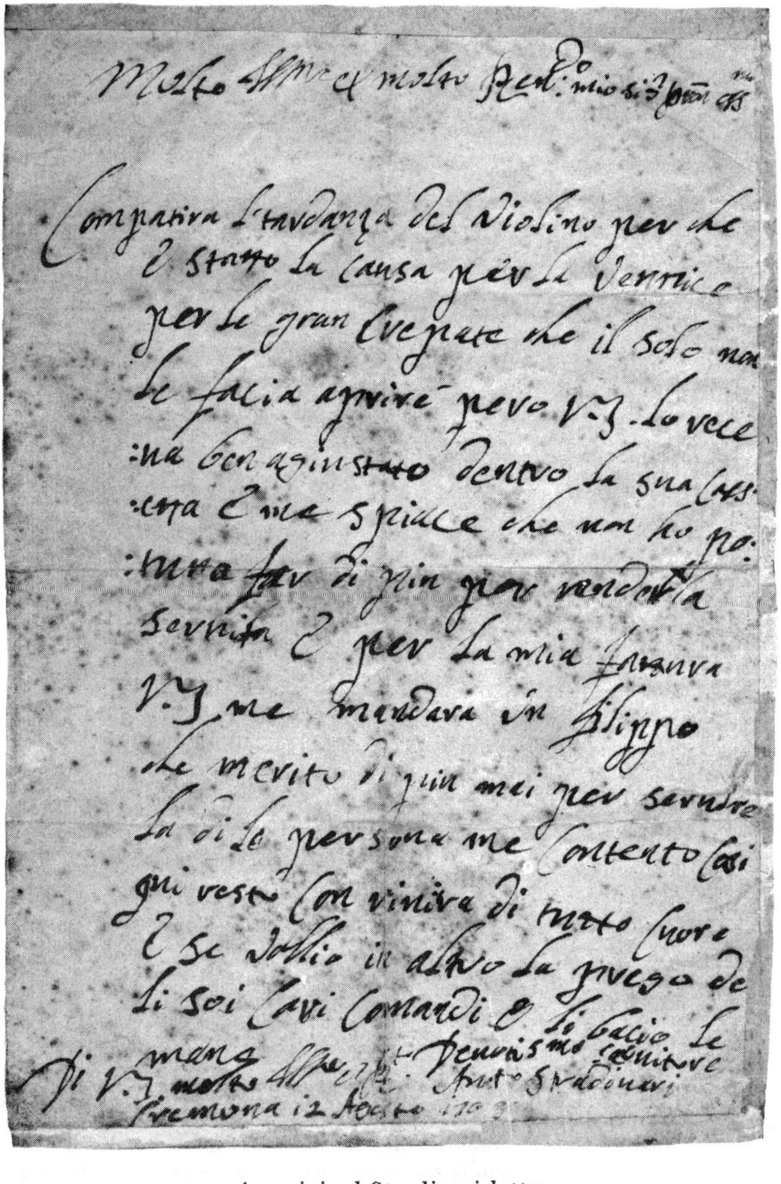
Molto Ill.re e molto Rev.do mio sig.r Pron Col.mo

Compatira l'induganza del violino per che
è statto la causa per la vernice
per le gran crepature che il solo non
le facia aprire pero V.S. lo rece
:vera ben agiustato dentro la sua cas
:seta e me spiace che non ho po
:tutto far di più per rendergli la
servitu e per la mia fatura
V.S. me mandava un filippo
che merito di più ma per servire
la di le persona me contento così
qui resto con riverirla di tutto cuore
e se voglio in altro la prego de
li soi cari comandi e le bacio le
mani

Di V.S. molto Ill.re e Rev.da Devotissimo servitore Anto Stradivari
Cremona 12 Agosto 1709

An original Stradivari letter

(reduced 27 per cent)

Non ho mandato il violino più presto a causa d'aspettare qualche persona sempre. Ora m'è capitato il Padre Scalzo di San Mauro al quale l'ho consegnato. Mi ha promesso di farlo aver subito a V(ostra) E(cellenza); la qual cosa prego V(ostra E(cellenza) perdonerà se non l'ho mandato più presto. Espero che sarà gradito—e resto per non tediar di più V(ostra) E(cellenza) e le baccio le mani e le faccio riverenza

Di V(ostra) E(cellenza)

Umilissimo e Devotissimo Servo

Antonio Stradivari.

Cremona, li 25 Agosto.

Most esteemed and very illustrious Sir,

I have not sent the violin sooner in consequence of having had to wait continually for some one (to convey it to you). Now I have the opportunity (by the departure) of the barefooted father of San Mauro, to whom I have entrusted it. He has promised to let you have it immediately. I therefore beg that you will forgive me for not having sent it earlier, and I hope you will be pleased with it. I will now finish, not wishing to weary you further, and kissing your hands and making obeisance,

Your Excellency's

most humble and devoted servant,

Antonio Stradivari.

---

* The transcription gives the letter as it should have been written. The original text is full of mistakes, omissions and transpositions, and is much interlarded with words of the Cremonese dialect. The omission of the article before " violino " is a great mistake ; the bad spelling and the use of so many dialectic words, such as " spetare " (for aspettare), " scarso " (for scalzo), ' consegnà " (for consegnato), " prumisso " (for promesso), " tedare " (for tediare), are striking. There was at the time a convent of bare-footed monks in the suburb of St. Mauro, outside the town of Cremona, and this fact *is in favour of the authenticity of the letter.*

Judging by the shaky handwriting and by the errors, which are more numerous than in the previous letter, we assume that this one was written some years later.

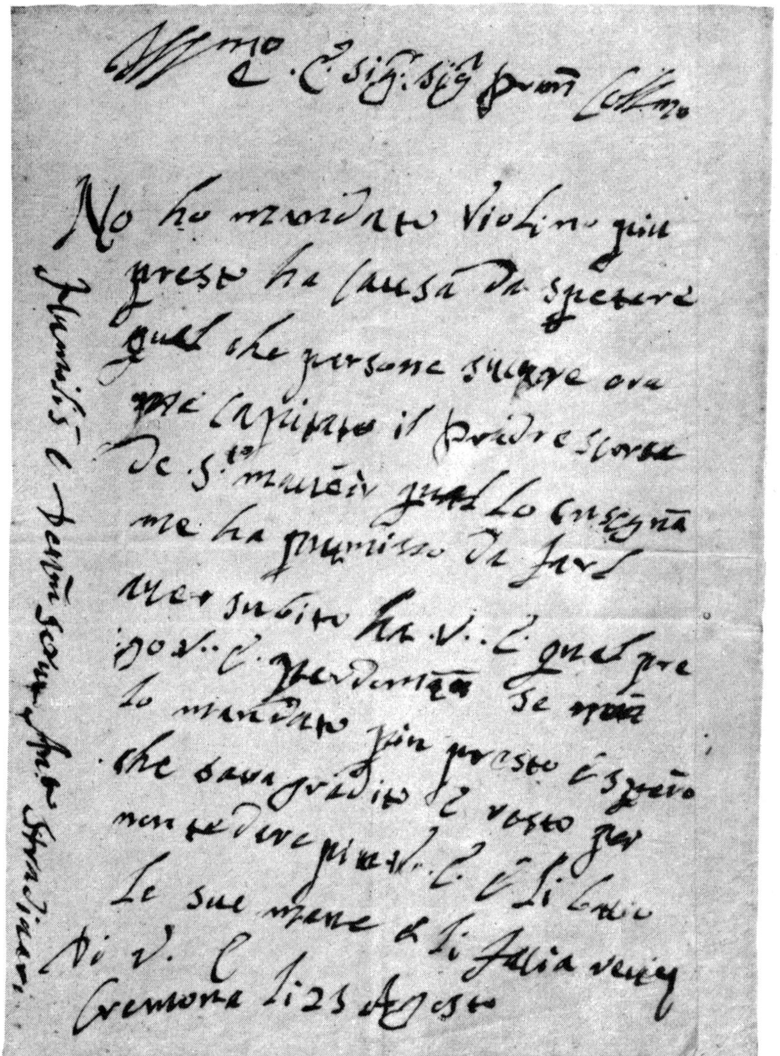

Ill.mo e R.mo Sig.r Sig.r Pron Col.mo

No ho mandato Violino piu
preste ha causa da spetare
qual che persone sicure ora
me capitato il Padre Sforza
de S.to Mattio qual lo consegna
me ha promisso de farlo
aver subito ha V. S.
... V. S. qual pre
lo ... perdonanza se non
lo mandato pin presto e spero
che sara gradito e vosto ...
non vedere piu V. S. e per
le sue mane e li bacio
Di V. S. ... li ...
Cremona li 25 Agosto

Humilis.o e Devot.mo Servitore Ant.o Stradivari

An original Stradivari letter

(reduced 30 per cent)

by the addition of other ingredients : it is needless to add that considerable judgment has to be exercised in fixing their relative proportions.

It is this question of colouring varnish which has proved the stumbling-block in the way of so many makers of the last century. If players would be content with instruments treated with colourless varnish, the difficulty of producing fine tone would be very greatly diminished, as the addition of many and various injurious colouring substances, or the artificial staining of the wood (at times accomplished by the use of acids) in order to please the eye, in the one case mars what would be a varnish favourable for tone, and in the other adversely affects the material from which the instrument is made. In fact, tone is, and has been, though often unintentionally, sacrificed by many through seeking to gratify the taste for mere outward appearance. The great effect wrought by gradual exposure to subdued light, and by the influence of time, is not sufficiently taken into account when the ordinary observer compares the newly varnished work with the old. As well try to change quickly new wine into old as try to obtain in a short time the richly matured and soft-toned appearance which age alone can impart to perfectly varnished violins.

Could we have seen the most brilliant works of Italian violin-makers fresh from their hands, we should have been not a little surprised by their bright and unsubdued aspect ; nay, in many instances, notably with regard to some of the violins of Joseph Guarnerius, we should have been struck by their positively crude appearance. The conditions for ulti-mately ensuring a fine appearance were certainly there ; but to the wonder-working effects of time and use, and to these alone, we unhesitatingly attribute all that charms us now. That the more ambitious of modern makers should have sought to rival the productions of the old masters in external appearance is readily conceivable—however injudicious at times their procedure—when we bear in mind the popular demand for a thing of beauty. An ugly or even plain instrument, though excellent in tone, is again and again rejected. Many may view this statement with incredulity; it is nevertheless strictly true, and the statement is the outcome of innumerable experiences.

How fascinating is the appearance of the varnish as now seen on fine examples of Stradivari's instruments! Lightness of texture, and transparency combined with brilliant yet subdued colouring, and above all, the broken-up surface, more especially that of the back, form a whole which is picturesque and attractive in the highest degree. Our illustrations admirably portray these features. It has often been asked whether this broken-up or chipped-off aspect of the varnish is solely the effect of usage, or whether Stradivari so treated it in order to lend additional charm to his work; for it cannot be denied that this appearance is more pleasing than the absolutely smooth surface presented by an instrument evenly varnished all over. That it is possible to attain this result artificially is conclusively seen by examination of the instruments of Vuillaume; and admirably he succeeded. We are of opinion, however, that in the case of Stradivari and the other Italian makers the appearance can only be ascribed to usage. Many a knock and rubbing against hard and gritty substances have the vicissitudes of time brought about; and then, in addition, must be borne in mind the effect of putting in and taking out of the old cases, especially of those opening at the end. It may also have been caused by contact with buttons and other articles of personal adornment.

The use of oil varnish, which was employed for so

many generations, was gradually abandoned as the art of instrument-making declined in Italy. Prior even to the death of Stradivari, several makers had strayed from the true road ; and the reason is not far to seek. New and easy methods of dissolving gum by means of spirit were being introduced, and they apparently fulfilled the conditions desired by instrument-makers, enabling them to varnish their works more speedily, and, above all, ensuring quick drying. That drying was at times tedious and troublesome, even under the favourable conditions of the Italian climate, is shown by the testimony of Stradivari himself. In one of the only two letters of the master known to exist, he apologises for delay about his work, *because of the non-drying of the varnish.* Very instructive is a letter written from Cremona in 1638, wherein we read, " The violin cannot be brought to perfection without the strong heat of the sun." * With Stradivari's death, the decay of the higher standard of instrument-making rapidly set in. Very probably the waning prosperity of the Church in Italy, coupled with the large number of fine instruments then existing, was the principal cause. Consequently circumstances favoured the use of varnishes which could be cheaply, and therefore quickly, put on. The spirit of artistic emulation which existed in Cremona in Stradivari's youth had died out. The two workmen, sons of the master, evidently enriched by their father's death, were content to rest ; while Carlo Bergonzi and Joseph Guarnerius, though the only serious workers left, gave but few signs of industry. Elsewhere the craft was still actively carried on, notably at Milan and Naples ; but works cheaply produced, rather than those of finished workmanship and fine varnish, seem to have been what the age required throughout Italy.

---

* See fourth letter of the Galileo correspondence, Chapter XI.

The demand, therefore, for slower-drying varnish no longer existed ; to use it meant extra cost, and its supreme importance passed either unnoticed or unheeded. To these causes, therefore, and to them alone, do we attribute the gradual disuse of the old varnish, and the final disappearance of the recipes for its concoction and for applying it employed by the great Italian violin-makers. From time to time generous patrons caused the old traditions to be revived, and we thus catch glimpses of the true recipe for Cremona varnish still now and then in use ; but as years rolled on these instances became rarer and rarer. They occurred at Milan until about 1760. We meet the true recipe again, and for the last time, at Turin, used occasionally by J. B. Guadagnini, no doubt under the auspices of Count Cozio, up till 1780–84 ; but by the end of the century it had died out of use and remembrance. If we of modern times really wish to regain the knowledge possessed on this subject by the old makers, we must begin by retracing our steps. Leaving behind us this very commercial age, we must seek to work under conditions more resembling those of the period when the grand old masters of violin-making flourished. Success will only come to those who, mindful of the old traditions, unhesitatingly return to them. The popular idea that somebody will some fine day shout " Eureka," and forthwith quickly produce instruments which, in point of varnish, will equal those of Stradivari, is in the nature of a dream. The materials he used exist now, as in his day ; but it will prove one problem to make the varnish, and quite another to utilise it with the perfect success of Stradivari.

We may here, before concluding our remarks on this subject, appropriately add a few words as to the influence of varnish. We think it is not either sufficiently known or recognised that in a great measure Stradivari instruments owe to it their distinguished quality of tone; in reality the future of any perfectly constructed instrument is determined by the coat it is clothed in. Fine varnish will not compensate for bad material or faulty construction; but that it makes or mars the perfectly formed instrument is, in our opinion, beyond dispute. It should be remembered that a violin must vibrate freely, yet not too freely,—as would be the case with a new unvarnished instrument when first in use. Now clothe it too thickly with even a good varnish, and the tone will be deadened, or with one too hard in texture, and the result will be that the tone will prove hard and metallic. Or again, cover it with a too soft oil varnish, and you will mute the tone of your instrument for a generation, if not for ever. Age and use will no doubt to some extent modify these effects, but never entirely. Many are the instructive examples of the influence of the varnish which could be furnished by comparison between various instruments of the different old masters of the craft. It is, for instance, known to not a few that Stradivari violins give forth a character of tone perfectly distinct from those of his great rival, Giuseppe Guarneri del Gesù. Why? The answer to the question is not to be found in the construction alone, as there exist Guarneris and Stradivaris built practically upon the same lines, yet each retains its own quality of tone. If construction alone is to account for peculiarity of tone, why do not respective copies of the one and of the other made by an experienced maker such as Vuillaume possess each the distinctive *timbre* of the original? It appears to us that those who are really competent, and in a position to make comparisons, can give only one answer. The methods of varnishing as practised by Stradivari and Guarneri were different. In some specimens the nature of the varnish also was different; and the tone was influenced accordingly.   Carlo Bergonzi affords us another example.   He was a pupil or assistant of Stradivari, and carried out more or less his master's principles of construction ; his varnish, however, is much more like that of Guarneri, and consequently the tone of his violins more resembles that of this master's works.   Vuillaume varnished all his violins alike, whether they were copies of Stradivari, Guarneri, or Amati, and accordingly the character of their tone varies but little.   Again, take the violins of J. B. Guadagnini and the finer specimens of the various members of the Gagliano family.   They are constructed on the principles of Stradivari, the material used is in many cases acoustically equal, yet they have by no means the same character of tone as a Stradivari.   And why ?   Because their varnish and their methods of applying it were in most cases very different.

Lupot, the French violin-maker, who is justly celebrated for his fine copies of Stradivari, furnishes yet another instance in support of our view, and it is all the more instructive in that he was the earliest maker who continuously, earnestly, and closely followed the models of the great master.   His varnish is, with certain exceptions, of a soft texture and laid on heavily, and the tone is consequently of a stiff and veiled character.

Let us now look at home, and we find the very interesting fact that one of our most meritorious makers, Daniel Parker, produced copies of a "long Stradivari" as early as 1720.   Form, construction, and material are often excellent; but the varnish is of a hard texture, and consequently the tone of his copies is of a more metallic *timbre* than that of a Stradivari.

Many other equally striking facts could be cited, but we think sufficient has been said to show that our views are well founded.

CHAPTER VIII.

Stradivari's Method of Construction.

O task is more difficult than that of defining precisely the features in Stradivari's work which are strictly original. In a broad sense the whole is so ; yet the more we analyse, the more do we discover that he was very deeply indebted to those who had preceded him. Perhaps one of his greatest merits was the possession of that power of perception which, as time passed on, allowed him to grasp and to profit by all that is excellent in the works of his forerunners, from Gasparo da Salò to Nicolò Amati.

That Stradivari was guided in his many and various changes by a knowledge of science as applied to the construction of instruments, we do not for one moment believe. That his intuition was great is unquestionable ; and what more natural than to assume that many of his deductions were the outcome of actual experience gained by comparing the numerous already-existing instruments made by the early Brescian and Cremonese makers ? It must be remembered that the art of instrument-making had been flourishing, first at Brescia, then at Cremona,

for close upon two centuries.   Stradivari was therefore in
touch   with   the   outcome   of   well-thought-out   experiments,
and   the   traditions   which   had   been   evolved   and   transmitted
by the different makers during this long period.   Time and
practical   experience   had   tested   various   methods   of   work,
and   thus,   in   our   opinion,   were   the   main   problems   of   construction   slowly,   but   surely,   solved.   Each   generation   added
its   link   to   the   chain,   and   Stradivari   finally   welded   the
whole   together.

Nothing   is   more   likely   than   that   Stradivari   often   came
into   contact   with,   and   heard   the   opinions   of,   the   different
musicians   of   his   day,   who   then,   as   now,   frequently   visited
the   violin-makers'   shops : for   instance,   J. B. Volumier * visited
Cremona   in   1715,   and   remained   there   for   three   months,
until   the   instruments   ordered   from   Stradivari   by   the   King
of   Poland †   were   finished.   That   a   large   part   of   this   time
was   passed   in   the   violin-maker's   shop,   we   may   be   sure.
Again,   Hart   mentions   that   Visconti,   a   distinguished   violinist,
follower   of   Corelli,   is   said   to   have   offered   his   advice   to   the
master   upon   the   construction   of   his   instruments.   These
players   were,   we   must   bear   in   mind,   at   that   time   in   possession   of   instruments   varying   in   age   from   a   hundred   to
a   hundred   and   fifty   years,   and   criticism   must   of   course
have   been   freely   expressed   with   regard   to   the   differences
of   tone   of   the   various   instruments,—those   of   Gasparo,   of
Maggini,   of   the   Amatis,   and   of   others   of   the   Brescian   and
Cremonese   schools.

These   simple   but   practical   views   will   not,   we   fear,   carry

---

* Jean Baptiste Volumier was Musical Director to Augustus, Elector of
Saxony   and   King   of   Poland.   He   resided   at   Dresden,   and   directed   the
Court Music in that city from the year 1706 until 1728, the year of his
death.

† Arisi MS., " The Violin " (G. Hart).

much weight with those who in the present, as in the past, have sought to represent Stradivari as

Fig. 41.—STRADIVARI'S CALLIPERS FOR THE ADJUSTMENT OF THE THICKNESSES.

an almost superhuman worker, taking every fresh step—be it change of form, of model, of proportions or material —only after mature reflection and calculation. Much has been written, and various more or less ingenious theories, based on scientific principles, have been propounded to account for the unsurpassed tonal qualities found in his instruments. We cannot agree with such deductions, and the views we express are the result of reflection founded on daily study of Stradivari's works, and on comparison of them with those of his forerunners, patiently carried on through a long period of years.

If we take the interior construction and examine more especially that important point —t h e t h i c k-nesses of the backs and bellies — we find that the principles left us by Stradivari are those of Gasparo, *plus* the result of a gradual progression, in which Maggini and the Amatis had a large share.

Maggini varied the thicknesses of the backs of his violins from $\frac{1}{8}$ to $\frac{11}{64}$ of an inch in the centre, graduating to $\frac{5}{64}$ at the flanks. The bellies vary from $\frac{7}{64}$ to $\frac{11}{64}$ of an inch in the centre, graduating to $\frac{5}{64}$ and $\frac{1}{8}$ at the flanks.

In Gasparo tenors—of the violins we cannot speak with any certainty—we note that the graduation of the thicknesses from the centre of the instrument is marked in the same decided manner. We see, therefore, that the importance, from a tonal point of view, of the extra thickness in the centre was recognised as early as Gasparo's time. Maggini's thicknesses are less irregular than those of his master, and his tendency was to diminish them.

> A violin of Andrea Amati, made in 1574, gives us: *back*, at the centre, $\frac{10}{64}''$ to $\frac{11}{64}''$, graduating to $\frac{1}{8}''$ at the flanks; *belly*, at the centre, $\frac{1}{8}''$, graduating to $\frac{6}{64}''$ at the flanks.
>
> An Andrea Amati violin (no date): back $\frac{11}{64}''$, flanks $\frac{1}{8}''$, diminishing to $\frac{7}{64}''$; belly $\frac{1}{8}''$, flanks $\frac{7}{64}''$, diminishing to $\frac{5}{64}''$ (thickness of belly rather irregular).
>
> A violin of the Brothers Amati, of the early date of 1596, gives us: $\frac{12}{64}''$ in centre of back, graduating to $\frac{1}{8}''$ at the flanks, and going off to $\frac{4}{64}''$ at the extreme of the flanks; the belly $\frac{6}{64}''$ in centre to $\frac{4}{64}''$ at the flanks.
>
> A Nicolò Amati, of the year 1648, gives: $\frac{10}{64}''$, graduating to $\frac{1}{8}''$ at the flanks, and $\frac{5}{64}''$ at extremes; the belly, at centre, $\frac{7}{64}''$, graduating to $\frac{5}{64}''$ at extremes.
>
> Another specimen of the last period (*i.e.* 1670-84) gives: back $\frac{11}{64}''$, diminishing to $\frac{6}{64}''$; belly $\frac{7}{64}''$ all over.

That Stradivari adjusted his thicknesses thoughtfully is apparent to anybody who has been privileged to examine very many specimens of his work; but we fail to find any indication whatsoever that he was guided by any other principle than that derived from the practice of his predecessors. He possibly tested by touch the resisting power of the back and belly when approaching the standard thickness, and, according to circumstances, he left them a little stouter or a little thinner, the back showing greater variation than the belly. Pieces of wood of equal thickness vary a good deal in rigidity; the curve of the model also influenced the decision. Neither do we find that Stradivari—or, in fact, any of the great makers—sought to obtain absolute precision in the working of the thicknesses; the whole is carefully wrought out, yet without any attempt at mathematical exactness. They were apparently of opinion that greater precision was unnecessary.

In Stradivari's earlier works we meet with the stoutest proportions he made use of; as he grew older his tendency was to lighten them. The following particulars, which are, without exception, of noted specimens, prove this statement:—

A violin, dated 1672. Back at centre $\frac{14}{64}''$, graduating to $\frac{5\text{-}6}{64}''$ at flanks; belly all over between $\frac{5}{64}''$ and $\frac{6}{64}''$.

A violin of the period 1680–84. Back $\frac{1}{4}''$, graduating to $\frac{6}{64}''$; belly $\frac{1}{8}''$, graduating to $\frac{7}{64}''$.

A violin of the year 1686. Back, centre $\frac{12}{64}''$, graduating to $\frac{6}{64}''$; belly centre $\frac{7}{64}''$, graduating to $\frac{6}{64}''$.

A violin of the year 1689. Back, centre $\frac{11}{64}''$, graduating to $\frac{6}{64}''$, and at extreme edge $\frac{4}{64}''$; belly varies between $\frac{5}{64}''$ and $\frac{6}{64}''$.

A violin dated 1690. Back, centre $\frac{11}{64}''$, graduating to $\frac{7}{64}''$; belly varies from $\frac{6}{64}''$ to $\frac{7}{64}''$.

A violin, "Long Strad," dated 1693. Back $\frac{12}{64}''$, graduating to $\frac{7}{64}''$; belly all over $\frac{6}{64}''$.

A violin dated 1698. Back, centre $\frac{11}{64}''$, graduating to $\frac{7}{64}''$; belly varies between $\frac{6}{64}''$ and $\frac{7}{64}''$.

A violin dated 1700. Back, centre $\frac{12}{64}''$, graduating to $\frac{8}{64}''$; $\frac{6}{64}''$ at extreme edges; belly $\frac{6}{64}''$ all over.

A violin dated 1704. Back, centre $\frac{10}{64}''$, graduating to $\frac{6}{64}''$; belly varies between $\frac{5}{64}''$ and $\frac{7}{64}''$.

A violin dated 1709. Back, centre $\frac{9}{64}''$, graduating to $\frac{6}{64}''$; belly varies between $\frac{6}{64}''$ and $\frac{7}{64}''$.

A violin dated 1711. Back at centre $\frac{10}{64}''$, graduating to $\frac{6}{64}''$; belly $\frac{6}{64}''$ all over.

A violin dated 1714. Back at centre $\frac{11}{64}''$, graduating to $\frac{6}{64}''$; belly between $\frac{6}{64}''$ and $\frac{7}{64}''$.

A violin dated 1715. Back at centre $\frac{10}{64}''$, graduating to $\frac{6}{64}''$ and $\frac{5}{64}''$; belly between $\frac{6}{64}''$ and $\frac{7}{64}''$.

A violin dated 1716. Back at centre $\frac{11}{64}''$, graduating to $\frac{6}{64}''$; belly $\frac{6}{64}''$ all over.

A violin dated 1722. Back at centre $\frac{10}{64}''$, graduating to $\frac{6}{64}''$ at flanks and $\frac{4}{64}''$ at extreme edge; belly $\frac{6}{64}''$ all over.

A violin dated 1727. Back at centre $\frac{9}{64}''$, graduating to $\frac{5-6}{64}''$; belly varies from $\frac{6}{64}''$ to $\frac{7}{64}''$.

A violin dated 1733. Back at centre $\frac{9}{64}''$, graduating to $\frac{6}{64}''$; belly varies from $\frac{6}{64}''$ to $\frac{7}{64}''$.

A violin dated 1736. Back, $\frac{9}{64}''$, graduating to $\frac{6}{64}''$; belly varies between $\frac{1}{8}''$ and $\frac{6}{64}''$.

It has at various times been asserted that Stradivari erred in the adjustment of his thicknesses, and made his instruments too thin. Fortunately, such statements invariably proceed from persons whose knowledge of Stradivari's work is very limited. The more thought we give to the subject, the more reason we see to hesitate in speaking positively for or against such a view. That the tone of different examples of Stradivari's work varies in degree of excellence is beyond dispute; but when we endeavour to find the cause of the disparity, many points have to be considered: thicknesses, model, dimensions, wood, and, last but not least, varnish, all play their part; each helps in its relative degree of importance to make or mar. Hence, where a theorist will condemn an unsatisfactory instrument because the thicknesses do not agree with his theory, quite another reason may be furnished for its shortcomings. We believe that the true cause of disparity lies in the most fitting relations of structure, wood, and varnish not having been attained. Stradivari, *we cannot too often repeat*, was not infallible; like all human workers he had his failings, although in the majority of his works he was eminently successful.

On the blocks and linings Stradivari bestowed more care and attention than did his predecessors. His principles were those of the Amatis, who before 1600 had the idea of mortising the linings of the bouts into the corner blocks, presumably to give greater strength to the sides, and at the same time to render the linings less liable to come unglued. The finish of these parts in many of the Amati violins, especially in those of the last period of Nicolò, gives the impression of having been hurriedly done—strangely in contrast with the exterior work. Often have we scrutinised these interiors with the hope of finding Stradivari's pronounced style, but up till now in vain. Stradivari seems to have hit the happy medium in his mode of finish,—no unnecessary polish, yet sound and clean, even though just as left by chisel, gouge, or knife : in fact, the interior forcibly illustrates his keen sense for trueness and squareness of work. He selected willow for the blocks and linings (generally of a deep brown-red colour), which is light and tough, and was easily obtainable in the neighbourhood of Cremona. The Amatis often utilised pine for their blocks and willow for the linings, but Stradivari invariably used the latter wood throughout.* He reduced his blocks to the exact limit consistent with

Fig. 42.—Stradivari's Callipers for the Adjustment of the Thicknesses.

---

* We have met with one exception, where the master used pine for the corner blocks of a violoncello.

strength—with the object, no doubt, of leaving the sides as free for vibration as possible. In the top block Stradivari inserted usually three rough-headed nails—we have seen blocks with four,—the use of which was to pass through into the base of the neck and thus aid to hold it securely in place.* The number of Stradivari violins retaining their original top block is very limited, their removal having been rendered necessary by various circumstances ; and the few which do still exist have had the nails removed, leaving the three holes and the impression made by the nail-heads in the soft wood plainly visible. This feature was evidently a very old practice with Italian makers, dating from the Brescians, and it continued in use till about 1800. Stradivari, as already stated, generally used three nails ; and so did the Amatis ; but some of the later makers dispensed with one, sometimes with two, while at other times they put in four. Had Stradivari mortised the base of the neck into the block instead of simply gluing it on to the sides, any such precaution would have been superfluous, but not until the dawn of last century was this improved method of mortising adopted. Our impression is that it originated with the French makers, about the period of Pique and Lupot, and not with the Italians.† These nails, varying from $\frac{3}{4}$ of an inch to 1 inch in length, penetrated from $\frac{1}{4}$ to $\frac{3}{8}$ of an inch into the base of the neck ; and, owing to the subsequent lengthening and re-shaping of the neck, especially at the base, which have taken place since the time of Stradivari, their points have come to the surface, and in the few violins and violas still possessing their original necks, the traces can be clearly perceived.

The interior of Stradivari's instruments serves to this

---

* See illustration of the linings and blocks. † See p. 204.

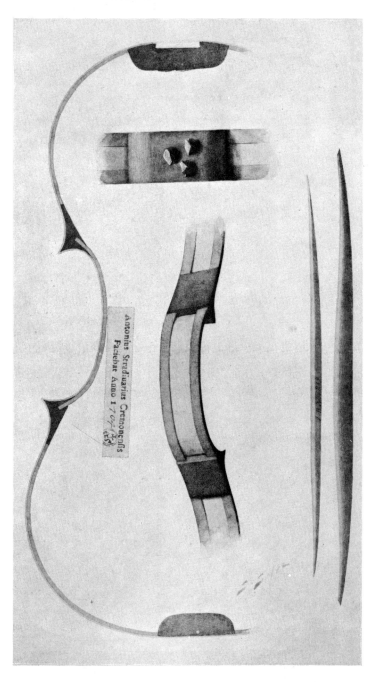

The linings and blocks as left by Stradivari—the position of his label—
the bass bar of Stradivari (the one taken out by J. B. Vuillaume
from the Betts Stradivari in 1859) and a modern bar.

day as our guide, and no modern maker of real ability has departed from it—putting on one side the bass-bar—except in some very small degree. Stradivari's bass-bar was, as is generally known, smaller in every way than those inserted by the more modern makers. There is, perhaps, no part of violin construction more full of interest than this slender piece of pine. Broadly speaking, its function consists in retarding the vibrations of the one side of the belly, thus materially helping to obtain the graver bass notes. To the question, who was the maker who first conceived the idea of utilising a separate piece of pine, which after being fitted to the curve of the belly is glued on to it, no certain answer can be given, and the scarcity of sixteenth-century instruments in their original state renders even a guess at the truth very difficult. We have nevertheless seen much to justify us in forming certain conclusions which we believe cannot be far from the truth. Our impression is that the earliest Brescian viol-makers simply made the bellies of stouter substance on the bass side, this being gradually so much accentuated as to assume the form of a ridge. That this ridge came eventually to be replaced by a detached bar was, we suggest, probably due in the first instance to an error in workmanship. In gouging out the interior of an instrument nothing is easier than to make it too thin before one becomes aware of the fact, and a good deal of Brescian work especially suggests a want of care and precision in the adjustment of the thicknesses. Hence the assumption is not too improbable that, in order to utilise an over-thinned belly, a detached bar was tried, and that the improved tone which resulted opened the eyes of the maker and insured the detached bar's permanent adoption. Whether or not this hypothesis be correct, we are convinced that the detached bar was not adopted till between 1550 and 1600. Maggini unquestionably glued in his bars, and Gasparo in some cases, we believe, did the same. The earliest bass-bar seen by ourselves is one which we took from a violin made in 1621 by Antonius and Hieronymus Amati; and a glance at its proportions, which together with those of others we now give, is not without interest. To facilitate comparison, we also give the average dimensions of a modern bass-bar :—

BASS-BARS.

Name.	Date.	Length.	Height in Centre.	Thickness.
		inch.	inch.	inch.
Modern Bar . . .	—	$10\frac{1}{2}$	$0\frac{7}{16}$	$0\frac{4}{16}$
A. and H. Amati . .	1621	$10\frac{5}{8}$	$0\frac{4}{16}$	$0\frac{3}{16}$
A. and H. Amati . .	Later	$9\frac{1}{4}$	$0\frac{4}{16}$	$0\frac{3}{16}$ bare
N. Amati . . .	1650	$8\frac{5}{8}$	$0\frac{4}{16}$	$0\frac{3}{16}$
N. Amati . . .	1665	$9\frac{1}{4}$	$0\frac{3}{16}$ full	$0\frac{3}{16}$
Stradivari . . .	168–	$9\frac{1}{2}$ & $\frac{1}{16}$	$0\frac{4}{16}$	$0\frac{3}{16}$
Stradivari . . .	1704	$9\frac{1}{2}$	$0\frac{4}{16}$	$0\frac{3}{16}$
Stradivari . . .	1710	$9\frac{5}{8}$	$0\frac{4}{16}$ full	$0\frac{3}{16}$
Stradivari . . .	1716	10	$0\frac{5}{16}$	$0\frac{3}{16}$
Stradivari . . .	1719	$9\frac{1}{2}$	$0\frac{4}{16}$ full	$0\frac{3}{16}$
Stradivari . . .	1721	$9\frac{3}{4}$	$0\frac{5}{16}$	$0\frac{3}{16}$
A. Gagliano . . .	1720	$10\frac{7}{8}$	$0\frac{5}{16}$	$0\frac{3}{16}$ full
Joseph Guarnerius, filius Andrea . . .	1711	$9\frac{1}{2}$	$0\frac{5}{16}$	$0\frac{3}{16}$
Carlo Bergonzi . .	174–	$10\frac{1}{4}$	$0\frac{5}{16}$	$0\frac{3}{16}$ bare
J. B. Guadagnini . .	1760	$9\frac{7}{8}$	$0\frac{5}{16}$	$0\frac{3}{16}$
Gagliano . . .	1780	$10\frac{1}{4}$	$0\frac{7}{16}$	$0\frac{4}{16}$
F. Gagliano . . .	1783	12	$0\frac{6}{16}$	$0\frac{4}{16}$ full
F. Gagliano . . .	1789	$10\frac{3}{4}$	$0\frac{11}{16}$	$0\frac{9}{16}$
Jacobs	1702	$9\frac{1}{2} \times \frac{1}{16}$	$0\frac{4}{16}$ full	$0\frac{3}{16}$
Albani	1700	$9\frac{1}{4}$	$0\frac{4}{16}$	$0\frac{3}{16}$ full

It will be noted that, with the exception of the year 1716, Stradivari adhered practically to one size of bar, that size showing a slight increase on the two bars of N. Amati, but not on that of A. and H. Amati; while those of Alessandro Gagliano of 1720, and of Carlo Bergonzi of 174–, as compared with Stradivari's, demonstrate the fact that bars of increased length and height were inserted at an early period. The later members of the Gagliano family adjusted at times bars of similar proportions to those of to-day, and even stronger ones, as can be seen by the instances given. In fixing the dimensions of his bars, Stradivari was evidently guided by past usage rather than by fresh experiments: in fact, the conditions which later on necessitated the substitution of a stronger bar did not then exist, consequently no change was called for. The standard of pitch was lower, hence the pressure of the bridge on the belly, which the bar helps to support, was less; and, further, more powerful tone production was only beginning to develop towards the end of the eighteenth century.* We may consequently assume that players were perfectly content with the results attained by the smaller bar. The proportions of the present bass-bar were more or less adopted about the beginning of the last century.

Let us now turn to the exterior work of Stradivari's instruments, commencing with the outline, which illustrates in a marked degree that refreshing originality ever present with the master, and never entirely absent from the work of the many other Italian makers who flourished both before and after this epoch: even the Milanese cheap-jacks† possessed it, although obviously inspired by Cremonese work. The recognition of this fact causes us to seek for an explanation to some extent in their system of construction,

---

* The improved bow must have had a considerable influence on the production of greater power of tone. Tourte was born in 1747, died in 1835.

† We here refer to such makers as Grancino, the several members of the Testore family, and their followers.

as it cannot for one moment be presumed that the greater
number of Italian workmen were other than men of ordinary
stamp, in no way possessed of the great powers of Stradivari.
Yet their instruments, however faulty they may have been
in other respects, have invariably a certain originality of
design, which is in many
cases remarkable : out-
line, sound-holes, model,
form of head—in fact,
every part shows it.   In
the case of Stradivari,
we know that he was a
fine draftsman and an
adept at designing, and
he turned his capabilities
to account when sketch-
ing out a fresh outline.
As will be seen on ex-
amining the illustration
we give of one of these
designs (fig. 43), his
practice was to draw the
curves *minus* the outer
edge all round—*i.e.* the

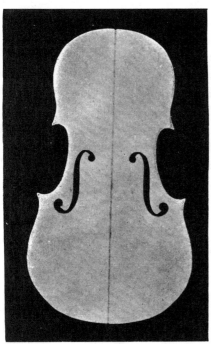

Fig. 43.—DESIGN BY STRADIVARI FOR THE OUTLINE
AND "*f*" HOLES OF A SMALL VIOLIN.

curves are those of the
sides.   The sides once
constructed, he placed them alternately on the slabs prepared
for the back and belly, and traced round them with an open
compass in order to obtain the margin of edge required.
Examine and compare the outlines of some of the principal
followers of Amati and Stradivari, such as Andreas Guarnerius,
Petrus Guarnerius of Mantua, his nephew of Venice, Joseph
Guarnerius *filius* Andreæ, the Rugeri family, Cappa, Carlo

Bergonzi, Lorenzo and Joannes Baptista Guadagnini, and you will find that each one struck out a form differing from that of his neighbour, although they were all indebted to the same source for the foundation of their ideas. Take Petrus Guarnerius of Mantua and Joseph Guarnerius, both sons as well as pupils of Andrea. Once set free from their father's workshop, each struck out in his own direction, and produced works which are stamped with originality—those of Petrus remarkably so. Even Carlo Bergonzi was not content with the unsurpassable designs of Stradivari, and seems to have taken the earliest opportunity of asserting his freedom. In fact, from the pioneer Brescians to the latest of the Cremonese, originality of form was ever one of the prominent merits of the many and various makers.

Were it not known that Stradivari made use of moulds for the building up of the sides, we would have suggested that he, after first settling upon his design for the outline, and tracing it—probably from a cartridge pattern—on the slabs of maple and pine prepared for back and belly, roughly cut it out by a bow-saw ; that then, after shaping the model, finally trueing up the curves of the outline and hollowing out the back to its correct thickness, he proceeded to glue on the six shaped blocks exactly in their respective places, and, when these were dry, bent the sides to them, thus dispensing altogether with a mould. This system, though obviously presenting greater difficulties, especially in the way of keeping the sides true, was that in use with all the old English makers (to whom we think moulds were unknown) ; and it certainly has the advantage of allowing unlimited freedom to continually alter the outline, a facility which is restricted by the use of a mould—*i.e.* if the same mould is utilised unaltered—as it cannot be too clearly understood that the outline has to follow the exact contour of the mould, and *vice versa*. That Stradivari did use moulds is proved by their existence in the hands of the descendants of Count Cozio, who purchased them direct from Paolo Stradivari, his son. Hence the question arises, how did he succeed in effecting, year after year, the continual and ever-varying modifications of the curves of outline? It is evident that he drew a fresh design, and made a new mould for each *decided* change of form, whether of larger or smaller dimensions; but at the same time we think he probably had

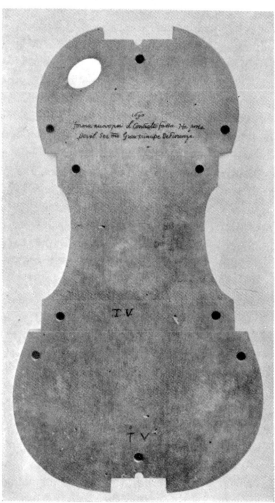

Fig. 44.—Mould made by Stradivari for the Contralto (Tenore Viola) of the Tuscan Set of Instruments.

(The inscription written on the mould by the master has been touched over in the reproduction in order to render it more legible.)

some simple plan which, by a slight alteration, permitted him to make use of the old mould while retaining a free hand to alter in a greater or lesser degree the curves, more especially those of the bouts and corners.

Examination of the moulds possessed by the Marchese Dalla Valle (there are nineteen, three of which are for tenors) furnishes us with no certain clue to any such method. All are of the most primitive type of interior moulds, made from planks about half an inch in thickness, similar to many actually in use at the various workshops in Mirecourt : several seem to have been frequently used, others but seldom. It may be that Stradivari continually re-shaped the existing moulds, and added to them thin strips of wood or canvas when necessary to suit the altered outline, eventually destroying them when too much patched. Failing some such plan, we can only conclude that he made new moulds for every change of form, however small that change may have been.

We may now turn to the purfling, which is connected with the outline. That this is so will be understood when it is borne in mind that it follows the contour of the instrument at an equal distance from the outer edge, and the perfection of its sweep depends in considerable measure on the accurate cutting of all the curves of the outline of the back and belly. It serves to throw into relief the elegance and truth or otherwise of the form ; and Stradivari, by varying the thickness of its substance, its distance from the outer edge, and the different treatment of the mitres at the corners, caused it to materially contribute towards effecting those various changes in the character of the edge and fluting which we all so much admire. His means and method of cutting the groove for the purfling were, as far as we can judge, those of to-day, and how admirably Stradivari handled the knife is shown by the accuracy of the cutting of these grooves. But the time of insertion is different, as the more general practice among modern makers is to insert the purfling immediately after the outline is cut and the model roughly shaped, whereas Stradivari and his brother makers did so only when the body of the instrument was glued together and so far finished. Recognition of this point is not without importance, as it left the maker a free hand to correct and alter the curves, should any inequality of the margin of the edge round the sides have required it; and Stradivari undoubtedly did so, as it is very rare to find the curves

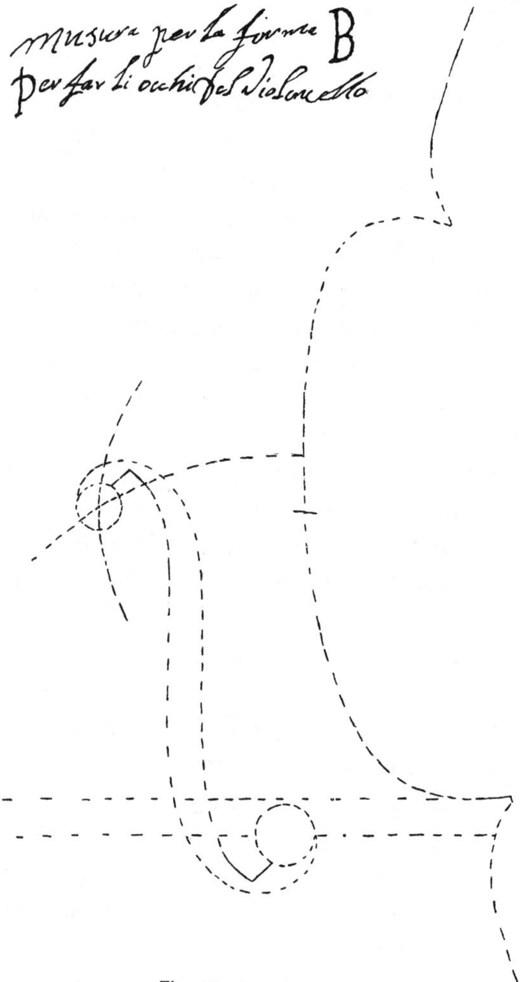

Fig. 45.

of the back and belly of any of his instruments in exact
agreement : in some, indeed, a considerable difference exists.
This method of purfling was that of all the old English
makers, and we believe of the various foreign ones also.

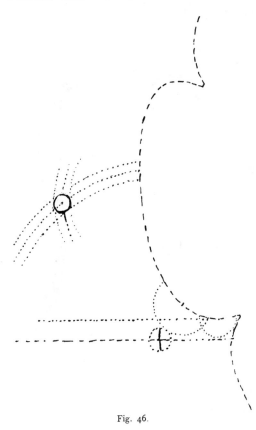

It unquestionably has
advantages ; but one
serious drawback to
it is that it presents
an obstacle to ob-
taining   absolute
accuracy   of   the
thicknesses,   as   it
necessitates finishing
the model and fluting
of the   edge   after
the thicknesses have
been adjusted.   We
are of opinion that
this fact accounts in
some measure for the
inaccuracy   and   in-
equalities   of   the
thicknesses of many
of   the   old   Italian
instruments.

Let us now pass
on   to   the   sound-
holes — that marked

Fig. 46.

feature of the violin which Stradivari designed and cut with
such consummate skill.   As in the outline, the same innate
originality is conspicuous, and it is difficult to meet with
two specimens of his work having sound-holes of identical
design.   His plan for placing them in correct position on

the belly (figs. 45 and 46) shows considerable ingenuity, and furnishes striking testimony to the freedom of the Italian system of violin-making. By a series of compass-made circles Stradivari fixed upon the exact position he desired for the top and bottom openings of the sound-holes ; then, aided by a small template (fig. 47) placed between the two holes, a small point at each end holding it in position, he

Fig. 47.   Fig. 48.

TEMPLATES FOR THE OPENING OF "*f*" HOLES, AND SKETCH OF COMPLETED "*f*" HOLE.

roughly traced the longitudinal opening, and thenceforward trusted to his unerring eye and command of the knife for the formation of the wings and the exact curve of the top and bottom holes.

We possess tracings of eight drawings which Stradivari termed " *Misura per gli occhi*," which were designed to decide upon the position of the sound-holes in violins of various dimensions, in tenors and violoncellos ; and, repeated scrutiny and comparison notwithstanding, we are still at a loss to discover either a fixed starting-point or a guiding rule in any of them.

This admirable method of forming the sound-holes evidently did not originate with Stradivari. It had been practised from the earliest period, and a template such as is now employed, to trace the entire sound-hole on the belly, was, if not unknown, at any rate not used. From Gasparo's time onward, succeeding generations of makers had been taught to trust to accuracy of eye rather than to any mechanical pattern, and a certain knowledge of drawing was probably an indispensable part of each maker's training. The result is that we are charmed by the ever-varying sound-holes of the greater Italian makers, and spared the sameness of design so characteristic of the more modern ones of all nations. Stradivari fixed upon the main features of the sound-holes at the commencement of his working career, and throughout his long life, although he varied the one set of curves in a number of ways, he always faithfully maintained the spirit of his design. Contrast Joseph Guarnerius del Gesù, who apparently, the position of the top holes once fixed, cut the remaining portion of the sound-holes at random—without, in fact, any effort to closely uphold a traditional design. The result is, in certain cases, magnificent ; in others, though intensely original, it is very ugly. An exceedingly curious feature is often noticeable in the sound-holes of many of Stradivari's instruments, and is more frequently met with in those dated later than 1720 : he placed the right-hand sound-hole slightly higher than the other. Often have we pondered over this strange fact, and we cannot but believe that it was due to defective vision, or perhaps to his method of tracing. We account for the right-hand hole always being higher by the hypothesis that he must invariably have traced and cut it before the other, or *vice versa*.

We now come to the modelling, a feature which Stradivari treated with his characteristic freedom. That he was
greatly influenced by the teaching of the several generations
of Amatis is clear, nor could it have been otherwise when
we recall the extreme grace and delicacy embodied in so
much of their modelling. Many of Stradivari's instruments,
notably the earlier ones, reflect Amati influence in their
modelling, more strongly perhaps than in any other part of
his work ; but as time passed on, doubtless seeking different
tone results, he reverted more frequently to the flatter and
less curved arching of the viols, and finally combined with
much of the grace of his predecessors the solidity and
bluntness exemplified in the instruments of the Brescians.
Now, at the period of which we write, arching templates or
models such as those generally, although not invariably, used
by makers of to-day, were unthought of and unknown.
Stradivari may possibly have had some gauge to indicate
the minimum or maximum thickness required at the highest
point of back and belly ; but we greatly doubt this, and
believe that all the old Italian makers were solely guided by
mind and eye. Thus unfettered, they could not but impart
to the archings of each instrument a something, however
slight, which avoided simple repetition. We must also
remember one important point which is apt to be over-
looked—namely, that the Italian makers, even Stradivari
himself, were often obliged to unduly flatten their model
because of the lack of substance in the material of back
and belly ; they were forced, in fact, to cut their fiddles
according to their wood.

The head, that all-important part of an instrument from
an artistic point of view, now claims our attention. Previous
to 1600 Maggini's efforts, assisted by those of Andrea Amati
and of his two sons, had succeeded in transforming the

rough, ill-shaped Brescian head into one of symmetrical curves and graceful appearance. The broad scope for originality of treatment offered by its component parts was duly perceived, and admirably taken advantage of by the Amatis and their contemporaries ; but Stradivari still found room to initiate small changes, often trifling in themselves, which in the majority of cases brought the head into harmony with the curves and proportions of the body for which it was destined. Stradivari transferred his design for the head to the block of wood, previous to carving it, by the aid of similar templates to those used nowadays by ourselves. A fixed pattern is practically indispensable in order that one side of the design may be the counterpart of the other. He probably traced round the outer curves from his pattern, and lightly pricked out the scroll with a fine point, removing all traces of the punctures in the carving. He invariably carved both faces of the scroll with strict accuracy, and also maintained absolute similitude between them. As he reached advanced age, we of course note slight failings in these respects from time to time. That a marking-point was used by the Italians for this operation is confirmed by the visible signs of its punctures round the tip of many of their scrolls, notably those of Joannes Baptista Guadagnini. It must not be understood that these means in themselves ensured that admirably accurate work which Stradivari's head so forcibly illustrates. Joseph Guarnerius del Gesù had, no doubt, similar patterns, yet it is quite exceptional to find in his instruments agreement and conformity between the two sides of the head : it is evident that in most cases he cast all rules to the wind, making first one side, then the other, without once comparing them. Many other Italian makers also worked with considerable inaccuracy in this respect.

Stradivari fluted his heads with the same freedom and

beauty as he carved the other parts; and it is not without
interest to note that he had recourse to the compass in order
to keep the line dividing the fluting exactly in the centre. The
marks made by the foot of the compass are often faintly
visible at a slight distance from each other. To effect this
purpose some makers, notably Lupot, ran a gauge-mark right
down the centre line.

The greatest change—indeed, with the exception of
the stronger bar, the only one which has taken place in
the construction of the violin since Stradivari's time—is the
altered proportions and position of the head and neck. The
necks of Stradivari's violins * were of the same dimensions
as those of the Amatis. In length they varied, from under
the nut to the edge of the belly, from $4\frac{3}{4}$ to $4\frac{7}{8}$ inches;
the width at the top of the finger-board was from 1 to
$1\frac{1}{16}$ inch; at edge of belly $1\frac{5}{16}$ to $1\frac{3}{4}$ inch, and the relative
proportions of to-day are: neck, length, $5\frac{1}{16}$ to $5\frac{1}{8}$ inches;
widths, $0\frac{7}{8}$ and $1\frac{1}{4}$ inch respectively. Thus we have lengthened
the neck from $\frac{1}{4}$ to $\frac{3}{8}$ of an inch and narrowed it about $\frac{1}{8}$ of
an inch. Our method of fitting the head and neck on the
body, and of obtaining the necessary angle to permit of the
finger-board carrying a given height of bridge, also differs
very materially from that of the old makers. In speaking of
the interior blocks, we mentioned that the base of the neck
was simply glued on to the top sides, and that the nails driven
through the block helped to hold it in position. This clearly
shows that Stradivari adjusted and fixed the head before
gluing the body together. How, then, did he determine
that the neck was placed straight?—as obviously, unless the
belly was in position, in order to correctly indicate the centre
between the sound-holes, the operation would be one of some

* See illustration.

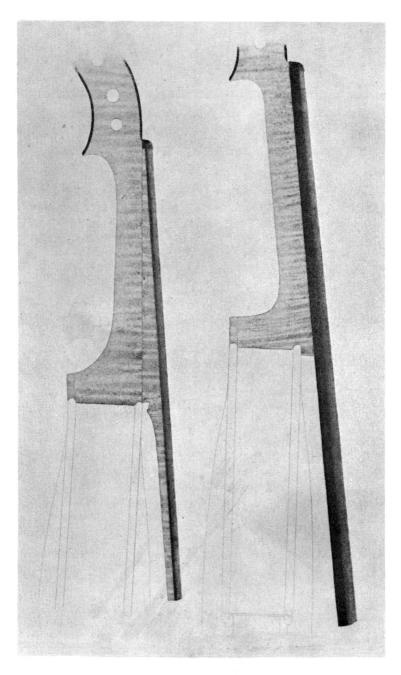

1. Neck and fingerboard as left by Stradivari.

2. Modern neck and fingerboard.

difficulty. Reflection has supplied the answer. Most
observers will have noted in Stradivari's instruments, as in
many other old ones, the existence of two small pegs, which
pass through the back into the top and bottom blocks; and
the generally accepted belief is that they were invariably
inserted exactly in the groove cut for the inlaying of the
purfling; in fact, we have had their position pointed out to
us by the learned as distinct evidence of the genuineness of
a *soi-disant* Stradivari. In the greater number of instruments
Stradivari did so place them, the purfling cutting them partly
through, leaving the inner half only showing; but in other
instances they are found entirely inside the purfling, or, again,
the halves remaining visible are on the outside. Now, similar
pegs were also inserted in the belly, and their object was
apparently to assist the glue in holding both back and belly
to the blocks; but in the case of the latter they evidently
served a double purpose, as they allowed Stradivari to fix
the belly exactly in its place upon the sides, then, after
adjusting and gluing on the neck, he removed the belly in
order to drive the nails through into the head. Our illustration
of the neck and finger-board as left by Stradivari, side by
side with those of to-day, clearly shows the very different
angle at which we now set the head. Observe that, instead
of canting backwards and the face of the neck standing up
from the belly about $\frac{3}{16}$ to $\frac{1}{4}$ of an inch, as seen in the case
of the modern one, Stradivari rather inclined it forward so
that the face of the neck came level with the edge, and
a small groove was cut in the neck to allow of the edge
passing over. We obtain our height at the bridge by means
of the more acute angle of the neck, whereas Stradivari
effected the same result by using a wedge-shaped finger-board.
The slighter proportions and the greater hollowing out of the
base of the modern neck will also be noted. Our modern

adjustment of the neck and finger-board certainly constitutes an improvement—small though it be—upon the methods of

Fig. 49.
DESIGN FOR A PEG.

the Cremonese makers; but, before taking credit to ourselves, we must remember that the change is entirely due to, and was brought about by, the altered conditions of playing. During Stradivari's lifetime no violin-player went beyond the third or fourth position, consequently the neck and finger-board as then fitted answered every purpose. It was only when players recognised the greater scope afforded them for more varied methods of execution by extending the compass of the instrument, that the makers realised the necessity of adapting the neck and finger-board to the altered circumstances, thus facilitating the shifting into higher positions. Lancetti * mentions that the brothers Mantegazza (living at the beginning of the last century) were often entrusted with instruments for the purpose of having the necks lengthened, *according to the fashion prevailing in Paris.*

Stradivari's violin finger-boards were of several different lengths. The shortest appears to have measured $7\frac{1}{2}$ inches, width at top $1\frac{1}{16}$, at bottom $1\frac{1}{2}$; in another we find the length increased to $7\frac{7}{8}$ inches (this pattern is dated 1685), and a third, dated 1715, on which the maker wrote "longer" and "broader," is $8\frac{1}{2}$ inches long by $1\frac{3}{16}$ and $1\frac{11}{16}$ wide. The modern finger-board

Fig. 50.
AN ORIGINAL PEG,
AS USED BY THE
MASTER.

---

* "Biographical Notices," Milan, 1823.

measures approximately $10\frac{1}{2}$ inches by $\frac{7}{8}$ and $1\frac{5}{8}$. Stradivari's were generally made from odd pieces of maple, cuttings from the slabs used for the backs; in some cases the top was veneered in ebony or an Italian wood. At times Stradivari inlaid a line of purfling or stringing composed of ivory and ebony along the edge, or inlaid the whole surface with a design in purfling. In the case of special instruments, such as the Tuscan set, in addition to the ivory and ebony lines, he inlaid the Medici arms, delicately executed in mother-of-pearl. The tail-pieces were made of similar material to that of the finger-boards, and invariably matched these as regards inlaying, etc.

Fig. 51.
DESIGN FOR A
TAIL-PIECE.

Stradivari's bridges were of various designs, but the same spirit pervades them all. They also appear to have been made from the odd cuttings of the backs, and were a little thinner and lower than those of to-day, as well as more open in design. Our modern tendency to leave more substance in the bridge has been rendered necessary by the increased strain put upon it since the time of Stradivari; otherwise it remains practically unaltered (figs. 52–55).

Before concluding this chapter, we will devote a few words to the unique collection of relics from Stradivari's workshop which have, thanks to the intelligent enthusiasm of Count Cozio de Salabue, fortunately been preserved to us. Of mechanical tools, with the exception of the callipers shown in our illustration, nothing of interest exists. Chisels, gouges, planes, knives, scrapers, cramps, and the other necessary appliances of a violin-maker's workshop, are all absent. In the correspondence that took place between the descendants of Stradivari and the Count, the word " tools "

Fig. 52.

is repeatedly used; we must therefore assume that the Count had them. Possibly one or other of the violin-makers with whom he was intimate, such as Joannes Baptista Guadagnini, or the brothers Mantegazza, may have begged or borrowed them. Vuillaume obtained several of Stradivari's moulds, which he presented to the Museum of the Paris

Fig. 53.

Conservatoire; and M. Chanot-Chardon possesses a set of small planes said to have belonged to Stradivari. We believe these things were taken to Paris by Tarisio, who, as stated elsewhere, had dealings with Count Cozio. Or it may be that Bergonzi, who had, we learn, the loan of certain patterns and moulds, also had a number of the working tools; and as less interest would be attached

Fig. 54.

to them—the majority being but the ordinary tools of the wood-worker of the period—than to drawings and moulds, their non-restitution probably passed unheeded, and they were then possibly used up or dispersed. As previously mentioned, the moulds number nineteen, of which sixteen are for violins and three for violas; those required for viols and for violoncellos are not extant. Several have Stradivari's writing or markings on them—the date when constructed, and letters such as S., L. or B., the object of which seems to have been to identify the patterns belonging to a given form, all of which were similarly lettered. Others bear remarks written on them by the Count—as, for instance, the mould dated 1692, on which he

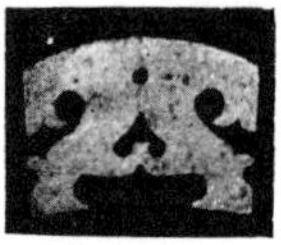

Fig. 55.

Figs. 52-55.—DESIGNS FOR THE BRIDGES.

records that it was utilised by Stradivari when in his ninety-second year to make a violin ; also on the mould dated 1705 the Count writes : "forma grande." Two of the tenor moulds bear Stradivari's interesting statement—"ha posta per il Gran Principe di Toscana," * that they were constructed expressly for the Grand Prince of Tuscany. Of the various drawings and patterns it is impossible to speak without enthusiasm. They bring us face to face with irrefutable evidence in support of the ideas we have formed of the man. Painstaking, thorough and careful to the smallest detail, we see him specially design-ing everything—even to bridge, pegs and tail-piece — for a given instru-ment, and then further embellishing these fittings with painted or inlaid designs. He also turned his atten-tion to the cases intended for the re-ception of his instruments, and carried his fervour to the point of making sketches for the locks and hinges (figs. 56 and 57). Nothing apparently was too unimportant for his attention,

Fig. 56.

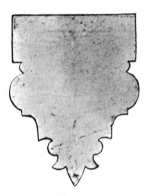

Fig. 57.
DESIGNS FOR CASE-HINGE OR LOCK-PLATE.

and the recognition of this veritable passion to leave nothing undone to ensure the success of the whole, throws a flood of light on his lifelong work.

Among other patterns we have those of a viol-da-gamba with five strings (small pieces of the strings used are

---

* Stradivari's orthography, as will be noted in the facsimile of this and of other specimens of his handwriting, was very imperfect.

Fig. 58.—Bow originally with the Stradivari Violins belonging to King Charles IV. of Spain. The Royal Arms are Inlaid on the Nut.

Fig. 59.—Bow Purchased by us at Cremona in 1884.

preserved) * made in 1684 for the Countess Christina Visconti; also the patterns of two violoncello heads respectively inscribed as that made in 1707 for the aforesaid lady, and as a "Violoncello da Venezia, 1707." There are numerous drawings for different types of bridges destined to the various instruments, a selection from which is given in our illustrations. For the sound-holes there are also many designs, all most carefully cut out in paper. Among them is a reproduction of the two sound-holes of an Amati violin cut out on a thin plate of copper. Count Cozio states that it came to him with the Stradivari tools, etc.

We also find in the collection the complete designs for a viol d'amore of twelve strings made in 1716; it is of the usual type of viol more generally met with—flaming-sword sound-holes, etc. It does not appear to have been inlaid, nor does Stradivari make any remark as to its having been specially executed for any grandee.

We have already spoken of the designs for the various inlaid instruments—on which Stradivari wrote: "Qui dentro questi designi che sono qui dentro sforati sono quelli che se fatto al Ill.ᵐᵒ Sig. Marchese Carbonelli di Mantova," †—as well as of those of the

---

* No doubt to preserve the sizes for future use.

† The designs (tracings and rubbings) that are contained herein (a packet), are those which were made for the Marquis Carbonelli of Mantua.

arms for the Medici and other instruments.   These are all of
surpassing interest.

A number of drawings for finger-boards and tail-pieces,
some quite plain, others with fancy designs, as well as
various patterns of minor importance, have likewise a place
in this collection.

We learn too for the first time, from this collection,
that Stradivari made bows.   There are a number of designs
for the nuts and several for the heads : all are of the
accustomed types of bow of that period.

We are somewhat surprised to note the absence from
the collection of anything relating to guitars, of which
Stradivari made several, also the absence of any templates
for the heads of violins or violas ; neither is there anything
connected with double basses.   Without doubt, the contents
of the workshop must have been laid under contribution
between the time of Stradivari's death and that of their
sale to Count Cozio—a period of close upon forty years.
In this way we can reasonably account for the disappearance
of the more useful patterns and tools.

That these mementoes are now in the hands of a
distinguished Italian nobleman is a matter for congratulation.
We venture to hope that the day is not far distant when
they will find their last resting-place in the Museum of that
city whence they came.   It is pathetic to think that Cremona
contains, with trifling exceptions, nothing which witnesses to
the glory of that splendid age of violin-making for which
her name will be ever famous.

CHAPTER IX.

Stradivari's Labels.

EFORE entering upon the subject of the labels inserted by Stradivari in his instruments, we think a short statement on the much-misunderstood question of the importance of those found in most old instruments will prove interesting. An impression largely prevails that the ticket found in a violin has little or no weight in deciding the question of the authenticity of the instrument. It is unfortunately true that labels, especially in the past, have been much tampered with, and this evil practice is carried on even to-day. This knowledge justifies to a considerable extent the mistrust created ; but, notwithstanding this, we assert that the majority of the productions of the famous makers still bear their original labels, and to him who would become a connoisseur, the study of them is indispensable. They alone furnish us with the knowledge of the periods at which the different makers flourished, confirm in many cases the relationship between master and pupil, and inform us as to the length of time the various makers worked ; in fact, they

are the test by which we recognise an instrument as being the work of a given maker. Again, they tell us, particularly in regard to the Italian schools, the cities in which many of the makers were born and in which they worked ; for they are the only sources of information concerning a number of minor makers, who were obscure citizens, of whose lives no record has been kept.

The Italians themselves were among the earliest to commence the practice of falsifying labels. Count Valdrighi, of Modena, in his work " Nomocheliurgografia," furnishes us with a very interesting instance. It is a petition to the Duke of Modena from one of his citizens in the year 1685, and runs as follows :—

" Your most Serene Highness,—

" Tomasso Antonio Vitali,* your most humble petitioner, now at the service of Your Most Serene Highness, bought of Francesco Capilupi, through the medium of the Rev. Ignazio Paltrinieri, a violin for the price of twelve pistoles because this violin bore the label of Nicolò Amati, a maker of great repute in his profession. Your petitioner has, however, discovered that the said violin was falsely labelled, he having found underneath the label one of Francesco Ruggieri, called ' *Il Pero*,' a maker of much less repute, whose violins at the utmost do not realise more than three pistoles. Your petitioner has consequently been deceived by the false label, and he appeals to Your Most Serene Highness for the appointment of a legal representative, who, without many formalities and judicial proceedings, and after ascertaining the petitioner's proofs of his assertions, should quickly provide, etc., etc. That God may long preserve Your Most Serene Highness's precious life, etc., etc.,

(Signed) " TOMASSO A. VITALI."

---

* Vitali was a violin-player attached to the Court of Modena. He had a violin school there. Senaillé was a pupil of his (" Nomocheliurgografia ").

On the back of this petition the Duke wrote the following in Latin : " Councillor Gagliani has to provide in reference to the above statement as he may deem convenient.

" From the Fortress of St. Agatha. 19th day of December, 1685." *

Here, then, is a proof that the practice of inserting false labels commenced in Italy, and at a very early period.

Now, without further explanation, the true significance of this incident of a violin made by Francesco Ruger being found bearing a label of Nicolò Amati as early as 1685 (a year after Amati's death) is apt to be lost sight of. It really tends to prove that which we have long recognised—namely, that certain pupils and followers of the great makers, who copied their masters' works, also in many cases inserted their masters' labels. For instance, all the members of the Rugeri family † frequently labelled their instruments with Amati tickets ; Giofredo Cappa almost invariably did so—in fact, only in one instance have we found his own label. Andrea Guarneri did likewise at times. The early Milanese makers and several members of the Gagliano family followed the same practice. These last copied not only the works of the Amati, but also those of Stradivari, and labelled them accordingly. Even the label " Sotto la disciplina d'Antonio Stradivari " was so inserted.

If we look at home, we find that as early as 1760–1770 the same practice existed. Both Joseph Hill and Richard Duke used the tickets of the Amati and of Stradivari for their somewhat feeble copies. In Germany the

---

* L. F. Valdrighi, " Nomocheliurgografia," p. 282.
† See note, p. 25.

number of eighteenth-century productions ticketed "Jacobus Stainer" is astonishing: in fact, various of this maker's followers rarely made use of their own labels.

Now, it must not be supposed that the object of this false ticketing was fraud. On the contrary, we are convinced that these old makers simply reproduced and offered to the world that which they considered to be *a faithful copy, label included.* That such was their view is proved by the fact of our having frequently found the true maker's own label inserted *elsewhere than at the usual place*;* sometimes, as in the case of the Ruger violin cited, it was covered by that of the master whose work was copied.† Vuillaume, the greatest of modern copyists, frequently inserted Stradivari and Guarneri labels in his instruments ; yet nobody who knew the man would suggest that he did so with a fraudulent motive. He invariably dated his Stradivari label 1717, and took no trouble to produce a really correct facsimile of the original—nor did the Italians ; and the labels are very often misspelt. In most cases Vuillaume, who numbered his productions consecutively, marked the number of the instrument in the centre of the back.

In justice to the earlier makers we have thought it right to deal at some length with the custom of inserting labels other than their own in the instruments they made. It is plain from the facts cited that they were entirely innocent of any wish to deceive. Their practice, injudicious and also objectionable as it was, was perfectly distinct from that of the unscrupulous dealer who inserts and withdraws labels for a very different reason. With this later and indefensible practice we will now deal.

---

* On the interior of the belly, on the top block, and on the sides.

† We have met with two other instances where Francesco Ruger covered his own label with that of his master.

Tarisio, the celebrated Italian dealer, who had more fine instruments passing through his hands than any other man of his time, must be credited with having resorted to this practice in a very fair number of cases; that is, if we are to judge by various instruments seen by us which were brought from Italy and sold by him bearing other than their original labels—labels, observe, which *could not have been put in by the makers.* The temptation for such evil-doing is not far to seek. At the beginning of the last century the Italian instruments most sought after were those of the Amati and Stradivari. The demand was an ever-increasing one, and the supply was not always equal to it; consequently it paid well to re-label the works of the lesser-known makers, and sell them as those of the above-mentioned masters. To the inexperienced buyers of those days the subtle distinctions existing between the works of master, pupils, and followers passed either unrecognised or unheeded. Again, the prices asked and given were exceedingly modest in comparison with those of to-day; hence the incentive to deeper research had not yet sprung up. That English and French dealers were not behind in following in the footsteps of Tarisio cannot, we fear, be denied, and so there ensued confusion worse confounded. When these facts are borne in mind, the difficulty of ascertaining what is an original instrument and what is not will be readily understood. To the casual observer, who has not the advantage of constantly examining instruments, the task is an impossible one.

We find, strangely enough, after long and careful observation, that it is quite the exception to meet with a genuine old label in a spurious instrument, and we account for this apparently singular fact in two ways: firstly, the principal sinners formed collections of labels, which are far from being without interest, and did not see fit to part with them when they could substitute a copy which would do equally well ; secondly, the removal of a ticket from an instrument (unless the instrument be in pieces) is a delicate operation, and in many cases the label, in the attempt to remove it, would be obliterated and destroyed.

Count Cozio di Salabue left a small collection of labels —amongst others, those of Stradivari, Amati, and Bergonzi ; and that they were removed from specimens of the works of these makers is certain. The Count also left a number of copies of genuine labels, especially those of Amati. It seems impossible to believe that the Count, who was such an enthusiastic admirer of old instruments, could have been guilty of taking the original tickets out of the instruments himself. Possibly Tarisio, who was in frequent communication with him, supplied them, and the copies were probably printed to the order of the dealers and makers living in Turin and Milan at the time. The Count's correspondence shows that he was particularly intimate with the Fratelli Mantegazza of Milan.

Charles Reade, who at one period of his life was an amateur fiddle-dealer, also left a small number of labels. He was intimately acquainted with Tarisio and had dealings with him, and from him some of the labels appear to have come, one of them being glued on part of a letter addressed by Reade to Tarisio. Nicolo Bianchi, a fairly well-known dealer and repairer who worked at Genoa, Paris, and Nice, at which latter place he died in 1880, formed a considerable collection of such labels. In connection with them an amusing incident was related to us by an English gentleman (an amateur violoncellist), who, when passing the winter in Nice, became intimate with Bianchi, and at his request arranged the collection in a book. In the course of time the Englishman confided his Ruger violoncello to Bianchi for repairs, and great was his surprise on its return to find that the label had been purloined—to aid, doubtless, in completing this collection.

Let us now return to the subject of the labels used by Stradivari himself. It is gratifying to be able to state that only a relatively small percentage of the tickets found in the master's instruments are other than those placed there by his own hands. The explanation is a simple one. The object generally aimed at in changing labels is to pass off the works of an inferior maker for those of a superior or more favoured one. But this could not apply to Stradivari, who represents the *ne plus ultra*; hence in most cases the original tickets have been suffered to remain, though we cannot add unscathed, for another phase of falsification here presents itself. Erroneous ideas and exaggerated statements have been disseminated with regard to the comparative merits of the various periods of Stradivari's work, and consequently an undue importance has often been attributed to the productions of certain years. Unscrupulous dealers have therefore sought to pass off examples of the early and late dates as those of the middle period of the maker's life, and the necessity of altering Stradivari's figures thus presented itself,—here, the figures to be entirely changed ; there, but partially. As usual, this has generally been done by bungling hands, and a careful study of the various reproductions of Stradivari's labels and groups of figures will enable even the uninitiated to decide for himself whether or not any given specimen has been tampered with in this respect. We were for some time in doubt as to the exact way in which Stradivari printed his labels, and examination of the still extant contents of his workshop did not enlighten us—the plates, blocks, or type which he used having evidently been cast aside as devoid of interest. Continued

Antonius Stradiuarius Cremonenſis Alumnus
Nicolaij Amati, Faciebat Anno 1666

Antonius Stradiuarius Cremonenſis
Faciebat Anno 1667

1672

1684

1688

1689

1693

Antonins Stradiuarius Cremonenſis
Faciebat Anno 1694

1698

1698

Facsimile labels (four plates)

Antonius Stradiuarius Cremonenſis
Faciebat Anno 1695

1700    1701

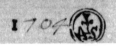
Prenisp a Carverto da me Antonio
Stradiuari in Cremona 1701

1703 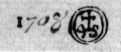   1704

1708    1709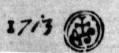

1711 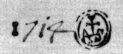   1713

1714

1715

1716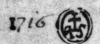

Antonius Stradiuarius Cremonenſis
Faciebat Anno 1717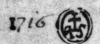

1718

R euiſto, e Corretto da me Antonio
Stradiuari in Cremona 1719
e fatto il Coperchio

1720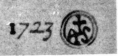

1722

1723

1727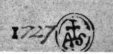

Antonius Stradivarius Cremonenſis
Faciebat Anno 1732
de Anni 9

Antonius Stradivarius Cremonenſis
Faciebat Anno 1736
D ANNI 92
92

Antonius Stradivarius Cremonenſis
Faciebat Anno 1736
D'Ao...
D'ANNi 92.

Antonius Stradivarius Cremonenſis
Faciebat Anno 1737
D'Anni 93.

Sotto la Diſciplina d' Antonio
Stradiuari F. in Cremona 1737

Omobonus Stradivarius Filius Antonij
Cremone Fecit Anno 1740. oTs.

Franciſcus Stradivarius Cremonenſis
Filius Antonii faciebat Anno 1742

observation at last furnished the information. We had noticed the somewhat inexplicable fact of "Antonius" being occasionally spelt "Antonins" (*i.e.* with three *n*'s), and finally the explanation dawned upon us that the third *n* was produced owing to the *u* being turned upside down, thus showing that the labels were printed from movable type.* This third *n* was therefore the result of error, and Stradivari does not appear to have thought the misspelling of his name of sufficient consequence to justify the label being wasted. We have met with a number of instances of this curious mistake, which occurs, however, only in the tickets of pre-1700 date. These remarks do not apply to the label dated 1666, printed in small type (see illustration), the use of which seems to have been quite exceptional ; in fact, we have only met with this one instance.

Stradivari's first label was set up in the sixties—we believe 1665 and 1666 to be the earliest years on record— and, as we shall see, he apparently committed the mistake of having the three figures, *166*, cut and printed from a single block, adding the fourth with his pen as required. The monogram by which the date is accompanied was also on a separate wood block, and Stradivari appears to have invariably impressed it at approximately the same position on the label,† as will be noted ; it is not found on the repairing tickets. It is frequently most irregularly formed, and one can at times easily discern where Stradivari completed with his pen those parts which the stamp failed to mark. (See illustrations.)

On reaching the seventies, the difficulty of the three

---

* See reproduction of label dated 1694.

† We have met with two instances in which Stradivari omitted the monogram altogether, and both were violins of his earliest period.

joined figures, *166*, presented itself. It is strange that he should not have had the superfluous *6* removed from the block ; but he may not have considered it worth while to do so, seeing the small use he made of his labels during these years. Instead, he simply erased the *6* (probably with a fine knife), and *wrote* in the *7* and the next figure.

In the eighties his ingenuity came into play, for, instead of erasing the second printed *6*, he formed it into *8* by adding the necessary top part only.* In the nineties he followed the same plan, removing the top part of the *6* and adding a tail to the lower part. As 1700 approached, he decided to make a change—possibly his prosperity had had effect—and we meet with a new type of label printed from letters of a coarser character than those hitherto in use ; the difference is very perceptible. He also decided to print henceforth only the figure *1*, adding the remaining three figures with his pen ; and from this rule he never again deviated, if we except his repairing label. We first find the new label in use in 1698, though he did not yet discard the old one, but used both contemporaneously until 1700. This ticket did service till 1729, and during that year and in 1730 came the third and last change.† The label is now printed with a still coarser type of letter, and Stradivari spells his name with a Roman *V* instead of a cursive one, as had hitherto been his practice. We believe that in one or two instances the maker did utilise the previous label during the years 1730 and 1731, but after that we invariably find

---

* We have seen several labels where he inked the printed part of the *6* over.

† We have met with one exception, that in which a violin, dated 1727, bore the last type of label.

the last type of ticket. It is curious to note that the type of the labels followed the same course as his work : the finer is found in the early work, the coarser in that of his old age. To some extent this may be attributed to the fact of Stradivari's hand losing the necessary steadiness for printing ; the very shaky monogram found on the labels of the late period affords striking evidence of this.

It is also not without interest to note that Stradivari, with extremely few exceptions, placed his labels— *i.e.* those of violins and violas—in position against the lining of the side. (See illustration of the interior work, Chapter VIII.)

In the reproductions given of labels and groups of figures, the following points are worthy of special remark :—

1.—The groups (of figures) dated 1698, showing both methods of forming the figures.

2.—The label dated 1717 has an inked line above the inscription, caused, we think, by the inking of the box which contained the type ; we have noted this on several occasions. It will also be seen that the letters, when compared with the label dated 1699, are coarser.

3.—The label of 1719 is interesting as showing that the master repaired instruments. He states that " he made the belly." (See also the manuscript label.)

4.—The explanation of the writing on the labels dated 1732-36 and 1737 will be found at the end of Chapter II.

5.—The Francesco Stradivari label comes to us from
the Marquis Dalla Valle. It was most probably
taken from one of the two violins purchased by
Count Cozio in 1775 from Paolo Stradivari.* We
may add that not a single authentic example of
Francesco's work has been hitherto identified
by us.

* See the Count's letter, " The Salabue Stradivari," London, 1891.

Fig. 60.—Carved Tail-piece of Early Italian Work.

CHAPTER X.

The Number of Instruments made by Stradivari.

O point in connection with Stradivari requires elucidation more than the question regarding the number of instruments he made during his lifetime. We have met with very few persons who possess an approximately correct idea on the subject. The prevailing belief is that the total number of his works still existing is comparatively small, and that consequently many instruments which are passing as his productions were never touched by the hand of the immortal master. That a certain number of instruments thus sail under false colours is undoubtedly true, but we venture to assert that this number is far smaller than is generally supposed. We take for granted that anybody who has mastered the rudiments of violin literature understands that the hundreds, nay thousands, of instruments bearing a *facsimile* (though never a correct one) of Stradivari's label in the interior do not pass in the world as original. Here of course we refer to old instruments for the most part of high merit, for

which a price has been paid that entitles the owner to believe he is in possession of an authentic example of the master's work.

The more we learn about Stradivari, the more are we impressed by his industry and devotion to his art. His powers of production seemed only to augment as the years rolled on ; his energy was apparently inexhaustible, and his fertility of invention equally unfailing. His art was his sole occupation ; and although we possess but meagre details of his actual life, we may safely assume that from morning till evening, week in week out, as year succeeded year, he was to be found peaceably seated at his work-bench, gouge, compass, or knife in hand, giving form to productions which were to prove models of perfection for future generations. His working life was a long one—unparalleled either before or since in the annals of instrument-makers—for he laboured, we may safely say, during upwards of seventy-five out of the ninety-four years of life allotted to him. Nicolò Amati also attained an advanced age, namely, eighty-eight years ; but we are decidedly of opinion that he ceased to take an active share in the construction of instruments some years before his death, while Stradivari continued to work up to the very last. How interesting would it have been had one or other of Antonio's sons approximately recorded the result of the old man's labours ! As far as we know, neither they, Arisi, Lancetti, nor Count Cozio refer to the subject, unless we except the general yet instructive statement of the last named : "In addition to the large number of Stradivari's violins scattered throughout Europe, ninety-one were in his possession at the time of his death." *

---

* We gather from Count Cozio's correspondence that Stradivari left at his death ninety-one violins, two violoncellos, and several violas, in addition

The "Rode" Stradivari, dated 1722.

In possession of MR. C. OLDHAM.

The "Rode" Stradivari, dated 1722.

The "Rode" Stradivari, dated 1722.

Nor have we any precise data as to the time devoted by Stradivari to the construction of his violins, violas, or violoncellos. The Arisi MSS. contain a letter written on September 19th, 1690, by the Marquis Ariberti, in which he requests Stradivari "to begin at once two tenors which are wanted to complete the Concerto"; and we learn in connection therewith the fact that the tenore (the larger-sized viola) was so far finished by the 20th of the following month as to permit of the master pencilling in the interior, "Prima 20 Ottobre, 1690, per S. A. da Fiorenza." Now, the necessary working drawings, together with the moulds, made, as the master tells us, "espressamente" for these instruments, still exist in the Dalla Valle Collection, and are dated by Stradivari "4 Ottobre 1690." We therefore infer that between this date and the 20th, a period of sixteen days, the body of one tenor was ready to be put together, and the second was possibly in an advanced state, as most probably the maker worked on each alternately.

Again, Arisi tells us that Giovanni Battista Volumier, Director of the Court Music of the King of Poland, went to Cremona in 1715 by special order of the King to await the completion of twelve violins which had been ordered from Stradivari. He remained there *three months*, and then took the instruments back with him to Poland. No conclusions of a definite nature can be deduced from these two statements, but they have nevertheless some bearing on this question of the time spent by the master in the making of an instrument. Oft-repeated examination of many examples

to the inlaid set of instruments, all of which passed into the hands of Francesco, the son, who died in 1742. Francesco had doubtless sold some of them, and the remainder passed to his brother Paolo, the cloth merchant, who appears to have gradually disposed of them.

of Stradivari's work justifies us in stating that he was an expeditious worker. Nothing executed by him bears the impress of having been laboured either in style or finish. He was a past master in handling the tools, and all his works bear the stamp of having been carefully, intelligently, but quickly carried out. In a warm climate, such as that of Cremona, we should scarcely presume that during the summer months Stradivari worked as many hours a day as the average workman in a colder land; but after duly weighing this point and making allowance for the time passed in striking out designs, constructing moulds, etc., we think that at the lowest computation he completed one violoncello or two violins in a month; say, an average of twenty-five violins or ten violoncellos in a year; and we believe, could it be only verified, that our estimate would be found to be rather below than above the actual number. Fétis* tells us that Polledro, the violinist, who died in 1853 at an advanced age, stated that his master knew Stradivari, and took pleasure in mentioning the fact. "He (Stradivari) was tall and thin in appearance, and invariably to be seen in his working costume, which rarely changed, as he was always at work." Whether this statement be fact or fiction we cannot say; but we are in a position to vouch for the actual existence of Stradivari instruments bearing their original labels, and dated from every year consecutively between 1682 and 1737, thus conclusively demonstrating that he kept to his work without a break of any duration for upwards of fifty-five years. It is equally clear to our minds that previous to 1682–3 Stradivari did not work on his own account with any continuity (a point to which we have referred in our chapter on the violins); and our

---

* "Antonio Stradivari," by Fétis, English Edition, p. 72.

proof of this statement rests on the fact of the rarity of his signed works—and the still greater rarity of unsigned ones—dated between 1665 and 1684, more especially before 1680. Were we to credit these earlier years with the same number of instruments as the later ones, we should be apt to overestimate the number of the master's productions Again, from 1725 onwards we cannot but assume that with advancing years the then octogenarian, though still sure of hand and eye to a marvellous degree, was slower of execution ; and therefore an average of twelve instruments per year up to 1736 agrees more nearly with our actual data. The year of his death, 1737, we do not include, believing that failing health must at last have all but stayed the master's hand.   Three examples only are known to us of this year. If we accept 1665 (Stradivari's twenty-first year) as the earliest date at which he used a label of his own, there are nineteen years before we reach 1684 ; and after giving the matter full consideration, we believe that his signed specimens during this period did not exceed on an average four per year—in all seventy-six instruments.   In our chapter on the master's violoncellos we state that fifty is the number known to us.   Assuming that Stradivari during his whole lifetime made as many as eighty of these instruments (we do not claim to know of every existing specimen, and some have been destroyed), and reckoning the time of construction at slightly over a month—ten a year—we thus account for eight years' labour.

If we now take the period from 1684 to 1725, a space of forty-one years, and deduct therefrom the above-mentioned eight years, we are left with a result for violin construction of thirty-three years, which gives, at an average of twenty-five violins per year, a total of 825 instruments.   The years between 1725 and 1736 give, at the reduced estimate of

twelve violins per year, 132 instruments. We thus arrive
at the following grand total :—

	Years.	Instruments.
From 1665 till 1684	19	76
,, 1684 till 1725 inclusive (less deduction of eight years for violoncello work)	33	825
,, 1726 till 1736 inclusive	11	132
The year 1737	1	3
Total of violins, violas, and kindred instruments		1036
Eight years' work on violoncellos and kindred instruments	8	80
Grand total of instruments		1116

That we should credit Stradivari with having made
over eleven hundred instruments will doubtless cause surprise
to many of our readers, yet we feel sure that we have
underestimated rather than overestimated the fruits of his
industry. Our calculations are based upon the results of
long years of observation.

Let us now turn our attention to the actually existing
instruments of the master, and see to what extent our
calculations are justified. Unceasing inquiry tends to
confirm our early impression that Stradivari's efforts were
principally, though not exclusively, concentrated on the
making of violins, violas, and violoncellos. Various writers
have stated that he made double-basses ; but, so far, our
researches do not enable us to confirm this assertion. On
the contrary, the instruments referred to by M. Gallay,[*] the
property of the Marquis de Pluvié, and the one belonging to
Count Ludovici Melzi mentioned by Mr. Payne,[†] are known

---

[*] Gallay, "Les Luthiers Italiens," Paris, 1869.
[†] E. J. Payne, Grove's "Dictionary of Music" : Art. 'Stradivari.'

to us. The former is of old French make, the latter
Italian, but of no special merit.   Among the various designs
and patterns made by Stradivari and now in the possession
of the Marchese Dalla Valle, nothing is to be found
referring to the double-bass, not even a design for the
bridge.   As already mentioned, we know of two viols-da-
gamba, since converted into violoncellos, also of a tenor
viol, since altered by J. B. Vuillaume to a viola by the
substitution of a modelled back instead of a flat one ; a
violin of a form without corners, though originally it was
of some type of small viol of different outline ; and we
also recall having seen in the possession of the late
M. Jacquot, of Nancy, another instrument which is also a
mutilated viol.   Two pochettes exist : one dating from the
later period is a most uninteresting specimen ; the other,
which is in the Paris Conservatoire Museum, is a very
charming example of Stradivari's early work.   For some
unaccountable reason a false label, dated 1717, has been
substituted for its original one ; it should be dated previous
to 1700.   Though a complete set of designs, dated 1716,
for the making of a viol d'amore of the usual form,
without projecting edge or corners, flaming-sword sound-
holes, and plain uncarved head, exist in the Dalla Valle
Collection, no such instrument has, to our knowledge, hitherto
been met with.   A tenor and violin, referred to by
Mr. Payne * as " a singular freak of the great maker "—the
outline, sides, form of sound-holes, and head consisting of a
series of straight lines—are not, we are happy to say, the
work of Stradivari.   Both instruments are intensely ugly, and
were made in Germany ; they are most probably of Mitten-
wald workmanship, dating from about 1750 to 1770.   The

* Grove's " Dictionary of Music " : Art. 'Stradivari.'

beautiful cistre originally owned by J. B. Vuillaume, now in the Paris Conservatoire Museum, has likewise, in our opinion, no claim to be regarded as the work of the great maker, though in this instance the instrument is quite worthy of him.*   Two guitars by Stradivari and the head

Fig. 61.—The Sound-hole, delicately cut out in wood, of a Guitar by Stradivari.

of a third (fig. 62) are known to us; both guitars are in singularly good condition, and date from the early years of the master's life.

---

* Illustrated in "Musical Instruments: Historic, Rare, and Unique," Hipkins & Gibb.

Here ends our list of Stradivari's works, other than those of the true violin form. Fétis, on the authority of Vuillaume, states that Stradivari made many viols of the various forms, besides lutes, guitars, and mandoras; but, judging by our own comparatively fruitless researches, we are inclined to regard this statement rather as an abstract opinion than as a positive assertion that specimens of these various types of instruments had been seen by him. Had Vuillaume been acquainted with many other instruments besides those already cited, several of which passed through his hands, they should still be in existence. The museums and private collections of antique instruments of any repute throughout Europe are known to us, and, with the exception of the Paris Conservatoire Museum, they contain not a single example of Stradivari's work; although viols, mandoras, and kindred instruments by earlier and also by contemporary makers are there to be found. Nothing is more likely than that the master did from time to time make one or other of these interesting instruments, although they were even then fast becoming obsolete. He, however, did not produce many, and the few he did make have been further reduced in number by the destructive hand of time.

With a view to obtaining a fairly complete list of Stradivari's existing violins, violas, and violoncellos, we have left no stone unturned which might aid us in arriving at a correct estimate : books, old papers, and catalogues have been consulted ; we have gone to every source likely to prove useful. We have corresponded with those in all parts of the world who were likely in any way to help us, and have sought the aid of those of our brother experts, both at home and abroad, who we thought could be of use in giving us information. In every instance we have taken steps to verify as far as circumstances would permit the authenticity of an instrument, never accepting the bare assertion of our informant.

Notwithstanding these efforts, we have to confess that we have found it impossible fully to attain our object : some reputed owners disdain even to answer our letters, others we are unable to find.   Again, instruments remain stowed away in old houses, especially in our own country, and great is the perseverance required to unearth them.   In giving figures, therefore, we wish them to be understood as only approximate, although our efforts to arrive at truth have

ANT.ˢ STRADIVARIVS
CREMON:F.ANNO 1675.

Fig. 62.—The Head of a Guitar made by Stradivari.

been most earnest.   Of the instruments made during the fifteen years of Stradivari's life dating from 1665, we are acquainted with but sixteen violins, one viola, and one violoncello altered from a viol-da-gamba ; we may also add the two guitars.   The years 1673, 1674, 1675, 1676, and 1678 do not, so far as we can learn from the labels, furnish a single example ; 1677 and 1679 but one example each ; 1680 to 1684 also give fifteen violins, one violoncello, and one transformed viol-da-gamba.   The years 1684 to 1690 —*i.e.* six years—furnish us with fifty-five violins and five violoncellos.   The increase should be noted.

The decade from 1690 to 1700 accounts for seventy-seven violins, five violas, and fifteen violoncellos.   Of the violins as many as fifty-two are of the "long" pattern, which includes all those of the years 1692, 1693,* 1694, 1695, 1696, and 1697.

The following decade, 1700 to 1710, gives ninety-eight violins, two violas, and five violoncellos. The years 1704, 1705, 1706 and 1707 are noticeable for the smaller output of eight, five, four, and eight violins respectively. The last year also gives a violoncello. On the other hand, 1709 is remarkable for its increased number: it accounts for no fewer than twenty-one violins and one violoncello.

The next decade, 1710 to 1720, gives the highest total of all : one hundred and twenty-five violins, and eleven violoncellos. No individual year, however, equals the total of 1709, which is, so far, the most productive on our record. 1710 approaches it, with nineteen violins and one violoncello, while 1711 gives but seven violins and three violoncellos. The years 1715, 1716, and 1717 yield respectively thirteen, fifteen, and thirteen violins, and three violoncellos. The remaining years are marked by a fair average.

The last decade, 1720–30, accounts for one hundred and four violins, one viola, a viol altered to a viola, and five violoncellos; the years 1720, 1721, 1722, 1723, and 1724 give respectively thirteen, fourteen, twelve, eleven, and twelve violins—the last year a violoncello also; the year 1725 gives but five violins and two violoncellos.

The remaining seven years, 1730 to 1736 inclusively, we can credit with forty-seven violins, two violas and six violoncellos. 1730 gives nine violins ; 1731, seven ; 1732, eight ; 1733, four ; 1734, five ; 1735, three ; and 1736, eight. The last year, 1737, gives three violins. We consequently arrive at the following total :—Violins, 540 ; Violas, 12 ; Violoncellos, 50.

---

* We have seen one exception of the year 1693.

The very limited number of the works of the early period, 1665–80, will be observed: an unaccountable fact unless our explanation be the correct one. The increase after 1684, the year of Nicolò Amati's death, certainly tends to give weight to our views regarding the working conditions of Stradivari's earlier years.*

A study of the above figures suggests the very natural question, "How near does this summary approach to the actual number of Stradivari's existing works?" In the case of the violins, we unhesitatingly express our belief that we have only succeeded in recording three-fourths of them, as we have traces, more or less clear, of quite one hundred more. Take, as an instance, the violin dated 1709, one of the instruments from the Plowden Collection, which was stolen from an attaché to the British Embassy at St. Petersburg in 1869–70. That violin is doubtless still in existence, and will in time probably reappear. Of violas, we doubt the existence of others than those recorded, but one or two more may possibly yet be brought to light. On the other hand, we think it probable that at least seven or eight violoncellos will sooner or later be forthcoming. We do not suppose most of these hypothetical instruments to be lying *perdus* in the hands of the ignorant, for during an experience extending over half a century we have met with scarcely any such cases; and even in these we have usually found Stradivari's productions associated with other worldly belongings of a similarly high order. That here and there an instrument has gone astray, is of course conceivable; in fact, several instances of this kind have come under our notice. That a portion of the results of Stradivari's labour has in various ways been destroyed is, we fear,

---

* See Chapter II.

only too true. It would otherwise be difficult to explain the falling off in number of the productions of certain years, such as 1704, 1705, 1706 and 1707,* when compared with 1708, 1709 and 1710. We cannot of course think that the hand of fate singled out the instruments of one year more than those of another; but it is very probable that whole sets of instruments made at one period shared a common lot, and were destroyed either by fire, pillage or otherwise. The upheaval among the Continental nations after 1790, coupled with the subsequent French invasions of Italy, Spain, and Austria, must have contributed to the general destruction, especially when we reflect that from the moment of their making Stradivari's instruments were destined to the palaces of noblemen and to churches. We have it from that ardent admirer of Stradivari, Count Cozio di Salabue, that when the French invaded Piedmont they ransacked his château at Casale, and this, added to the heavy war-taxes imposed upon the land, forced him to try and sell his collection in order to live. His Stradivari treasures probably escaped dispersal and destruction at the hands of the invaders through being at his house in Milan.

Another instance is furnished by the instruments belonging to the Spanish King, Charles IV., including violins by the Amatis, by Joseph Guarnerius, by Stainer, and the quintet of inlaid Stradivaris, besides other

---

* 1705 and 1706 were not tranquil years for the citizens of Cremona. A war was being waged with great stubbornness between the Austrians, French, and Spaniards, which terminated late in 1706 by the occupation of the Castle of Santa Croce—the fortress of Cremona. The Austrians then armed the fortress with one hundred heavy guns, and thus rendered it for the time being one of their strongest bulwarks in Lower Lombardy. It is computed by historians that the cost of fortifying the town in that year amounted to eleven million francs, of which sum the poor Cremonese had to pay their share by taxes and impositions of all kinds.

examples.   In 1790 they were still in the Royal Palace
at Madrid.   Local tradition says they were dispersed during
the French occupation, and if any were saved it is due to
their having been secreted.   Of the whole collection only
four good instruments remain—two violoncellos (one being
that of the quintet) and the two violins.   Both tenors of
the set vanished : one was found in Paris in 1819, where it
was purchased by Mr. F. C. Rivaz, a well-known English
amateur of those days ; the other has never since been
seen or heard of.   Researches carried out on our behalf in
the archives of the Medici family at Florence show that
the set of five instruments made by Stradivari for the
Tuscan Court in 1690 were in safe keeping up to 1734.
Prince Ferdinand, for whom they were specially made, died
in 1713 ; and from inventories of the musical instruments
left by the Prince, dated up to 1734, together with various
vouchers and receipts, we learn that the Stradivari
instruments were lent to various players—presumably with
the result that both violins and the smaller viola were finally
" borrowed," never to be returned, the large-sized viola
and the violoncello alone remaining in Florence.   The only
violin of the pair now existing, so far as we can learn, was
purchased by Mr. David Ker at Florence in 1794.*   Our
impression is that since 1815, when Europe was once more
restored to peace, very few Stradivari instruments have
been destroyed.   Here in England we only know of one
solitary instance : W. Ware, the leader of the orchestra at
Covent Garden, played upon a Stradivari violin, which was
lost at the burning of the theatre in 1808.   Even during
the terrible experiences of Paris in 1871, as far as our

* See its history : " The Tuscan Stradivari," a short account of a Stradivari
violin, 1889.

inquiries among our French colleagues show, no Stradivari instrument—and a good many were there—shared the fate of the city's fine buildings and treasures.

It is, of course, a matter of rejoicing that so many of Stradivari's works have been hitherto spared to us; but we should fail in our duty were we to neglect to add a serious word of warning as to the urgent necessity for greater care and thought being brought to bear upon the question of the preservation of these noble instruments, in order that we may not only enjoy their possession ourselves, but may honestly feel that we are doing our best to hand them on unimpaired to future generations. Ah! if those of last century interested in the subject, more especially players and makers, had been more prudent—nay, conscientious—in this matter, what a different result should we have been able to chronicle to-day! Our total as regards numbers might possibly have been no greater, but what of their condition? When we come to examine each example critically, we are grieved to find so many showing traces of wounds which are not honourable ones—scars attesting bad treatment at the hands of owners and, worse still, at the hands of would-be restorers. By consent of the former, at the instigation of the latter, most dire acts of vandalism have been per- petrated: in fact, of much of this kind that has been done in the past we cannot speak without positive horror. Violon- cellos and violas have perhaps suffered most, owing to their size and proportions not being in accordance with the ideas of the day—ideas in many cases absolutely erroneous. They have been cut down and mutilated in the most ruthless manner; and this was done by violin-makers who, then as now, considered themselves thoroughly competent! Charles Reade very aptly refers to this subject in his letters

addressed to the *Pall Mall Gazette* in 1872.* Speaking of
the instruments at the Loan Collection of that year, he
says: "The brothers Amati are represented in this collection,
first, by several tenors that once were noble things, but
have been cut on the old system, which was downright
wicked. It is cutting in the statutory sense—*i.e.* cutting
and maiming. These ruthless men just sawed a crescent
off the top and another off the bottom, and the result is
a thing with the inner bout of a giant and the upper and
lower bout of a dwarf. If one of these noble instruments
survives in England uncut, I implore the owner to spare it ;
to play on a £5 tenor, with the Amati set before him to
look at while he plays."

Alas! how true are these words! What more shock-
ing evidence of the truth of the charge could present itself
than is afforded by the fate of the unique violoncello made
by Stradivari for the ornamental set which he intended to
present to the Spanish monarch, Philip V.!† With how
much love and pride must the master have laboured during
weeks upon such an instrument! and how grievous it is now
to contemplate the destruction wrought by a man who
proved himself to have been devoid of the slightest feeling
which is inborn in the true craftsman! We regret to have
to add that the culprit, Ortega, who as a mere workman
was very good, was in this respect not one whit worse than
the majority of his brother-makers in other countries.

The equally fine violoncello made for Cosimo de' Medici
in 1690 has not escaped unscathed. In consequence of
slight ravages by worms,‡ it was sent some years ago to

---

* Reprinted in "Readiana."
† Chapter II., page 73.
‡ Strictly speaking, these ravages are due to the beetle known as
Anobium domesticum in its caterpillar state.

Vienna for restoration (we know not to whom), when its original neck was unhesitatingly sacrificed, and the charming inlaid finger-board and tail-piece were dealt with in true Philistine manner. The pearl cupids which adorned them were, in order that they might be preserved, removed and re-inlaid on a new finger-board and tail-piece of the crudest modern make. The absolute incongruity can be noted by comparison with the tenor which hangs in the same case, *fortunately not restored.* Both these instruments, together with the fine violin dated 1716, are to be seen at the Musical Institute in Florence.

A third instance, equally glaring, is furnished by a fine Stradivari, the sides of which were lowered by an Italian violin-maker, who added insult to injury by inserting his own label stating : *"Revisto e corretto da me !"* Very many similar instances are known to us, but nothing would be gained by recounting them now. The point we desire to bring home to all who are interested in the preservation of the many still existing admirable examples of our art, is that the present generation has profited but little by the knowledge of the miserable misdeeds of the past. True, violoncellos and tenors requiring to be thus drastically operated upon no longer exist ; but in other directions plenty of scope is left for the present-day vandal. The matter is now perhaps more subtle, and the injuries inflicted less apparent ; but under the cloak of restoring and improving, vandalism goes on as actively as ever. Will it be believed that within recent years, notwithstanding the boasted enlightenment of so many of those who aspire and claim to be considered worthy followers of the great traditions of violin-making, things have been done which call for the sternest condemnation ! What have we to say to the complete revarnishing of Stradivari and Guarneri violins

in order to renovate the old varnish ? to the cutting
down of a Gasparo tenor to the proportions of an
oversized violin ? to the replacing of the back of a fine
violoncello by a new one in order to remedy a wolf-note ?
to the cutting down of a Guadagnini violoncello—already
of small size—to satisfy the caprice of its owner, who,
still dissatisfied, had it enlarged again ? These instances
are but a few of those that from time to time come under
our notice.

Would that we could succeed in impressing on all
owners of fine instruments, more especially on professional
players, *the paramount necessity of giving more thought to the
care and preservation of these valuable possessions !* Under
mistaken ideas of " improvement," consent is continually
given with fatal light-heartedness to all kinds of pernicious
changes, which we do not hesitate to affirm are in the
majority of cases unnecessary, and therefore uncalled for.
The poor instruments are ripped open without further ado :
we know only too well how many show the sorry traces of
the bad performance of this ever-delicate operation. More
than one fine Stradivari instrument bears the mark where
the knife has passed right through the belly ; and many are
the cracks and fractures one could point to as having been
similarly produced. B cheerfully undoes that which but a
few years—or even months—previously had been thoughtfully
carried out by A. Then C, the sounds of whose trumpeter
have fallen on sympathetic ears, is called upon to set A and
B right. The climax is reached when D, a workman with
a telling long grey beard and gold spectacles— his sole
credentials—is recommended to the unfortunate owner by a
distinguished artiste, and undertakes without a moment's
hesitation to undo the bungling of A, B and C, and to substitute his own work founded on his own fallacious theories.

Mark, readers, we beg you, that during this time the real stamina of the instrument is being steadily impaired.

We have drawn a sad picture ; yet the sadness is not exaggerated, and it is difficult to say whether the violin-maker or the player be the more to blame. The former is at times swayed by mercenary motives, and very often by a sense of self-importance mingled with a certain amount of curiosity ; for he imagines that he can by studying the interior of a celebrated instrument enrich his store of knowledge. Players have yet to learn that they themselves are more often at fault. They should administer treatment to themselves, and not to their instruments, when these seem irresponsive.

As an example, on the other hand, of the way in which a violin may be preserved, though kept in continual use, we would cite the Stradivari dated 1724 of Señor Sarasate— a violin which has been the solo instrument of that distinguished player for upwards of thirty years. Known to us for twenty years, the condition of this instrument is as fresh to-day as when we first had it in our hands. Alard, Sarasate's master, seems also to have taken care of his violins in a similar manner ; but we are sorry to say that this cannot be affirmed of most players. Thoughtlessness and indifference seem to reign supreme.

To close,—one most earnest word. Instruments by continual use are apt to become weary. They may even virtually be killed. Give them rests. We feel it a duty to urge most strongly that fine instruments should not be brought to premature death by ceaseless use.

CHAPTER XI.

The Prices Paid for Stradivari Instruments.

I T may be useful to commence this chapter by giving the information we have been able to glean concerning prices paid for Cremonese instruments previous to the time of Stradivari.

Vidal quotes the following :— "In 1572 Charles IX. of France ordered to be paid to one Nicolas Dolivet, a Court musician, the sum of *fifty livres tournois* to enable him to purchase a Cremona violin for his use." * The livre tournois, a nominal not actual coin, was approximately equivalent to the franc of to-day, and fifty of them thus represented £2 of our money. We believe that the purchasing power of the livre tournois then was six times that of the franc now. The price paid, therefore, by Dolivet for his Cremona, was approximately equal to £12 ; and we may reasonably assume that the instrument was by Andrea Amati, as he was the only Cremonese maker of repute at that time.

Again, very interesting and instructive is a correspondence which took place in 1637–38 between the astronomer Galileo and his former pupil the Servite monk, Fra Fulgentius

---

* Cimber et Danjou, "Archives de l'Histoire de France," t. viii., p. 355.

Micanzio, concerning a violin which Galileo wished to procure for his nephew.

Galileo writes to Father Fulgentius Micanzio, in Venice, as follows :—

ARCETRI,* *Nov. 20th,* 1637.

. . . When you receive the amount of my small pension, please keep it until my nephew Alberto, who is in the service of His Serene Highness the Prince of Bavaria, and is now staying with me here, passes through Venice on his return journey to Munich and pays his respects to your Most Reverend Paternity. He wishes to purchase a violin there, either of Cremonese or Brescian make, being a very good performer on that instrument ; and the said small pension will help to pay for it. I suppose that these instruments, though made elsewhere, can be found in Venice ; but should that not be so, and it becomes necessary to obtain one from somewhere else, you will greatly oblige me by making arrangements so that some competent musician shall select one from Brescia, an instrument of the highest order. . . .

In reply Father Micanzio writes :—

VENICE, *December 5th,* 1637.

I have received your most kind letter of the 20th of last month, and I have already obtained the amount of your small pension by inducing the Most Illustrious Baitello to give an assurance to that scamp Arisío that you are still alive. Concerning the violin which your nephew on passing through here wishes to buy, I have spoken to the Musical Director of the Concerts of St. Mark's (Maestro di Concerti di S. Marco), who tells me that I can easily find Brescian violins, but that those of Cremona are incomparably the better—in fact, they represent the *non plus ultra* ; and by the medium of the Cremonese Signor Monteverdi, Chapel-Master of St. Mark's, who has a nephew living in Cremona, I have given the order for a violin to be sent here. The difference in the price will show you the superiority, for those of Cremona cost at the lowest *twelve ducats* each, whilst the others (Brescian) can be had for less than *four ducats.* As your nephew is in the service of His Highness of Bavaria, I think he will prefer by far the one ordered to be sent to Venice as soon as possible. . . .

---

* Near Florence.

A second letter from Father Micanzio, dated Venice, January 16th, 1638, says :—

If I have delayed writing to you it is only because I am still awaiting that blessed violin from Cremona, for which Signor Monteverdi assures me he has made so many repeated applications ; yet, notwithstanding, it does not appear. . . .

A third letter, dated Venice, March 20th, 1638, says :—

I am still pining for that blessed violin. Every day I am shown letters which explain that in order to construct a perfect instrument it has been found necessary to wait until the cold weather has passed away, and that in a couple of days it will be ready ; still, there is no end to the delay. You may rest assured that I do not cease from pressing them. . . .

A fourth letter, dated Venice, April 24th, 1638, says :—

Concerning the violin, Signor Monteverdi has recently shown me a letter in which his nephew writes him that the new one is in progress, but as he wishes to send an instrument of exquisite work, it cannot be brought to perfection without *the strong heat of the sun* ; he can, however, offer an old one of superlative merit, but the price asked is two ducats more—that is, fourteen. I have requested him to have this one sent at once, irrespective of the price ; he has promised to do so, and I am expecting it from day to day.

Having been obliged to negociate this matter through other hands, you must excuse me (for the delay). I give you my word of honour that I have not neglected it ; on the contrary, I have left no stone unturned. And now, kissing your hands, believe me, etc., etc.

A fifth letter, dated May 28th, 1638, says :—

. . . As regards the violin, Signor Monteverdi read me a letter which he had received from his nephew, in which he wrote that he had the violin, and that it proved on trial to be a singularly successful instrument ; that he had consigned it to a boatman who lay at anchor, and was on the point of starting for Venice ; that he had not been able to get it for less than fifteen ducats, besides the expenses of the carriage and the case. I replied that I would settle everything, and begged the gentleman not to delay any longer, as too much time had already been wasted over such a trifle. As soon as it arrives I will at once consign it to the Illustrious Signor Residente Rinuzzini. . . .*

It is again to be regretted that throughout this correspondence the Cremonese violin-maker's name is unmentioned ; as in the previous instance, we cannot but assume that he was one of the Amati family,—most probably Nicolò, who at this date had reached his maturity as a craftsman.

Now, the ducat was a Venetian gold coin of the value of eight shillings ; and, on the assumption of its purchasing power being three times that of to-day, we find that the price for a new Cremona violin, as quoted by Fra Micanzio, was equivalent to £14 8s., whilst a Brescian instrument could be had for £4 16s. It is instructive to remember in this latter connection that Maggini had been dead but six years.

Our next record is that cited by Forster and Sandys, obtained from the Warrant - books of the time of King Charles II., preserved at the Record Office. The warrant is dated October 24th, 1662 :—

"To John Bannister,† one of his Maj[ies] Musicians in Ordinary, for two Cremona Violins by him bought and delivered for his Maj[ies] Service £42."

The purchasing power of the above sum to-day would be approximately double ; the violins, therefore, cost not less than £40 apiece. Once more our curiosity to learn who was the actual maker is baffled, though, as in the previous instances, he was doubtless one of the Amatis.

Our last record bearing upon the prices paid for early violins is furnished by Vitali's petition, presented to the Duke of Modena in 1685 (see Chap. IX., p. 211).

---

* "Opere di G. Galilei," Firenze, 1842–56. The letter of May 28th, 1638, is an unpublished one in the Galileian MSS. in the Bib. Nat., Florence : Vol. XII., 1st Part, leaf 62.

† John Bannister, violinist, born 1630, died 1679.

Vitali therein says that he had paid for the violin, on the assumption of it being a genuine Nicolò Amati, the sum of *twelve pistoles*. The pistole, or double ducat, was a Spanish gold coin of the approximate value of sixteen shillings, and its equivalent purchasing power to-day is £2 8s. The price paid would thus be equal to £28 16s. The value Vitali set upon the violins by Francesco Ruger, *three pistoles*, was equivalent to £7 4s. of to-day.

If we now summarise, we arrive at the following conclusions :—

1. In 1572 a Cremona violin (Andrea Amati ?) cost approximately £12.
2. In 1637 a Cremona violin (Nicolò Amati ?) cost approximately £14 8s. ; an *old* one cost £16 16s.
3. A Brescian violin at the same period could be purchased for £4 16s.
4. In 1662 two Cremona violins (Amatis ?) cost £40 each.
5. In 1685 a violin accepted as a Nicolò Amati (it should be remembered Amati died in 1684) cost £28 16s. The violins of F. Ruger were valued at £7 4s.

From the publication of the Arisi Manuscripts, we learnt definitely that which had previously been but a matter of conjecture. Far from being an obscure, unheeded man, Stradivari is held up to us as one of the notable citizens of Cremona, recognised far and wide as the most distinguished violin-maker of his time. Indeed, we find that kings, princes, noblemen, the dignitaries of the Church, and the most renowned musicians of the day were among his patrons, and all were unanimous in their testimony to the unsurpassed merit of his productions. This subject, and that of the remuneration Stradivari received for his instruments, and their ever-increasing value reckoning from early times, are of considerable interest, and will, we feel sure, justify us in dwelling more at length upon them than has been done by writers in the past. Up to the present time we

The Title of Appointment granted to Stradivari by the Archbishop of Benevento.
(reduced 16 per cent)

Brother Vincent Maria Romanus Orsini, of the Order of Preachers, by Divine Providence, Cardinal, Priest of the Holy Roman Church, of the title of St. Xystus, Archbishop of the Church of Benevento.

Considering the faithful service and kindly affection which Antonius Stradivarius, of Cremona, has shown us when opportunity offered, we have determined to show him in return our good will, and we desire to rank him among our familiar friends, in order that he may always be a partaker of the privileges, prerogatives, and exemptions which those enjoy who are actually engaged in our service. And therefore we exhort all and every one, that they show him the same favour, esteem, and due honour; and we on our part promise in return our best thanks. In testimony of all and everything above mentioned, we have commanded this writing to be drawn up, . . . signed by our own hand and certified with the impression of our own seal.

Given at Benevento this 25th day of the month of June, 1686.

Brother Vincent Maria, Cardinal Orsini, Archbishop of Benevento.

Note.—Notwithstanding various inquiries, we have not been able to ascertain the present ownership of the original of this document. The late Sig. Giacomo Stradivari informed us that it had always been retained in the family until he himself presented it to Vuillaume, of Paris; yet strangely enough we find that the only document known to have been in the possession of Vuillaume, and which in turn was presented to us by his family, is a reproduction. We have, however, reason to believe that the original is in existence, that it was Count Castelbarco, of Milan, who had it reproduced, and that this copy is the one now in our hands. Possibly the original may yet come to light!

Vincentius Maria Romanus Ordinis Praedicatorum Miseratione Divina
Tituli S. Praxedis S.R.E. Presbyter Cardinalis Ursinus Ecclesiae Beneventanae Archiepiscopus.

Dilectus Dilectam Servientibus, atque amori Comitatum suam Antonium Antonianam
Comitensis ergo Nos, ut occasio poterantur emptor ostendi: Eidem nos sui beneventani
nostro Cultuam praesentam Uruxinus significationum, ac votorum inter accuratae familiari
eam Communicandi gratiam, ut ipsam fructus privilegii, prerogativis et exemptionibus,
quas ateni apud Nos nostro actualis Dilecti servitus fortibus. Neque sortuam
omnes et singulis ut eundem favoribus provenient existimet, et Vobis venerit,
honoris. Nostram eum omnibus precibum Condonis animi gratis videamus. Et quos
omnium, et singulof fidem tuo praesens faciendi mandamus, nostro proprio
manu subscripta, nostroque impressione sigillo munita. Dat. Beneventi hac die
XXV mensis Junij M.DCCXXXVI.

Vincentius Cardinalis Ursinus Archiepiscopus

have been baffled in our efforts to discover some
authentic document giving the actual price paid
to Stradivari for one of his instruments (on this
point all writers are silent with the exception
of Fétis), and so far our own researches in the
different archives of Italy have proved futile.

Fig. 63.

On ascertaining that in 1715 the Elector of
Poland ordered twelve violins from Stradivari and sent
Volumier—the director of his music—to Cremona to await
their completion, we turned our attention to the Dresden

Fig. 64.

archives (there are none at Warsaw), but with
the same negative result. Arisi refers to this
question of payment in the two following entries,
but, unfortunately, gives us no precise information. He states that in the year 1685 Cardinal
Orsini, Archbishop of Benevento, ordered a
violoncello and two violins, which were sent as
a present to the Duke of Natalona in Spain,
and adds that the Cardinal, besides paying liberally for the
work, expressed his appreciation by conferring upon Stradivari
a title of appointment. Again, under
date 1686, he tells us that Stradivari
was requested by the Duke of
Modena to make a violoncello and
deliver it in person to him. The
Duke not only expressed the pleasure
it gave him to make his personal
acquaintance and highly praised his
work, but marked his gratification by
making him a present of thirty pistoles in addition to paying the price

Fig. 65.

Figs. 63-65.—Designs for the Arms of Stradivari's various Patrons, intended most probably for Inlaying on Finger-board or Tail-piece.

agreed upon. Thirty pistoles was approximately equal to
£24, and, as we have already seen, its purchasing power
then was equal to three times that of to-day. The present
thus represented £72—under the circumstances a princely
gift.

Now, although these references afford us no information
of a precise nature, they yet offer valuable evidence in
support of our firm belief that Stradivari obtained for the
majority of his instruments more than the ordinary prices
given to his working colleagues. He must have received
good remuneration, otherwise it is impossible to think
that he would have so unremittingly maintained that high
standard of excellence, carried, as we have elsewhere
shown, into the smallest details. We believe that Stradivari
varied his prices according to circumstances. Then as now,
no doubt, violin-makers had to meet the wishes of their
customers; hence his use at times of plainer and less costly
material. Fétis states, on the authority of La Houssaie, the
violinist (born 1735, died 1813), who visited Cremona not
many years after Stradivari's death, that the price fixed by
the master for a violin was four louis d'or; also that in
Cremona he bore the reputation of being a prosperous
citizen. Forster * incidentally mentions that the elder
Cervetto, violoncellist (born 1682, died 1783), had actually
traded personally with Stradivari and brought a consignment
of his instruments over to England, but returned them, as
he could not get as much as £5 for a violoncello; but he
does not enlighten us as to how much was really asked.
If the story of the return of the instruments be true—
which we strongly doubt—it only shows how unappreciative
were the musicians here at that period. On the other

---

* "The History of the Violin, etc.," by Forster and Sandys. 1864.

hand, we find that William Corbett, the violinist (born 1668, died 1748), went to Italy in 1710, and brought back a collection of Cremona instruments. In the correspondence left by Count Cozio, and communicated to us by the Marquis Dalla Valle, we have the copy of a letter written to the Count by Paolo Stradivari (son of Antonio), dated June 4th, 1775, wherein he states that a certain Signor Boroni was willing to sell his Stradivari violin for eleven

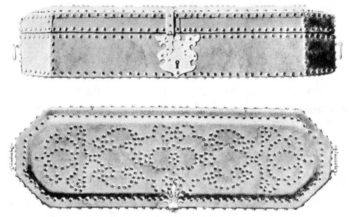

Fig. 66.—An Original Stradivari Case, made to contain a Violin.

"gigliati." In another letter, dated June 25th, he writes that the Rev. Father Ravizza has succeeded after some trouble in obtaining the violin for ten gigliati. A third letter, written to Signor Briatta, the Count's agent, by Signor Giuseppe Morandi on July 6th, 1775, says: "The present is to tell you briefly that we have come across a genuine Amati violin of large pattern, intact, as intact as if it were new, without a single defect, and with a fine tone, speaking freely, with an original label—Nicolaus Amatus—etc., etc., dated 1656. Forty gigliati is the price asked—I say forty—including a fine and well-made case. You must tell me precisely what you think about it. I am always at your command," etc.

We also learn from this correspondence that Antonio, the son of Paolo Stradivari, sold the inlaid quintet * of instruments, together with two other violins, in 1775, to the Padre Brambilla for one hundred and twenty-five "gigliati." From the above information we glean certain facts : first, that an Amati violin was more highly valued than that of Stradivari—nearly four times more highly valued ; secondly, that thirty-eight years after Stradivari's death the sums asked and accepted for one of his violins at Cremona was eleven and ten gigliati respectively ; thirdly, that the grandson of Stradivari, who must have heard his father mention the approximate value the maker set upon these instruments, sold a special quintet of them—i.e. a violoncello, a contralto viola, a tenor viola, and two violins—besides two additional violins, for one hundred and twenty-five gigliati. We should apportion this sum thus : thirty-five gigliati for the violoncello, forty for the two violas, and fifteen each for the violins ; twenty for the two additional violins.

A gigliato † was a Tuscan gold coin of the value of 9s. 5d. of our money, and assuming that its purchasing

---

* See Chapter II., p. 75.

† It may be convenient here to give a list of the coins referred to in the text, with their values :—

1572.—*Livre Tournois.* A nominal, not actual coin, equal in 1572 to 10d. of our money. Its relative purchasing power at the present time would be six times the above amount, viz. 5s. of our money.

1634.—*Ducat.* A Venetian gold coin, equal in 1634 to 8s. of our money. Its relative purchasing power at the present time would be equal to £1 4s. of our money.

power was three times that of to-day, we arrive at the following results :—

The price asked for the Amati represented approximately £57 ; the sum accepted for the Stradivari, *i.e.* ten gigliati, was approximately £14 ; that for the quintet of instruments, £148 (the violoncello about £50, the two violas about £56, the two violins £21 each).

If we now return to the statement of Fétis, and similarly multiply the purchasing power of four louis d'or, we get two hundred and forty francs—let us say £10 ; and as we do not believe any decided rise in the value of Stradivari instruments had taken place within thirty-five years of his death—the period of the transactions just mentioned—since their superiority was still keenly contested by those of the Amati and of Stainer, we may, with considerable probability of being correct, conclude that the sum Stradivari charged for a violin or viola was approximately equivalent to from £10 to £15 of our money of to-day ; for violoncellos, £25 to £35, the variation between the lower and the higher figures depending upon the individual merits

---

1685.—*Pistole,* or Double Ducat. A gold coin equal in 1685 to 16s. of our money. Its relative purchasing power now would be equal to £2 8s. of our money.

1775.—*Gigliato,* or Zecchino Fiorentino. The sequin of Tuscany was a gold coin equal in 1775 to 9s. 5d. of our money. Its relative purchasing power now would be approximately equal to £1 8s. of our money. The *gigliato* was so named because it bore the device of the Florentine *giglio,* or iris (fleur-de-lys), the emblem of the Republic, as it is to-day of the Commune of Florence.

It is extremely difficult to speak certainly as to the value of money in the past. The estimates as to the relative purchasing power, used in the text and given above, are based upon the standard of *payment for labour;* and in making them the advice has been sought of such experienced experts as the Keeper of the Coins in the British Museum, and M. Salvioni, Professor of Statistics in the University of Bologna.

of a given instrument. For such exceptional specimens as those forming the inlaid quintet an exceptional price was paid. Any question as to the master having been but poorly remunerated can, we think, be dismissed without further discussion. No better proof to the contrary can be forthcoming than that given us by Arisi, who writes under date 1702 : "Stradivari made a complete set of bow instruments which he intended to present to Philip V. of Spain on the occasion of the King's passage through Cremona, and he had prepared a memorial to that effect, but he was dissuaded and the instruments are still in his possession." The making of such a set of instruments represented the work of several months, and a poorly-paid worker would hardly contemplate such a costly present. The fame of Stradivari's instruments spread surely, if at first slowly. How interesting it would have been had the early writers, such as Burney, left on record who were the makers of the violins and violoncellos then in the hands of the foremost Italian players ! The little we are able to glean from various sources points to Amatis and Stainers being reputed above all others, and it is consequently probable that these were the instruments upon which the majority of the renowned violinists of the early and middle part of the eighteenth century played. Burney mentions that Veracini (born about 1685, died 1750) used two famous Stainers, which he christened " St. Peter " and " St. Paul," and that they were lost when he was shipwrecked. The same writer, referring to his visit to Signor Mazzanti, a distinguished musician in Rome, says : " He plays pretty well on the violin, and is in possession of the most beautiful and perfect Stainer I ever saw." * William Corbett, already mentioned,

---

* "The Present State of Music in France and Italy," p. 282.

who bequeathed his collection of instruments to Gresham College, enumerates them in his will. There were specimens of the Amati, Stainer and Albani—this last-named, he adds, was the violin of Corelli. We also find in an old note-book in our possession, compiled at the beginning of last century, an entry concerning an Andrea Amati formerly the property of Corelli.*

Corbett died in 1748, and unfortunately Gresham College refused his gift on the ground that there was no room in the College fit for its reception ; the instruments were therefore subsequently dispersed by public sale in 1751.† Some years before his death—in 1724—Corbett had already offered both his collections of music and of instruments for sale by public auction. The following is an extract from the *Daily Journal* of May 16th, 1724, announcing the sale :—

"Mr. Corbett's choice collection of musick, to be sold this day, the lowest price being fix'd upon each lot, at his lodgings near the Nag's Head Inn in Orange Court, by the Mewse : viz., A series of the finest Instruments made by the famous Amatuus's,‡ and *old Stradivarius* of Cremona, by Gio. P. Maggini, Gasparo da Salò of Brescia ; the noted Albani and Stainer of Tyrol, with two fine-toned Cyprus Spinnets, one of Celestini, and the other by Donatus Undeus of Venice. Wherein are the celebrated violins of

---

* Corelli, in his will, which is dated the 5th January, 1713, says : "To Signor Matteo Fornari I leave all my violins." Unfortunately, neither in the will nor in the inventory of the contents of his house is any mention made of either the value or the makers of these said violins. We also learn from his will that Corelli died on the 9th day of January, and not on the 18th as stated by his biographers.

† We have failed to discover any record of this public sale.

‡ Two of Corbett's Amatis are known to us.

Gobo, Torelli, N. Cosmi, and Leonardo of Bolognia, which those deceased virtuosos generally played on. Several hundreds of original Manuscripts of Latin Psalms, Operas, Cantatas, Solos, and Concertos never heard or seen in England; all composed by the most eminent Masters. A small Collection of Pictures, Medals, and some Drawings, with valuable books of the Theory of Musick, and others in different Languages. Attendance will be given each day from Nine in the Forenoon till Seven in the Evening, till all are sold."

Curiously enough, the following numbers of the *Daily Journal**** are silent as to the result of this highly interesting auction—presumably they did not think the matter of sufficient importance to chronicle. However, as Corbett still possessed a certain number of the instruments at his death, we must conclude that the prices offered for these lots did not reach the reserve, and that they were withdrawn. The mention of "Old Stradivari" is extremely interesting. Corbett may possibly have visited Cremona, and met and conversed with the master, who was apparently then spoken of as "Il vecchio Stradivari." Corbett, it will be remembered, visited Italy in 1710; and this date is instructive as showing that the master was then called "Old Stradivari." He was 66 in 1710, and 80 in 1724, when the instruments were offered for sale.

There can be but little question that at this period Stradivari's productions were, so to speak, on their trial; and unquestionably the easier production and lighter character of tone of the Amatis and Stainers, as compared with

---

* The following extract is not without interest: "Thursday an old Cremona Violin sold for thirty-six Guineas at the private sale of a deceased Gentleman's Effects in Bond Street, esteemed the finest toned Instrument in England."—*Daily Journal*, 1756.

those of Stradivari, especially in the earlier years of the existence of the latter, carried the day in favour of Amati and Stainer. In a book entitled "Advice on Violin-playing, with Practical Examples," written by George Simon Lohlein, Leipzig, 1774, we read as follows: "One finds that Stradivari worked his bellies and backs almost the same thickness, still he left a little more wood in the middle near the bridge than at the edges; in addition, his instruments are rather large and of a flat model, clumsy head and corners, peculiar sound-holes, and thick in wood. They have therefore a light, penetrating, oboe-like, but at the same time thin tone. On the other hand, Jacobus Stainer of Absam, like his master Amati (*sic*), worked with a high model—it is fairly thick in the middle, but in the cheeks (flanks), *i.e.* towards the edges of the instruments, the wood is very thin. This able man even surpassed his master, although one finds very good instruments of Amati." The author then sings the praises of Stainer, one of whose violins he possesses; and later states that the Amatis, then the Stainers, and after that the Stradivaris, are the most famed; finally he says that Stainer has always this peculiarity, "that his tone is full and soft like a flute," and he gives his violins the preference above all makers' for solo-playing. With the exception of the conclusion, which gives Stainer preference over the Amatis, such appears to have been the generally accepted opinion concerning the comparative merits of the makers named until well on towards the close of the eighteenth century.

Hawkins, in his "History of Music," published in 1776, says: "There were two persons of the name of Stradivari of Cremona, admirable artizans; the latter was living at the beginning of this century,"—and he concludes his remarks as follows: "The violins of Cremona are exceeded only by those of Stainer, a German, whose instruments are remarkable for a full and piercing tone."

We are enlightened as to French opinion by the following extracts from a work published in 1785,* which treats fully of the construction, etc., of various musical instruments. The writer, after minutely describing the process of making violins, adds: "The violins of the greatest reputation are those of Jacob Stainer, who, during the middle of last century, lived in a small township in the Tyrol, by name Absam, near Innsbrück, the capital of the country. This celebrated artist, who worked during upwards of seventy years, aided by a number of workmen whom he had trained, finished every violin with his own hands, and made a prodigious number, as he lived to the advanced age of nearly one hundred years. The violins, still in their original state, of this famous craftsman—those, namely, of which the interior has not been altered by any modern maker—are very rare and much sought after. The violins of Cremona are also renowned: there are two kinds—those made by the Amatis, and those which are the work of Stradivari. Those who excelled among the Amatis were, firstly, Andrea Amati, the master of Stainer, and his violins, though of ungraceful form, were much sought after at the beginning of last century by those who preferred a quality of tone soft and pleasing; secondly, the brothers Antonius and Hieronymus, contemporaries of Stainer, who made admirable violins now much sought after and very expensive; thirdly, Nicolò Amati, who made excellent violins, but of varying merit, and not all possessing equal goodness of tone. Among the skilled makers of more recent date we find Antonio Stradivari, who, like Stainer, was long-lived, and made a very large number

---

* "Encyclopédie Méthodique," Paris, 1785.

of good violins; the merit of his instruments consists in their masculine, powerful, and melodious tone. The Amatis made their violins of high build, Stradivari on the contrary nearly flat, yet these opposite methods have both furnished instruments of an equally perfect description.

"Among the fiddle-makers working in France stand out Bocquay, Pierray, Castagnery, and others, who have made violins which will bear comparison with those of the celebrated makers whom we have just mentioned."

As a further proof that such was the prevailing opinion, we have only to look at the different schools of violin-makers, men who were living during the latter part of Stradivari's life or immediately afterwards. The work of Romans, Venetians, Florentines, Genoese, Mantuans, and Neapolitans—especially the earlier work—was all strongly touched by a mixed Amati-Stainer influence; and it took years to eradicate their errors and to return to the earlier teachings upheld and emphasised by Stradivari. In England, France, Germany, and Holland it was the same; especially in England, as Stainer influence was early imported here—soon after 1700. How much richer we should be in old English instruments of merit had Stradivari's precepts obtained the firm footing acquired by those of his rivals! That Stradivari violins were early brought to our country is certain. We have the instructive fact that Daniel Parker—a maker who was working as early as 1714, and who was probably a pupil of Barak Norman—made instruments in which are reproduced more or less correctly the main features of the "Long Strad"; he even picked out the outline of the head and scroll in black. With the possible exception of Nathaniel Cross, none of the other contemporary makers seem to have been impressed by this worthy example; all soon became completely Stainerised! One of the few Continental makers, if we except those of Italy, who early recognised the merit and did his best to reproduce the character of Stradivari's violins was De Comble of Tournay, who worked from about 1720 to 1750. He was forthwith dubbed pupil of the great master by Fétis, on what authority we know not. Probably, as with Parker, De Comble had simply been fortunate enough to see a Stradivari, and the sight bore fruit. The earliest intimation hitherto met with by us affording evidence that Stradivari was coming to the front in England, is furnished by Richard Duke and Joseph Hill inserting a copy of his label in certain of their new violins made as early as 1750–60, instruments which they no doubt considered fairly good reproductions ; * and in 1780–85 John Betts intimates on his business cards that he "makes in the neatest manner violins after the patterns of Antonio Stradivari, Hieronymus Amati, Jacobus Stainer, and Tyrols." It should be observed that Stradivari is mentioned first.

Count Cozio's correspondence again furnishes us with an interesting item of news bearing on this subject. Paolo Stradivari, writing under date June, 1775, to the Count's agent, concludes his letter as follows : "An English gentleman, a person of rank, passed through Cremona, and wanted to buy two violins by Stradivari. I had not the courage to ask him his name, but I told him about you, and that you collect instruments by all the best and most renowned makers. I gave him your name and address, and he then wished to know if you had any instruments made by Stradivari, and I informed him that you had many, as I had sold you some a short time ago."

It is impossible to say whether we or our French

---

* See Chapter IX., p. 212.

neighbours were the first to recognise the superiority of Stradivari's instruments. We were certainly not behind them, and it is probable that conviction was brought home to both nations at about the same time, and that both were primarily indebted to Italian players for the impulse. In " Les Luthiers Italiens " * Gallay states that the arrival of Viotti in the French capital in 1782 (not in 1796 as given), his admirable playing, and the fine tone he produced from his Stradivari instrument caused quite a sensation, and from that moment a keen interest in the hitherto but little known master was evinced. Viotti's visit to England a few years later, and his subsequent prolonged residence among us, must have equally influenced the opinions of our musicians and amateurs. We obtain a very instructive insight into this change of opinion through the very able comparison between Stainer and Stradivari found in a letter addressed by the Rev. Thomas Twining, M.A., to Dr. Burney, dated May 4th, 1791.† He says : " I have lately had a sort of fiddle mania upon me, brought on by trying and comparing different Stainers and Cremonas, etc. I believe I have got possession of a sweet Stradivari, which I play upon with much more pleasure than my Stainer, partly because the tone is sweeter, mellower, rounder, and partly because the stop is longer. My Stainer is undersized, and on that account less valuable, though the tone is as bright, piercing and full as that of any Stainer I have ever heard. Yet, when I take it up after the Stradivari, it sets my teeth on edge. The tone comes out plump all at once ; there is a comfortable reserve of tone in the Stradivari, and it bears pressure, and you

---

* " Les Luthiers Italiens aux XVIIième et XVIIIième Siècles," Paris, 1869.
† "A Country Clergyman of the Eighteenth Century," p. 149. John Murray, 1882.

may draw upon it for almost as much tone as you please. I think I shall bring it to town with me, and then you shall hear it. It is a battered, shattered, cracky, resinous old blackguard, but if every bow that ever crossed its strings from its birth had been sugared instead of resined, more sweetness could not come out of its belly."

At the opening of last century Stradivari's transcendent merit was being widely proclaimed. The Abbé Sibire, an intimate friend and admirer of Nicolas Lupot, from whom he is understood to have received the information incorporated in his charming little book entitled, " La Chélonomie, ou le Parfait Luthier," published at Paris in 1806, expresses the prevailing sentiment there when he writes: " Antoine Stradivarius! À ce nom auguste et vénérable je m'incline profondément devant le patriarche des luthiers." With but few exceptions, all the notable players of the day had acquired and were playing upon his instruments; amongst others, La Houssaie, Kreutzer, Rode, Baillot, Habeneck, Lafont and Bouchet; in England, Viotti, Mori, Kiesewetter, Loder, Salamon, Libon, Raimondi, Cotton Reeve and Alday. The violin-makers, equally impressed, threw over their lingering Stainer-Amati sympathies, some not without a considerable struggle, and vied with each other in adopting Stradivari's principles and form. In France, Fent, Aldric, Pique and Lupot were the principal makers who did so with success ; in England, Dodd, Fendt, Tobin and Panormo ; in Germany and Austria the best copyist of Stradivari of the period known to us was Geissenhof, of Vienna; in Italy the craft was in a declining stage—in fact, it had all but ceased to exist. A slight revival took place later with the advent of Pressenda, Rivolta, Gibertini and, lastly, Rocca. The brothers Mantegazza, who were capable workmen, appear to have turned their attention more to repairing. Lorenzo Storioni, Joannes Rotta, the elder Ceruti, and Carlo Bergonzi (the last fiddle-maker of that family *), all of Cremona, just managed to keep alive the embers of that city's former ardour, and maintain there, though imperfectly, Stradivari's teachings.

Now, France was unquestionably favoured in her intercourse with Italy : her geographical position, the intimate relations between the two peoples, the fact that most of the cultured musicians generally wended their way first to Paris, where, at the period of which we write (the early part of last century) all the most brilliant executants were to be met with, and, lastly, the advantageous dealings early commenced between the indefatigable Tarisio and the principal Parisian luthiers, soon brought into their country a far greater proportion of Stradivari's instruments than were possessed by other nations. We gather from various sources that, previous to the Napoleonic upheaval, Spain also was particularly rich in Stradivari and other high-class Italian instruments. Arisi mentions several orders received by the master from the Spanish monarch and other grandees ; and no doubt the distinguished Italian musicians, such as Manfredi, Brunetti and Boccherini, who held appointments at the Spanish Court, did their best to foster the taste for their great countryman's work. Guillelmi of Barcelona and Contreras of Granada, surnamed "il Grenadino," both highly meritorious makers, who were working during the latter half of the eighteenth century, had clearly seen and appreciated Stradivari's instruments ; their productions, especially the violoncellos, were excellent—decidedly Italian in character : in fact, to-day we generally find them passing as Italian, needless to add minus their original labels. As with Italy, so with Spain : war and

---

* Grandson of the first Carlo Bergonzi.

its accompanying evils played sad havoc with the country's prosperity, and early in the century its Stradivaris began to migrate to more prosperous lands. We may mention here that no fewer than six violoncellos by Stradivari have to our knowledge been brought to France and England from Spain. Old records in our possession enable us to throw an interesting light on the introduction of many of Stradivari's instruments into England, and on dealings in them during the early part of last century.

The Betts family, whose business premises were situated at the Royal Exchange, were the foremost dealers of their day; the others were Dodd, Forster and Davis. Whether Betts was in direct communication with similar firms in Paris, such as Pique, Lupot, Köliker or Gand (Köliker was especially reputed as a dealer), we know not; but we do know that an active intercourse was kept up with the Continent, either through the medium of well-known city merchants of those days, such as the Cazenoves and the Rivaz—members of which families were distinguished amateurs, keenly interested in the subject, and brought several fine instruments to our shores—or through the foreign players who were constantly visiting us. Arthur Betts, who was an excellent violinist, was taught by Viotti; and what more probable than that the intimacy between the two may have been the means of inducing the Italian to obtain from Italy Stradivari instruments, which were then sold for their mutual benefit? At all times there have been well-known musicians who have found both pleasure and profit in combining playing and dealing in instruments.* Dragonetti brought several

* Parke, in his "Musical Memoirs," speaking of Giardini, the celebrated Italian violinist (born 1716, died 1796), says: "Giardini, when in his zenith, produced on the violin a tone more powerful and clear than any of his

The "Betts" Stradivari, dated 1704.

In possession of MR. R. D. WADDELL.

Stradivari and other violins from Italy, and at his death in 1846 he left by will to the then well-known lady player, Teresa Milanollo, a fine specimen dated 1728; also a violin by A. and H. Amati to Sivori. Paganini also bought and sold a number of instruments, and Ole Bull was quite notorious for such dealings in his day.

A certain J. N. Durand *—a city merchant—appears to have been particularly active, and brought—or had consigned to him—Stradivari instruments from France and Germany. His correspondent in the latter country was a person named Kreutzer, who lived at Mannheim.

Mr. Dowell and Mr. Harper, both merchants of Cadiz, were instrumental in bringing several Stradivaris from Spain; to the former we are indebted for the fine violoncello which belonged to Signor Piatti, and was brought here in 1818.

George Astor, who kept a music shop in Cornhill, and was brother of the famous John Jacob Astor, founder of the well-known American family of that name, also brought several specimens from Germany; two of them, dated . respectively 1699 and 1706, were imported about 1809. Besides these instances, various individual cases could be cited, such as that of Mr. Kerr, who purchased the " Tuscan " violin at Florence in 1794; General Kyd, about the same period, brought several

---

contemporaries; and even on an indifferent fiddle he displayed nearly the same admirable qualities. This knack, if I may be allowed the expression, proved very profitable to Giardini, enabling him to sell his inferior instruments at a large price to gentlemen who, in his hands, admired the powerful tone, though they found afterwards, to their great surprise, that they could draw forth very little, apparently not aware that the tone came from the skill used, not from the fiddle."—"Musical Memoirs," by W. T. Parke, London, 1830, Vol. I., p. 155.

* We possess a letter addressed by Mr. Durand to Lupot in 1821. The writer is sending a banker's acceptance for 300 fr., on account of the purchase of two Stradivari violins and a Joseph Guarnerius.

fine instruments from abroad, amongst others the violoncello now in the hands of the well-known player, Leo Stern, and a violin dated 1720. In fact, members of most of our wealthy families who travelled on the Continent, and especially in Italy, invariably brought back examples of the different arts: hence, at times, fine instruments.

With the prolonged peace in Europe after 1815 came, as years passed on, increased prosperity, which further stimulated the demand in this country for Stradivari and other fine instruments—a demand which has ever since steadily grown. From 1830 onwards, and more especially in the forties, fifties and sixties, a more intimate trade-relationship was established with our French neighbours, nor can we learn that any of our dealers went farther afield in search of Stradivaris. The principal dealers in England during this period were A. and J. Betts, Corsby, John Hart, Davis, Fendt and Purdy, John Alvey Turner and W. E. Hill. The foremost was Hart, but perhaps the most enterprising was Turner, who, taking John Lott* with him as adviser (Lott had the reputation of being a connoisseur, and understood French), paid periodical visits to Paris to make purchases. The corresponding dealers in Paris were Aldric, Thibout, Bernardel *père*, Gand *père*, and, later, his sons Adolphe and Eugène, J. B. Vuillaume and Georges Chanot *père*. The brothers Silvestre, of Lyons, also had many dealings with Tarisio, who generally halted there with his precious cargo *en route* to Paris. On the death of this remarkable man, in 1854 (he had during nearly thirty years brought into France many of the finest Italian instruments), Vuillaume and Chanot

---

* John Lott, the violin-maker (born 1804, died 1871), was especially clever as an imitator of Joseph Guarnerius. His life, which was not without a touch of romance, has been written by Charles Reade.

determined to explore Italy for themselves, which they did, often with excellent results. Georges Chanot also travelled in Spain. The story of Vuillaume's purchase of the priceless treasures left by Tarisio has already been told. A small yet interesting detail in connection therewith was related to us by M. Van der Heyden, of Brussels, an ardent admirer of fine instruments, who by chance met Vuillaume in Turin when returning from his now historic journey. They dined together, and Vuillaume related how he found the "Messie" Stradivari and the "Alard" Guarneri. Both were in the bottom drawer of a poor rickety piece of furniture, and Vuillaume experienced considerable difficulty in opening it without damaging the instruments. When his eyes rested on the contents, he gazed on them for some moments without making a movement. It was Tarisio's sister who accompanied Vuillaume to the village where the instruments were. M. Van der Heyden knew Tarisio, having met him on various occasions; and says he was a man of common appearance—that he looked what he was, a peasant; he spoke French indifferently, dressed badly, and wore heavy, rough shoes. He was tall and thin, and had features of an ordinary Italian type. He used to relate that he walked to Spain when he went to that country to purchase the Stradivari violoncello, the story of which is told by Charles Reade.*

Giacomo Stradivari, one of the direct descendants of the great maker—he died in Milan in January, 1901, and was in his youth a follower of Garibaldi—told us that during one of the campaigns in the south of Italy his mother wrote to him from Cremona saying: "There lately came to our

* "Letters addressed to the *Pall Mall Gazette* in 1872," reprinted in "Readiana."

house a Frenchman, who actually offered 500 lire for the old fiddle hanging up in the kitchen, and I immediately accepted it." Our friend knew not whether it was one made by his ancestor, but did not think so. In Madrid we heard a similarly amusing incident from the Count de Villares, whose father possessed a small collection of Italian instruments, including two violins and a violoncello by Stradivari. The Count was on several occasions greatly pressed by a Frenchman who came to Madrid in search of instruments—presumably Chanot—to sell him one of these violins; and at last, to get rid of his somewhat troublesome guest, he determined to ask what he thought would be an inordinate price for such a person to pay, the equivalent, namely, of 4,000 pesetas (about £160); but, to his intense dismay, the Frenchman immediately took him at his word! M. Chanot-Chardon, of Paris, still possesses the double violin-case with hidden pockets in which old Chanot secreted his gold during these ramblings.

Charles Reade, during a number of years between 1840 and 1860, took a keen interest in old instruments. He travelled a good deal in France, where he frequently met Tarisio, and purchased there Italian instruments, including Stradivaris and Guarneris, which he resold to the London dealers, principally to Hart and Corsby. He also had transactions with Mr. Gillott, the pen-maker,* whom he materially aided in forming his collection. The late Andrew Fountaine, of Narford Hall, was also an enthusiastic admirer of Stradivari, and at about the same period he brought from the Continent at different times several fine Stradivaris— notably that dated 1709, which he presented to Ernst, and which is now in the possession of Lady Hallé; that of

---

* The Gillott collection was dispersed at Christie's in 1872.

Habeneck, dated 1736; the "Gillott," dated 1715; that of the year 1734 belonging to Lord Amherst of Hackney, and the " Hausmann" violoncello of the year 1725. Of recent years, *i.e.* from 1865 to 1885, we have been more particularly indebted to the late Mr. David Laurie, of Glasgow, for the introduction to our shores of some of the finest existing examples of Stradivari's genius. Though in no way connected by tradition with our calling, Mr. Laurie developed a taste for high-class instruments, which, added to a keen business capacity and rare energy, he soon turned to good account. Profiting by commercial connections which necessitated frequent visits abroad, he sought out and came to be on intimate terms with various foreign luthiers, notably with J. B. Vuillaume, Gand & Bernardel *frères*, of Paris, and N. F. Vuillaume, of Brussels; and in the course of time he also became acquainted with many of the owners of Stradivari instruments residing on the Continent.

Mr. C. G. Meier, an amateur, and ardent admirer of Stradivari, also brought over several noted examples: amongst others the " Betts " (which Vuillaume had purchased in London and afterwards sold to Wilmotte), the " Ames," the " Dolphin," and the " De Barrau," one of the violins upon which Joachim now plays.

The following records of prices paid for Stradivari instruments will be read, we are sure, with considerable interest.

Our earliest information—excepting that obtained from the extracts already given from Count Cozio di Salabue's correspondence—commences at the year 1792.

We may here give the following extract, which refers to a Stainer violin: it furnishes an interesting record of the higher prices paid for that maker's instruments as compared with those of Stradivari.

1791. At the sale of instruments belonging to the late Duke of Cumberland, held by Christie's, Feb. 17th, a violin by Stainer realised 130 guineas. This same violin was sold at Messrs. Puttick & Simpson's in 1895, and realised £87.

Instruments by Antonio Stradivari.

1792. A violin dated 1692, which had been sold by Richard Duke, the violin-maker, to a Mr. Rawlins, was purchased by Betts for 72 guineas, and resold by them to a Mr. Herington, who still possessed it in 1834.

„   A second extract is extremely interesting. It refers to the celebrated " Macdonald " viola, which was purchased in 1792 by Betts from the Marquis dalla Rosa, an Italian nobleman, and then sold by them to Captain Coggan. Later it again passed into their hands, and was resold to Mr. Champion, a well-known amateur. Between 1820 and 1830 it was sold by auction at Messrs. Phillips', and realised 105 guineas. It shortly afterwards passed into the hands of General Boswell (afterwards Lord Macdonald), then found its way to John Hart, who sold it to Mr. Goding, at whose sale, in 1857, it was purchased by Vuillaume on behalf of the Vicomte de Janzé for £212. From the Vicomte it passed in 1886 to the Duc de Camposelice at the increased price of 30,000 francs = £1,200.

1793. In this year Betts purchased from Mr. Menel a violoncello for 50 guineas, and then sold it to Colonel Leslie of Dublin.

„   The same year a violin dated 1688 was sold by auction at the Custom House, and was bought by Mr. Norborn, of Holborn, from whom it passed to Mr. Rivaz, senior ; in August, 1821, it was purchased by Betts for 60 guineas ; in 1846 it was owned by Mr. Abbot, and some years later was purchased by W. E. Hill, who sold it in 1862 to the present owner, Mr. F. A. Forbes, for £105.

1794. A violin (the " Tuscan ") was purchased in Florence for 50 zecchini, approximately equivalent to £40 of to-day. This instrument was sold in 1875 for £250, and purchased by our firm in 1888 for £1,000.

1803. A viola dated 1690 was bought by Mr. Bright from the Cavaliere Giantighazzi of Florence and sold to Betts for 45 guineas; later it passed into the hands of Mr. Glennie, and subsequently of Mr. F. de Rougemont.

„ The same year a violin dated 1693 was purchased from Libon (violinist) by Betts for £80, and was sold to Mr. Glennie. A few years later it passed into the hands of Lord Arbuthnot for the sum of 200 guineas.

1805. A violin dated 1690, originally bought from William Forster, senior, passed into the hands of Betts in 1805 for 40 guineas. In 1831 the same instrument was purchased by Mr. Austin for 90 guineas.

„ A violin, broad pattern (no date given), sold by Betts to J. P. Salamon for 65 guineas; resold by auction in 1810 at Phillips' in Bond Street for 95 guineas and purchased by Mr. Hunter.

1806. A violin dated 1704, bought by Betts from Mr. E. Stephenson in 1806 for £100; sold to Mr. A. Glennie for £120 in 1808.

1808. A violoncello dated 1711, sold by Crosdill to Betts for £100; it then passed to Mr. Champion for £150, and was resold by auction at Phillips' in 1810 for 200 guineas, the purchaser being General Boswell. About 1860 it became the property of Mr. Whitmore Isaacs, of Worcester, at the price, we believe, of £300.

1809. A violin, sent from Cadiz by Mr. A. Dowell, was purchased by Betts for £50.

„ A violin dated 1694, sold by Betts about 1809 to Mr. T. Keene of Bishopsgate Street for 100 guineas, passed in 1820 into the hands of Mori for £120. Mori parted with it in the same year to an amateur (Mr. Golding) at the price he himself had paid; purchased from Mr. Golding's widow in 1866 by the Rev. Frank Hudson, of Cambridge, who retained it until 1882, when he sold it for £300. This instrument was sold by our firm to the present owner in 1888 for £500.

„ A violin dated 1699, the property of a French dancing-master, was sold by auction in 1809 at Phillips', and was purchased by Betts for 106 guineas.

1812. A violin dated 1690, bought in Venice by Mr. Pybus, of Bond Street, and sold in 1812 to Mr. Cary for 100 guineas; purchased in 1817 by Betts for 80 guineas and sold to Lord Arbuthnot. This instrument was sold by our firm in 1894 for £450.

1814. A violoncello (no date given) was purchased in 1814 by Betts from Mr. Roper Head for 80 guineas. The instrument is described as having the back and sides made from lime-tree wood, the head of beech.

    ,,   A violin dated 1660 (?), belonging to Sir John Twisden, was purchased in 1814 by Betts for £45; in June, 1816, it passed into the hands of Mr. Saunders, of Palace Yard, at the enhanced price of 100 guineas.

1816. A violoncello dated 1698, sent from abroad to Clementi (the musician), was purchased by Betts for £50. This instrument was much damaged.

1818. A violin dated 1702, brought from abroad by Mr. J. N. Durand, and sold in 1818 to Dodd, of St. Martin's Lane, who resold it to Mr. Cotton Reeve for 100 guineas. At Mr. Cotton Reeve's death the violin was purchased by W. E. Hill, and sold in 1866 to Mr. Mongredien for £130; bought back in 1876 for £200, and resold for £225, it again passed into W. E. Hill's hands the following year, and was then sold for £255. It subsequently passed into the "Hawley" collection, of Hertford, U.S.A.

    ,,   A violin dated 1700, purchased in 1818 from Dragonetti by Mr. F. Rivaz, for 200 guineas.

1819. A violin belonging to Sir Patrick Blake was sold by auction at Phillips' in March, 1819, and purchased by Mr. C. Holford for 85 guineas.

    ,,   Another specimen of the early period, which had belonged to Salamon, the musician,* sold for £40. It subsequently passed into the possession of Dr. Hague, of Cambridge.

---

* J. P. Salamon, who died in 1815, bequeathed his Stradivari, formerly the property of La Motte, to Sir Patrick Blake.

1819. A viola dated 1696, purchased by Mr. F. V. Rivaz in 1819
from Koliker, of Paris, passed in 1825 into the hands of
Sir William Curtis for £120. In 1876 this instrument was
purchased by Mr. John Adam; and at the dispersal of
his fine collection in 1881 it was sold to the Duc de Camposelice for £800. We purchased it in 1891 for £900.

1821. A violin dated 1720 brought from Spain in 1821 by Mr.
G. Champion, was sold at Mr. Crane's sale in 1848 for
116 guineas, and purchased by Mr. Woolhouse, at whose
sale, in 1893, it fetched £623.

1825–30. Violin dated 1704 bought by Arthur Betts for £1 1s. (the
famous "Betts" violin), was sold by him, about 1852, for
£500, to Mr. John Bone, of Devonport—an amateur much
addicted to the malady of continually exchanging instruments. He parted with his treasure about 1859 to J. B.
Vuillaume, through John Lott, for approximately £200.
Vuillaume sold it to M. Wilmotte, of Antwerp, in 1861, for
7,000 francs = £280 ; he in turn retained it until 1873,
when Mr. C. G. Meier became its owner at the increased
price of 15,000 francs = £600. In 1878 George Hart bought
it from the last-named amateur for £800, and not until
1886 could he be induced to sell it. In that year the Duc
de Camposelice became its possessor at the price of £1,200.
We purchased it in 1891 at an increased price.

From these records our readers will be able to form
a fairly correct idea of the sums paid in England for
Stradivari instruments shortly after their fame had become
established. Once and for all they shatter the illusion
entertained by many that in those days such instruments
were to be picked up for a mere song. We have unfortunately not been able to obtain as much information
regarding the prices ruling on the Continent at the same
period. Owing to the unsettled times, it may possibly have
been here and there less, though we know that the margin
could not have been great. From Count Cozio's correspondence we learn that early in the century he sold a

Stradivari violin to Pique, the French luthier, for 200 louis d'or, approximately £160.

1770-80. Gallay informs us * that the price paid by Duport for his famed Stradivari violoncello was 2,400 francs = £96, and that it was purchased from Cousineau, the harp-maker. No date is given, but we should presume this transaction took place between 1770 and 1780.

1803. A violin dated 1727 was bought by the late M. Luce, of Douai, for 70 louis d'or = 1,400 francs, £56. After his death it was put up for sale by auction in 1854, and was repurchased by the family for 2,630 francs = £105.

1808. A violin ("Le Messie"), valued by Count Cozio in the inventory of his instruments at 150 louis d'or, approximately £120 ; purchased by Tarisio from the Count in 1827 ; purchased by Vuillaume from the heirs of Tarisio in 1855. Vuillaume offered the violin to M. Fau, a French amateur, in 1865 for 10,000 francs = £400. On the death of Vuillaume, in 1875, it was valued by the family at 12,000 francs = £480, at which price it was offered and refused by N. F. Vuillaume, of Brussels (the brother). In 1877 Mr. David Laurie submitted an offer of £1,000, which sum Vuillaume's daughters were disposed to accept, had not Alard, the violinist, husband of one of the daughters, decided to buy the instrument himself. Bought by our firm in 1890 for 50,000 francs = £2,000.

1817. From a letter of Paganini in our possession we learn that Count Cozio sold him a Stradivari violin in the year 1817 for 100 louis d'or = £80 approximately.

1824. Viotti's fine violin was sold after his decease at the Hôtel Bouillon in Paris (the then auction mart, as the Hôtel Drouot is to-day) for 3,816 francs = £152 12s. approximately. In 1860 it changed hands at the price of 5,500 francs = £220.

„   Habeneck bought a Stradivari from Lupot for 2,400 francs = £96. Some years later this instrument was purchased by Andrew Fountaine and brought to England.

---

* "Les Luthiers Italiens aux XVIIième et XVIIIième Siècles."

1831. Gand *frères* purchased from Tarisio a violin dated 1736 for 2,000 francs = £80 ; they sold it in 1832 for 2,500 francs = £100. In 1862 it again passed into the hands of the firm of Gand, and was resold to Wilmotte, of Antwerp, for 5,000 francs = £200 ; five years later it fetched £240. In 1874 it was again resold by Gands for £320 to Mr. H. M. Muntz, of Birmingham, who in 1886 sold it to us. Its next owner was Lord Wilton, who paid £650, and in 1889 it again passed into our firm's hands.

1838. From a letter written in 1838 by Alard, the celebrated French violinist, and communicated to us by M. Croste, of Bayonne, we extract the following: " Si je vais à Bayonne cet été, comme j'ai l'espoir, je te ferai entendre un véritable Stradivari ;* il m'a coûté plus de mille écus (3,000 francs = £120), mais au moins je suis persuadé de sa realité et de plus de sa qualité de son, qui est admirable. Si j'avais voulu le vendre, j'en aurais tiré il n'y a pas longtemps quatre mille francs, mais j'y suis trop attaché pour m'en défaire."

1836-9. The " Rode " violin, dated 1722, was purchased from the Duc D'Olbreuse, who had obtained it from Rode, by M. Norès, a musician, for 4,000 francs = £160. M. Norès sold his violin in 1873 to MM. Gand & Bernadel *frères* for 5,000 francs, who resold it to M. Lamoureux for 6,000 francs = £240. In 1890 it passed into our hands at the increased price of £1,200.

1845. The " Sasserno " violin, dated 1717, was sold by the elder Gand for 3,700 francs = £148. In 1884 it was purchased from M. Sasserno for 20,000 francs = £800, by Mr. David Laurie, who immediately sold it for 25,000 francs = £1,000. It again changed hands in 1887 at the price of £1,000, and was brought to England by Mr. David Johnson (an amateur player), who parted with it in 1894 at an increase of price.

1846. A fine violin dated 1689 was sold at Milan by Signor Carli to the Duc de Litta for the equivalent of 3,000 lire = £120. The Duc presented this instrument to Signor Arditi.

---

* This does not refer to the celebrated Stradivari known as the ' Alard."

1849. Joachim purchased his first Stradivari, dated 1714, for 250 louis d'or = £200 (he was then nineteen) from Herr Müller, of Bremen. The price asked was 300 louis d'or = £240; but his uncles, who had agreed to find the money, considered this sum excessive. In the dilemma Joachim offered to make up the difference himself, but they would not consent; and finally the owner, seeing the artist's anxiety to possess the violin, consented to accept the reduced price.

Reverting to England, we have the following extracts about this time from the sale of the late Duke of Cambridge's instruments :—

1850. A Stradivari violin, dated 1723, was sold for £115 10s. Another, dated 1700, and described as being in beautiful preservation, fetched £140. The former of these two violins was in the possession of the late Duke of Edinburgh, and is now owned by Mr. D. J. Partello.

1851. "La Pucelle" violin, dated 1710, was bought from Vuillaume by M. Leroy de Chabrol, a Parisian banker, for 6,000 francs = £240. A few years later it passed into the possession of M. Glandez, after whose death it was sold at the Hôtel Drouot in 1878 for 22,100 francs = £884. In a letter written in 1851 regarding the sale of a Stradivari violin, M. Adolphe Gand, the luthier, says : "Le prix est de 2,000 francs, ce qui est extrèmement bon marché pour un Stradivarius, dont vous savez, Monsieur, que les prix montent à trois, quatre, et cinq mille francs."

1853. At the sale of the instruments of the Earl of Falmouth, a violin, dated 1692, of the long pattern, realised £110. Another violin was sold for £140.

In the same year a violin dated 1712 was sold for £240 (both sales held by Messrs. Puttick & Simpson).

1855. At another sale held by the same firm in 1855 a violin dated 1710 realised £149.

1857. At the Goding sale a violin dated 1722 was sold for £200; another specimen, dated 1700, realised £125. The former violin was purchased by Vuillaume on behalf of the Vicomte de Janzé, who retained it until 1886, when he sold it to the Duc de Camposelice, per the intermediary of George Withers, for 30,000 francs = £1,200.

1860. A violoncello dated 1730, the property of the Hon. Mr. Greaves, was offered for sale by auction at Messrs. Phillips'. It was bought in, and subsequently sold in 1866 to W. E. Hill, who resold it for £230 to Mr. Frederick Pawle. Purchased back in 1877 for £380, and resold to Mr. Edward Hennell in 1878 for £500. Again repurchased in 1880 for £475, and sold a few months later to Mr. C. G. Meier for £525. The instrument now migrated to Paris, and was there bought in 1882 from MM. Gand & Bernardel *frères* for £600 by Mr. David Johnson, and brought back to England, to be once again purchased by our firm in 1885 for £650.

1862. At the sale of the collection of instruments formed by Count Castelbarco, of Milan, held in London in 1862, the highest prices paid for Stradivari instruments were : A viola, transformed from a viol, dated 1715, £120; a violin dated 1701, £135; another dated 1685, £135; two violoncellos, dated respectively 1687 and 1697, were sold for £115 and £210.

1862. The violin known as the "Dolphin" was purchased from Vuillaume by Mr. C. G. Meier for 6,500 francs = £260; he retained it until 1868, when he parted with it to George Hart for the equivalent of £200. Hart sold it to the late Louis D'Egville, but soon after repurchased it, and the violin remained in his possession until 1875. In this year it was sold to John Adam for £625, and at the dispersal of the Adam collection the "Dolphin" passed to Mr. David Laurie, who sold it in 1882 to Mr. Richard Bennett for £1,100. In 1892 it came into our hands at an enhanced price.

These prices may be accepted as the average ones more generally ruling both here and abroad up to about the year 1870. Even at the sale of the Gillott collection, in 1872, which included, among other instruments, seven violins by Stradivari, the highest sum realised was £295, paid for an example of the year 1715 (the " Gillott " Strad), the others selling for smaller sums, £200 being the maximum. Obviously at all times there have been instruments which for various reasons commanded quite exceptional prices: such as, for instance, the " Betts " Stradivari, sold by Arthur Betts about 1852, as previously mentioned, for £500; and the " Duport " bass, purchased by Franchomme in 1843 for 22,000 francs = £880. From 1870–75 onward, the ever-increasing admiration for Stradivari's instruments has caused their value to rise by leaps and bounds—owing of course in a very great measure to the immense strides that music, and especially violin-playing, has made in this country. Instruments which we have cited as selling at comparatively moderate prices have doubled, trebled, and even quadrupled in value; and to-day an average specimen of violin cannot be purchased for less than from £600 to £1,000, while a fine specimen is worth from £1,000 to £1,200. The examples which command a still higher figure are of quite exceptional merit: their value is a fancy one, fixed most often by arbitrary circumstances, and they are invariably in the possession of wealthy owners, who as a rule can only be induced to part with them—if at all— by tempting offers. Nevertheless the Stradivaris for which sums greater than £1,000 have been justifiably paid are fewer by far than is popularly believed.

We will now add a few words as to collectors of instruments, more especially of those by Stradivari. We may safely assume that the love of forming a collection of instruments with a view to playing on them, comparing and contrasting their various and diverse qualities and features, has existed since the time of the earliest makers. Of recent years some writers have with considerable vehemence recorded their views for and against the forming of such collections, and there is doubtless something to be said on both sides. We, however, who have daily brought under our notice the ravages which time, and above all *injudicious usage*, have wrought upon so many fine instruments, cannot but pronounce in favour of those collectors who, by their care and reverence, have preserved, and are preserving for present and future generations, some of the masterpieces of the past. There must have been many such collectors, both here and on the Continent, during the last century; but unfortunately no one deemed it worth while to chronicle their existence.* Count Cozio di Salabue appears to have been the first really ardent admirer of Stradivari's works,

---

* Parke, under date 1802, says : " Mr. E. Stephenson, the banker, had perhaps the best and most valuable collection of Cremona violins of any private gentleman in England. I am, however, inclined to think that these are frequently more estimated on account of their scarcity (like strawberries in January) than their valuable qualities. As the appellation of ' Cremona fiddles ' may not be generally understood, I will take this opportunity to explain it. These instruments were made by two Italians, named Amati and Stradivarius, of Cremona in the Milanese ; and, like the well-known Sedan-chairs, originally made in France, go by the name of the town in which they were first manufactured. That there exists a sort of mania amongst certain connoisseurs in fiddles (as in regard to pictures) is not to be doubted, as the following fact will show. Mr. Hay, a former excellent leader of the King's band of musicians, produced on his favourite violin, made by Klotz, a German, a tone so sweet and powerful, that he had been frequently solicited to part with it, and was on one occasion offered for it by a noble lord three hundred pounds in cash, and an annuity, ' durante vita,' of one hundred pounds ! Mr. Hay, however, possessing a handsome independence, and not being desirous to part with his instrument, rejected the offer, and dying some years afterwards, this ' rara avis,' at the subsequent sale of his effects, produced but forty pounds !"—Parke's " Musical Memoirs," Vol. I., p. 301.

and we learn from his correspondence that in 1775 he purchased *en bloc* from Paolo Stradivari no fewer than eleven violins—in fact, all that remained in the hands of the family of those left by the great maker at his death. From an inventory of the Count's instruments made in Milan in 1808, we learn that he still retained, among other violins, five by Stradivari, including the " Messie." The troubled times in Italy, caused by the French invasion, had in 1800 forced the Count to realise some of his possessions ; and his printed announcement in both French and English, which we give, will be read with interest. Count Cozio died in 1840, at the age of eighty-five years, and left but few instruments, the best of which—a Nicolò Amati—is still in the possession of his descendant, the present Marquis Dalla Valle. Before his death he had parted with all those by Stradivari.

Count Archinto, of Milan, who died about 1860, was the possessor of a quartet of Stradivari instruments, afterwards purchased by Vuillaume for, we believe, 15,000 francs. The tenor of this quartet is the fine example now owned by Mr. Rutson ; the violoncello is that of the late M. Delsart.

Count Castelbarco, also of Milan, formed a collection of instruments, which included five violins, one viola, and two violoncellos by Stradivari ; but with one exception they were not of the first rank.

The late Count Valdrighi, of Modena, informed us that the Marquis Menafoglio of that city possessed a quartet of Stradivaris, but they were dispersed some years ago. He also mentions a violin purchased by Tarisio from Count Forni for 2,000 lire = £80.

Paganini had a quartet of Stradivaris, which were sold, after his death, we believe, to Vuillaume. We can trace three of these instruments.

AUX AMATEURS
DE MUSIQUE

Un amateur de musique aïant fait depuis plusieurs années avec beaucoup de soin et de dépense une ample et choisie collection de Violons des plus célébrés Auteurs Crémonois qui aïent jamais été, tels que ANTOINE, JEROME, et NICOLAS AMATIS Pere, onc e et Fils, ANTOINE STRADIVARIO, RUGERI dit le Per, ANDRÉE et JOSEPH GUARNERIO, CHARLES BERGONZIO, et JEAN BAPTISTE GUADAGNINI, et étant disposé à vendre cette collection tant en gros, qu'en détail ici à Milan, avant de satisfaire aux demandes qu'on lui a faites hors du païs, cet amateur invite tous ceux qui en voudront faire acquisition de s'adresser dans l'espace de 20. jours à dater du 22. prairial tous les jours ouvriers depuis les onze heures du matin jusqu'à midi, et depuis les trois heures après-midi jusqu'à cinq, au portier de la maison 1295. dans la Rue del Gesù peu loin du mont S. Thérese, qui leur sera voir cette collection aux heures et jours ci devant marqués.
Cet amateur se flatte que non seulement ils admireront la rareté de cette collection, mais qu'ils trouveront encore très-discrets les prix qui y sont fixés, en égard aux qualités de ces instrumens.
Milan ce 22. Prairial An. IX. Republicain. (8. Juin 1801. v. s.).

To the Virtuosos of Violins.

A Virtuoso having done a large, and choice collection of *V*iolins of most famous ancient Cremone's Authors, viz. of A'NTHONY, JEROM, and NICOLAS AMATIS, A'NTHONY STRADIVARIUS, FRANCIS RUGER, called PER, ANDREAS and JOSEPH GUARNERIUS, CHARLES BERGONZI, and JOHN BAPTIST GUADAGNINI, and being now disposed to sell that collection both by wholesale, and separately here into Milan, at discret price, invites all virtuosos who will buy them, to apply in this City to Merchant A'nthony Clerici at house Cavanago in the street of that name, N. 2334 since twelve o'clock until two, and since four, until six.

Count Cozio di Salabue's Announcement offering his collection of instruments for sale.

(reduced 15 per cent)

Of more recent years the only notable collections formed abroad were those of the late M. Wilmotte, of Antwerp, who died in 1893; and of the Duc de Camposelice, who died in Paris in 1887. The former had owned as many as twenty instruments during his lifetime, and the latter possessed at his death eight violins, two violas, and two violoncellos, all by the great master.

The Count de Chaponay, who died in Lyons in 1877, was also an enthusiastic collector of fine instruments, and possessed several Stradivaris.

The late Vicomte de Janzé may also be mentioned as a former owner of a quartet of Stradivaris.

The late M. de St. Senoch was the last French amateur to possess a quartet of the master's instruments. They were dispersed after his death in 1886 at the Hôtel Drouot, and realised the following prices :—

Violin, dated 1737	.	.	15,100 francs	= £604
,, ,, 1704	.	.	7,000 ,,	= £280
Viola ,, 1728	.	.	12,900 ,,	= £516
Violoncello, dated 1696	.	10,200 ,,	= £408

Hart states that our own early collectors were the Duke of Hamilton, the Duke of Cambridge, the Earl of Falmouth, the Duke of Marlborough, and Lord Macdonald. Later came Messrs. Andrew Fountaine, Goding, Plowden, and lastly Gillott. More recently still, the most enthusiastic collector was Mr. John Adam, who owned, in addition to other instruments of the first rank, a quartet of Stradivaris and seven additional violins, all examples of great merit. He dispersed his collection in 1881.

In concluding this chapter, we may state that the enhanced prices now paid for all fine instruments act as a powerful deterrent to the formation of collections. We are acquainted with only three amateurs who possess a quartet of Stradivari's instruments: Mr. Charles Oldham, Baron Knoop, and Mr. R. E. Brandt.   The Messrs. Mendelssohn, of Berlin (two brothers), own a quartet between them.

CHAPTER XII.

A Supposed Portrait of Stradivari.

OME twenty years ago our attention was drawn, in Paris, to a photograph which passed as a reproduction from a portrait of Antonio Stradivari. The photograph greatly interested us, and we obtained it from the possessor; but in answer to our inquiries as to the whereabouts of the original picture, he could tell us nothing. The photograph had been presented to its then owner by J. B. Vuillaume. So matters rested for ten years, when in 1891 we made the acquaintance of the late Signor Giacomo Stradivari, and, in the course of conversation, learnt that it was he who had years previously presented Vuillaume with an old portrait, which he stated had been one of the relics of his family, and which represented his famed ancestor, Antonio Stradivari.

In order to clear up any doubt as to the identity of our photograph, we sent it to Signor Stradivari; at the same time we ventured to touch upon certain doubts which had arisen in our minds as to this portrait really representing

Stradivari.   In replying to us Signor Stradivari stated that
the photograph was a faithful copy taken from the original
painting, which had always been accepted by his family as
undoubtedly a portrait of his ancestor (fig. 67) ; and, as
further proof of the correctness of his belief, he sent us
a small bank-note of the face value of fifty centesimi issued
by a Cremonese Bank in 1870, on which the said portrait
was reproduced.   So far, then, we had gathered the family
history of the portrait ; but these mere assertions of

Fig. 67.

Signor Stradivari could not settle the authenticity of the
portrait.   The question again rested for some years.   Nobody
in Paris knew what had become of the original oil painting,
nor could the descendants of Vuillaume give us any assistance, until we submitted the photograph to the surviving
daughter of J. B. Vuillaume, an elderly lady who lives
retired in the country.   She immediately recognised it as
taken from a painting in her possession.   Not attaching
particular value to it, to our great satisfaction she most
willingly consented to our becoming its owners.
    We are indebted to Lady Huggins for the following
discussion of the portrait :—

It was extremely natural there should have been doubts as to what personage is represented in this picture. Everything about the portrait not only points to a date considerably earlier than the time of Antonio Stradivari, but to an original who was a musician. In short, it seems absurd to suppose the portrait could represent Stradivari.

The reproduction gives a good idea of this most interesting picture in everything except the colouring. This has been injured by unwise cleaning, and some very valuable details have unfortunately been quite obliterated.

The costume of the figure is that which was in use among the upper and professional classes in the west of Europe from the latter part of the sixteenth to the earlier part of the seventeenth century. A portrait of Michael Prætorius of the year 1614 shows a costume strikingly similar; and so does the portrait of Galileo Galilei attributed to Sustermans in the Pitti Palace at Florence, painted, one may suppose, when its subject was about fifty, and therefore about the year 1614.

The artist of our picture, following a custom common among early portraitists—one which is well worthy of being kept alive—tried to indicate by the accessories of his picture the calling of his subject. On the wall we are shown an alto viol with its bow. A viol-da-gamba is being used; while on a table is displayed a piece of vocal music, an ink-bottle with a quill pen in it, and a case for music. All these things indicate the latter part of the sixteenth century, or a little later.

The painting represents a young man of about twenty-five, with light brown hair somewhat curly, a promising moustache, and indications of whiskers and beard. The well-opened brown eyes have a thoughtful, far-away look very characteristic of great musicians ; the complexion has a pleasing ruddiness ; the mouth is slightly open, as if the musician were in the act of singing. The dress consists of a close-fitting doublet of a dull greenish cloth—probably brighter once. The doublet has a number of small buttons close together down the front, and its short skirt is tabbed. The sleeves are cut close, and have a line of decorative braid down the inner sides. On the shoulders there are epaulet pieces tabbed to match the skirt. The neck of the doublet is cut rather loose, and there folds over a broad, stiff white collar rising almost ruff-wise behind, which has evidently been edged with lace-work of an early kind, though unfortunately injudicious cleaning has removed most of it. The cuffs have white ruffles of softer material than the collar.

Returning to the accessories, which are important, the body of the viol on the wall is obviously that of a sixteenth-century instrument—suggestive of the Brescian school. The sound-holes are vigorous and well-defined, the finger-board has a geometrical (probably) inlaid pattern, and below this is a lozenge-shaped geometrical quatrefoliate ornament. The belly is double purfled. The body of the viol-da-gamba in the hands of the player is almost wholly hidden by the table ; but the pegs are sixteenth-century pegs, except the highest one, which has been badly repainted. It is difficult to feel certain whether the instrument had six or seven strings ; apparently (?) it had seven.

The bows of both viols seem to be of pre-Corelli type, but in neither case can the tip be seen. The music represents the first line of a song apparently in the *ut* clef. It is written in black and white notes, is unbarred, and has a direct at the end of the line. The hands deserve attention, for undoubtedly they are the hands of a musician, not of a craftsman. The picture is painted rather thinly in oil, on canvas, and measures 2 ft. 5 in. by 1 ft. $9\frac{1}{2}$ in.

The costume, the *personnel* of the portrait, its accessories—all tell that the picture represents not Stradivari, but some musician who lived towards the close of the sixteenth or the earlier part of the seventeenth century. Three names at once suggested themselves—Claudio Monteverdi, Giulio Caccini, and Bardello (Antonio Naldi). Peri was not considered, because his long hair was a well-known peculiarity.

Caccini was a performer upon the lute, but the instrument which he used for accompanying his recitatives was the theorbo. The theorbo it was, too, to which Bardello sang. As the instruments in the picture are certainly viols, they point to some musician who was not only a composer, but an accomplished performer on them. " It must be Monteverdi!" I exclaimed. He began his musical life as a violist, and indeed was very young when he showed ability enough to become one of the Duke of Mantua's violists. Born at Cremona, what more likely than that a painting of him as a young man should be there? though after a time its identity, as has happened in countless cases, was forgotten. All the details of the costume would fit the last decade of the sixteenth century, when he would be about the age of the subject of the picture.

It remained to prove in some way that the above conjecture was well founded. A copper-plate engraving of Monteverdi is given by Caffi in his work ; * but it represents the great musician as a middle-aged man, and although there is some resemblance between the engraving and the painting, it is not strong enough to form a satisfactory proof of identity of subject.

* "Storia della Musica Sacra nella già Capella Ducale di San Marco in Venezia dal 1318 al 1797."

Fortunately there is another print, published in 1644, the year after Monteverdi's death, in a volume * now very rare, of which I heard through Signor F. Sacchi. This print bears much more closely upon the portrait. There is no copy of Marinoni's rare volume in the Library of the

Fig. 68.—MONTEVERDI.

British Museum; but the engraving of Monteverdi has been fairly well reproduced as the frontispiece of a pamphlet which is obtainable † (fig. 68.)

---

* "Fiori Poetici" raccolti da G. B. Marinoni, e stampato in Venezia nel 1644.
† "Claudio Monteverdi a Cremona" da Giorgio Sommi Picenardi. (G Ricordi e C. Milano.)

The Supposed Portrait of Stradivari.

A comparison of this reproduction with the portrait—allowance being made for some twenty or five-and-twenty years' difference of age—affords reasonably satisfactory proof that the portrait does represent Claudio Monteverdi, All the details of the picture being borne in mind, the likeness is too striking to be accidental. It should be mentioned that the dress of Monteverdi in the prints is probably that of his office as Maestro di Capella of St. Mark's, Venice.

The painting thus discussed is therefore of quite exceptional interest, as in it we have a portrait hitherto unknown of the great Monteverdi as a young man ; and the story of its fortunes, while forming a romantic tale, points more than one important moral.

It must, however, be accepted that there exists no authentic portrait of Antonio Stradivari. For knowledge of his personal appearance we must rest content with the few words of description handed down by Polledro : "*He was tall and thin in appearance, invariably to be seen in his working costume, which rarely changed, as he was always at work.*"

APPENDIX I. (TO CHAPTER I.)

CENSUS RETURNS.

CASA DEL PESCATORE (HOUSE OF THE FISHMONGER).

1668. M. Antonio Stradivari, (years) 28.

M. Francesca, wife   ,,   26.

Giulia Maria, daughter, (months) 3.

1669. Stradivari's age given as 22.

1672.   ,,   ,,   ,,   ,,   25.

1675.   ,,   ,,   ,,   ,,   28.

1676.   ,,   ,,   ,,   ,,   30.

1677.   ,,   ,,   ,,   ,,   29.

1678.   ,,   ,,   ,,   ,,   29.

1680. Antonio Stradivari, with his family, removed during this year to the parish of S. Matteo, and settled in the house he had bought of the family Picenardi.

(In the intervening years the census returns are wanting.)

1681. *Signor Antonio Stradivari*, P.F. (paterfamilias), aged 32, has been confirmed, has confessed, and received the Holy Communion.

Francesca Feraboschi, wife, aged 35.

Emily (*sic*), daughter   ,,   11 (her real name was Giulia Maria).

Francesco, son   ,,   8.

Caterina, daughter   ,,   6.

Alessandro, son   ,,   4.

Omobono   ,,   ,,   1.

1687. Francesco received the Holy Communion for the first time.

1689. Giulia Maria is no more mentioned ; she had married in another parish in the preceding year.

1695. Omobono received for the first time the Holy Communion.

1696. Alessandro was admitted to Holy Orders.

1699. There is no mention of Francesca Feraboschi, wife of Antonio, as she died in the month of May of the preceding year.

1700. Antonio's first wife being dead, he married, on August 24th, 1699, Antonia Maria Zambelli, daughter of Antonio, aged 36, of the parish of S. Donato, so that under this year begin the entries with the name of the second wife.

1701. A girl, born in the preceding year, is mentioned, to whom the name of the first wife, Francesca Maria, was given.

1702. In the previous year a boy came into the world, who was christened with the names Giovanni Battista Giuseppe.

1703. Giovanni Battista Giuseppe having died in 1702, his name is omitted from the yearly list.

1705. A new son is registered, named Giovanni Battista Martino.

1706. Alessandro is ordained a priest. There is an entry of another son, named Giuseppe Antonio.

1708. The family receives another addition by the birth of a son, named Paolo Bartolomeo.

1720. Death of the girl Francesca Maria.

1726. The son Giuseppe Antonio is accepted a clerk in Holy Orders.

1727. Giovanni Battista dies.

1729. Giuseppe Antonio is ordained a priest.

1732. The Rev. Alessandro dies.

1737. Fatal year for the Stradivari family. On March 3rd Antonia Maria Zambelli, the second wife, dies, and on December 18th Antonio Stradivari, the head of the family.

1738. In Stradivari's house we find Francesco, Caterina, Omobono, Paolo Bartolomeo, his wife, Elena Templari, of the late Giorgio, aged 30, and the Rev. Giuseppe.

1739. The marriage of Paolo Bartolomeo is blessed by the birth of a son, to whom is given the grandfather's name, Antonio.

1740. Paolo has a daughter, Francesca; she afterwards became a Carthusian nun, and died in 1809.

1742. A third child is born to Paolo, a son named Carlo Andrea Francesco, who became a Carmelite monk, was appointed Professor of Physics at Florence, and died in 1808.

1743. Omobono is left out, having died on June 8th of the preceding year.

1744. Another son of Paolo is entered, named Francesco Gaetano Faustino Omobono, born on February 11th.

1746. Paolo Stradivari's family removed from their house and went to live in another parish, letting the house and the shop to the violin-maker Carlo Bergonzi, pupil of Antonio Stradivari, and they settled in the parish of the cathedral, Quartiere Maggiore, in the house owned by a certain Berzi, together with Paolo's brother, the priest Giuseppe.

1746. Stradivari's house occupied by Carlo Bergonzi, of the late Michele, aged 60 years. } Received Confirmation, made Confession, and Communion.

Gertrude, his daughter, aged 29 years.	,,
Francesca, his daughter, aged 27 years.	,,
Zosimo, his son, aged 21 years.	,,
Michele (Angelo), his son, aged 24 years.	,,
Barbara Berselli, daughter of the late Alfonsa, wife of Michele (Angelo), aged 27 years.	,,

The Bergonzi family had the house up to the year 1758.

In 1759 it was tenanted by Giacomo Caraffi.

In 1761 it was tenanted by Caterina Ceresa, and up to 1777 by Giuseppe Paleari and others.

In 1777 Antonio Stradivari, son of Paolo and grandson of the great maker, sold the house to Signor Giovanni Ancina.

APPENDIX II. (TO CHAPTER I.)

ANTONIO STRADIVARI was married on July 4th, 1667, to Signora Francesca Feraboscha. The following children were issue of this marriage:—

    I. *Giulia Maria*, born on December 21st, 1667.

    II. *Francesco*, born on February 6th, 1670; died on the 12th of the same month.

    III. *Giacomo Francesco*, born on February 1st, 1671; died a bachelor on May 11th, 1743.

The last-named followed his father's calling, for which reason we add the certificate of his birth, death, and burial.

In the Baptismal Register of S. Agata, vol. vi., p. 251:—

"On the 2nd day of February, 1671, Jacomo Francesco, son of Signor Jacomo Antonio Stradivari, and of Signora Francesca, his wife, was born on the 1st of this month, and was christened by me, Don Michel Zaldino, Parish Priest of the illustrious and Collegiate Church of S. Agata, the godfather being Sig. Michele Rodeschino,* of the Parish of S. Leonardo, and the godmother Signora Maria Elisabetta Poggi, of the Parish of S. Agata."

In the Register of Deaths of S. Matteo, vol. iii., p. 34:—

"In the year of our Lord one thousand seven hundred and forty-three, Sig. Francesco Stradivari, of the late Antonio, died, aged about seventy, fortified by the Sacraments of Penance, Holy Eucharist, and Extreme Unction, on the 11th day of the month of May, a bachelor, with the regular prayers for his soul; and his corpse was conveyed, with a suitable funeral, by the Rev. Rocco de Gambarine, Parish Priest of S. Nicolo, by instruction of the Vestry of that Church, to the Church of the Father Preachers of the Order of S. Dominic, in which he was buried on the 12th of May."

The burial is registered also in the Book of Deaths of S. Dominic, at p. 40:—

"On May 13th, 1743, took place the burial of the late Sigr. Francesco Stradivari, who was interred in the Chapel of the Rosary, in the tomb of Sigr. Francesco Villani, of the Parish of S. Matteo."

---

* This person was evidently the Marquis Michele Rodeschini, the same for whom Stradivari in 1686 made a viol da gamba, to be sent to King James II. of England. (See Hart, art. Stradivari, p. 181.)

IV. *Catterina Annunciata*, born March 25th, 1674; died a spinster on June 17th, 1748.

V. *Alessandro Giuseppe*, born on May 25th, 1677; entered Holy Orders, and died on January 26th, 1732.

VI. *Omobono Felice*, born on November 14th, 1679, and died a bachelor on June 8th, 1742.

As he followed his father's profession, we give the certificates of his birth and death.

In the Baptismal Registers of S. Matteo, vol. vi., p. 349:—

"On the 15th day of November, 1679, in Cremona, Omobono Felice, son of Antonio Stradivari and of Francesca Feraboscha, man and wife, was born on the 14th of this month, at 23 o'clock, and was christened by me, Francesco de Cherubelli, Parish Priest, the godfather being Signor Gian Giacomo Sperlasca, of Lugano, residing at S. Leonardo, in testimony of which I have written this," etc.

In the Register of Deaths of S. Matteo, vol. iii., p. 33:—

"In the year of our Lord one thousand seven hundred and forty-two on the 9th day of June, Sigr. Omobono Stradivari, of the late Sigr. Antonio, died a bachelor yesterday, aged about fifty-seven years, fortified by the Holy Sacraments and prayers for his soul, and to-day his body was conveyed by me, Domenico Antonio Stancari, to the Church of the Fathers Preachers of the Order of S. Dominic, in which he was buried."

And in S. Domenico's Register of Deaths, p. 39:—

"On June 9th, 1742, took place the burial of the late Sigr. Omobono Stradivari, whose body was interred in the Chapel of the Rosary, in the tomb of Sigr. Francesco Villani, in the Parish of S. Matteo."

On August 24th, 1699, Antonio Stradivari married Signora Antonia Maria Zambelli as his second wife. The following children were issue of this marriage:—

I. *Francesca Maria*, born September 19th, 1700; died a spinster, February 12th, 1720.

II. *Giovanni Battista Giuseppe*, born November 6th, 1701; died July 8th, 1702.

III. *Giovanni Battista Martino*, born November 11th, 1703; died November 1st, 1727.

IV. *Giuseppe Antonio*, born October 27th, 1704; died December 2nd, 1781.

V. *Paolo Bartolomeo*, born January 26th, 1708; died October 14th, 1775.

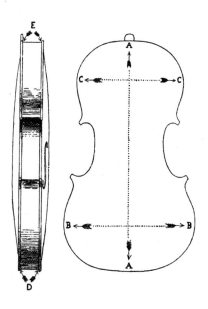

APPENDIX III. (TO CHAPTER II.)

TABLE OF MEASUREMENTS.

Grand Amati, 1648.

Length A to A .	14 inches full	
Width B to B .	$8\frac{1}{4}$,, ,,	
,, C to C .	$6\frac{3}{4}$,, bare	
Sides D to D .	$1\frac{3}{16}$,,	
,, E to E .	$1\frac{1}{16}$,,	

Grand Amati, 1682.

Length . . .	$13\frac{15}{16}$ inches
Width . . .	$8\frac{1}{4}$,,
,, . . .	$6\frac{11}{16}$,,
Sides . . .	$1\frac{3}{16}$,, full
,, . . .	$1\frac{1}{8}$,,

Grand Amati, 1658.

Length . . .	14 inches
Width . . .	$8\frac{1}{8}$,, full
,, . . .	$6\frac{5}{8}$,,
Sides . . .	$1\frac{3}{16}$,, full
,, . . .	$1\frac{3}{16}$,, bare

Stradivari, 1667.

Length . . .	$13\frac{3}{4}$ inches
Width . . .	$7\frac{13}{16}$,,
,, . . .	$6\frac{1}{4}$,,
Sides . . .	$1\frac{3}{16}$,, full
,, . . .	$1\frac{1}{8}$,, ,,

Small form Amati, 1671.

Length . . .	$13\frac{7}{8}$ inches
Width . . .	$7\frac{15}{16}$,,
,, . . .	$6\frac{3}{8}$,,
Sides . . .	$1\frac{3}{16}$,,
,, . . .	$1\frac{1}{8}$,,

Stradivari, 1669.

Length . . .	$13\frac{7}{8}$ inches
Width . . .	$7\frac{7}{8}$,,
,, . . .	$6\frac{1}{4}$,, full
Sides . . .	$1\frac{3}{8}$,, full
,, . . .	$1\frac{3}{8}$,, bare

Stradivari, 1672.

Length . . . 14 inches
Width . . . 8 ,, full
,, . . . $6\frac{1}{2}$,, bare
Sides . . . $1\frac{1}{4}$,, ,,
,, . . . $1\frac{1}{8}$,, full

Stradivari, 1677.

Length . . . $14\frac{1}{16}$ inches
Width . . . $8\frac{1}{8}$,,
,, . . . $6\frac{1}{2}$,,
Sides . . . $1\frac{1}{4}$,, bare
,, . . . $1\frac{1}{8}$,, full

Stradivari, 1679 (The Hellier).

Length . . . $14\frac{1}{8}$ inches
Width . . . $8\frac{3}{8}$,, full
,, . . . $6\frac{13}{16}$,, ,,
Sides . . . $1\frac{1}{4}$,, ,,
,, . . . $1\frac{3}{16}$,, ,,

Stradivari, 1683.

Length . . . $13\frac{13}{16}$ inches
Width . . . 8 inches less $\frac{1}{16}$
,, . . . $6\frac{3}{4}$ inches bare
Sides . . . $1\frac{1}{4}$,,
,, . . . $1\frac{3}{16}$,,

Stradivari, 1684.

Length . . . $13\frac{3}{4}$ inches
Width . . . $7\frac{7}{8}$,,
,, . . . $6\frac{5}{16}$,,
Sides . . . $1\frac{1}{4}$,, bare
,, . . . $1\frac{3}{16}$,,

Stradivari, 1684.

Length . . . $14\frac{1}{8}$ inches
Width . . . $8\frac{5}{16}$,,
,, . . . $6\frac{3}{4}$,,
Sides . . . $1\frac{1}{4}$,,
,, . . . $1\frac{3}{16}$,,

Stradivari, 1686.

Length . . . 14 inches
Width . . . $8\frac{1}{4}$,,
,, . . . $6\frac{5}{8}$,, full
Sides . . . $1\frac{3}{16}$,,
,, . . . $1\frac{1}{8}$,,

Stradivari, 1687.

Length . . . $14\frac{1}{16}$ inches
Width . . . $8\frac{3}{8}$,, bare
,, . . . $6\frac{3}{4}$,,
Sides . . . $1\frac{3}{16}$,, full
,, . . . $1\frac{3}{16}$,,

Stradivari, 1688.

Length . . . 14 inches
Width . . . $8\frac{1}{8}$,,
,, . . . $6\frac{1}{2}$,,
Sides . . . $1\frac{3}{16}$,,
,, . . . $1\frac{3}{16}$,,

Stradivari, 1689.

Length . . . $14\frac{1}{16}$ inches
Width . . . $8\frac{1}{4}$,,
,, . . . $6\frac{3}{4}$,,
Sides . . . $1\frac{1}{4}$,,
,, . . . $1\frac{3}{16}$,,

Stradivari, 1690.

Length . . . 14 inches
Width . . . $8\frac{1}{8}$,,
,, . . . $6\frac{1}{2}$,,
Sides . . . $1\frac{3}{16}$,,
,, . . . $1\frac{1}{8}$,,

Stradivari, 1690.

Length . . . 14 inches
Width . . . $8\frac{1}{4}$,,
,, . . . $6\frac{11}{16}$,,
Sides . . . $1\frac{1}{4}$,,
,, . . . $1\frac{3}{16}$,,

Stradivari, 1690.

Length	.	.	$14\frac{1}{4}$ inches
Width	.	.	$8\frac{1}{4}$,,
,,	.	.	$6\frac{11}{16}$,,
Sides	.	.	$1\frac{3}{16}$,,
,,	.	.	$1\frac{1}{8}$,,

Maggini (Small Pattern).

Length	.	.	$14\frac{1}{4}$ inches
Width	.	.	$8\frac{3}{16}$,, full
,,	.	.	$6\frac{5}{8}$,, bare
Sides	.	.	$1\frac{1}{8}$,,
,,	.	.	$1\frac{1}{8}$,,

Stradivari, 1690 (Typical long pattern).

Length	.	.	$14\frac{5}{16}$ inches
Width	.	.	$8\frac{1}{16}$,,
,,	.	.	$6\frac{7}{16}$,,
Sides	.	.	$1\frac{1}{4}$,, bare
,,	.	.	$1\frac{3}{16}$,,

Stradivari, 1691.

Length	.	.	$14\frac{1}{4}$ inches full
Width	.	.	$8\frac{1}{4}$,,
,,	.	.	$6\frac{11}{16}$,,
Sides	.	.	$1\frac{1}{4}$,,
,,	.	.	$1\frac{3}{16}$,, bare

Stradivari, 1694 (Typical long pattern).

Length	.	.	$14\frac{5}{16}$ inches
Width	.	.	8 ,,
,,	.	.	$6\frac{7}{16}$,,
Sides	.	.	$1\frac{3}{16}$,,
,,	.	.	$1\frac{3}{16}$,, bare

Stradivari, 1698.

Length	.	.	14 inches full
Width	.	.	$8\frac{1}{4}$,, full
,,	.	.	$6\frac{11}{16}$,,
Sides	.	.	$1\frac{1}{4}$,,
,,	.	.	$1\frac{3}{16}$,,

Stradivari, 1698.

Length	.	.	14 inches bare
Width	.	.	8 ,,
,,	.	..	$6\frac{5}{8}$,,
Sides	.	.	$1\frac{1}{4}$,,
,,	.	.	$1\frac{3}{16}$,, bare

Stradivari, 1698.

Length	.	.	$14\frac{1}{16}$ inches
Width	.	.	$8\frac{5}{16}$,, bare
,,	.	.	$6\frac{11}{16}$,, full
Sides	.	.	$1\frac{3}{16}$,,
,,	.	.	$1\frac{1}{8}$,,

Stradivari, 1699.

Length	.	.	14 inches
Width	.	.	8 ,,
,,	.	.	$6\frac{7}{16}$,, full
Sides	.	.	$1\frac{3}{16}$,,
,,	.	.	$1\frac{1}{8}$,, full

Stradivari, 1700.

Length	.	.	14 inches full
Width	.	.	$8\frac{1}{4}$,,
,,	.	.	$6\frac{11}{16}$,,
Sides	.	.	$1\frac{1}{4}$,,
,,	.	.	$1\frac{3}{16}$,,

Stradivari, 1702.

Length	.	.	14 inches
Width	.	.	$8\frac{3}{16}$,, full
,,	.	.	$6\frac{5}{8}$,,
Sides	.	.	$1\frac{1}{4}$,, bare
,,	.	.	$1\frac{3}{16}$,,

Stradivari, 1703.

Length	.		14 inches
Width	.		$8\frac{3}{16}$,,
,,	.		$6\frac{5}{8}$,,
Sides	.		$1\frac{3}{16}$,,
,,	.		$1\frac{1}{8}$,, bare

35

Stradivari, 1704.

Length	.	.	14	inches
Width	.	.	$8\frac{1}{4}$	,,
,,	⸱	.	$6\frac{11}{16}$	,,
Sides	.	.	$1\frac{1}{4}$	,,
,,	.	.	$1\frac{3}{16}$	,,

Stradivari, 1707.

Length	.	.	14	inches	
Width	.	.	$8\frac{1}{4}$	,,	
,,	.	.	$6\frac{5}{8}$	,,	full
Sides	.	.	$1\frac{3}{16}$	,,	
,,	.	.	$1\frac{3}{16}$	,,	bare

Stradivari, 1708.

Length	.	.	$14\frac{1}{8}$	inches
Width	.	.	$8\frac{1}{4}$	,,
,,	.	.	$6\frac{11}{16}$	,,
Sides	.	.	$1\frac{1}{4}$	,,
,,	.	.	$1\frac{3}{16}$	,,

Stradivari, 1709.

Length	.	.	$14\frac{1}{8}$	inches
Width	.	.	$8\frac{1}{4}$	,,
,,	.	.	$6\frac{11}{16}$	,,
Sides	.	.	$1\frac{3}{8}$	,,
,,	.	.	$1\frac{1}{4}$	,,

Stradivari, 1709.

Length	.	.	14	inches	
Width	.	.	$8\frac{1}{4}$	,,	full
,,	.	⸱	$6\frac{11}{16}$	,,	bare
Sides	.	.	$1\frac{1}{4}$	,,	
,,	.	.	$1\frac{3}{16}$	,,	

Stradivari, 1709.

Length	.	.	14	inches	bare
Width	.	.	8	,,	
,,	.	.	$6\frac{1}{2}$	,,	
Sides	.	.	$1\frac{1}{4}$	,,	
,,	.	⸱	$1\frac{3}{16}$	,,	

Stradivari, 1710.

Length	.	.	14	inches
Width	.	,	$8\frac{1}{4}$	,,
,,	.	.	$6\frac{11}{16}$	,,
Sides	.	.	$1\frac{1}{4}$	,,
,,	.	.	$1\frac{3}{16}$	,,

Stradivari, 1711.

Length	.	.	$14\frac{1}{8}$	inches	
Width	.	.	$8\frac{1}{4}$	,,	
,,	.	.	$6\frac{11}{16}$	,,	
Sides	.	.	$1\frac{3}{16}$	,,	
,,	.	.	$1\frac{3}{16}$	,,	bare

Stradivari, 1712.

Length	.	.	$13\frac{15}{16}$	inches
Width	.	.	$8\frac{1}{4}$	,,
,,	.	.	$6\frac{5}{8}$	,,
Sides	.	.	$1\frac{1}{4}$	,,
,,	.	.	$1\frac{3}{16}$	,,

Stradivari, 1713.

Length	.	.	$14\frac{1}{16}$	inches
Width	.	.	$8\frac{1}{4}$	,,
,,	.	.	$6\frac{5}{8}$	,,
Sides	.	.	$1\frac{1}{4}$	,,
,,	.	.	$1\frac{3}{16}$	,,

Stradivari, 1714.

Length	.	.	14	inches	
Width	.	.	$8\frac{1}{4}$	,,	
,,	.	.	$6\frac{5}{8}$	,,	full
Sides	.	.	$1\frac{3}{16}$	,,	
,,	.	.	$1\frac{3}{16}$	,,	

Stradivari, 1716.

Length	.	.	14	inches
Width	.	.	$8\frac{1}{4}$	,,
,,	.	.	$6\frac{5}{8}$	,,
Sides	.	.	$1\frac{1}{4}$	,,
,,	.	.	$1\frac{3}{16}$	,,

Stradivari, 1716.		
Length .	.	. $13\frac{15}{16}$ inches
Width .	.	. $8\frac{1}{4}$,,
,,	.	. $6\frac{5}{8}$,,
Sides	.	. $1\frac{1}{4}$,,
,,	.	. $1\frac{3}{16}$,,

Stradivari, 1727.		
Length .	.	. 14 inches
Width .	.	. $8\frac{3}{16}$,,
,,	.	. $6\frac{5}{8}$,,
Sides	.	. $1\frac{1}{4}$,,
,,	.	. $1\frac{3}{16}$,,

Stradivari, 1718.		
Length .	.	. $14\frac{1}{8}$ inches
Width .	.	. $8\frac{1}{4}$,,
,,	.	. $6\frac{11}{16}$,,
Sides	.	. $1\frac{1}{4}$,, bare
,,	.	. $1\frac{3}{16}$,,

Stradivari, 1732.		
Length .	.	. $14\frac{1}{8}$ inches
Width .	.	. $8\frac{1}{4}$,,
,,	.	. $6\frac{11}{16}$,,
Sides	.	. $1\frac{1}{4}$,,
,,	.	. $1\frac{3}{16}$,,

Stradivari, 1720.		
Length .	.	. $14\frac{1}{16}$ inches
Width .	.	. $8\frac{1}{4}$,,
,,	.	. $6\frac{5}{8}$,,
Sides	.	. $1\frac{1}{4}$,,
,,	.	. $1\frac{3}{16}$,,

Stradivari, 1734.		
Length .	.	. $14\frac{1}{8}$ inches
Width .	.	. $8\frac{5}{16}$,,
,,	.	. $6\frac{3}{4}$,,
Sides	.	. $1\frac{5}{16}$,, bare
,,	.	. $1\frac{1}{4}$,, ,,

Stradivari, 1722.		
Length .	.	. $14\frac{1}{16}$ inches full
Width .	.	. $8\frac{1}{4}$,,
,,	.	. $6\frac{11}{16}$,,
Sides	.	. $1\frac{1}{4}$,,
,,	.	. $1\frac{3}{16}$,,

Stradivari, 1736.		
Length .	.	. 14 inches
Width .	.	. $8\frac{1}{16}$,, full
,,	.	. $6\frac{1}{2}$,, bare
Sides	.	. $1\frac{1}{4}$,, full
,,	.	. $1\frac{3}{16}$,, ,,

Note.—The measurements given in these tables were all taken with a rule over the modelling —*i.e.* exterior to the instruments.

APPENDIX IV. (TO CHAPTER III.)

TABLE OF MEASUREMENTS.

VIOLAS OF LARGE SIZE.

Gasparo da Salò.

Length A to A	.	$17\frac{1}{2}$ inches
Width B to B	.	$10\frac{1}{8}$,,
,, C to C	.	$8\frac{5}{8}$,,
Sides D to D	.	$1\frac{9}{16}$,,
,, E to E	.	$1\frac{1}{2}$,,
Stop .	.	9 ,,

A. and H. Amati, 1620.

Length .	.	$17\frac{3}{4}$ inches full
Width .	.	$10\frac{7}{16}$,,
,, .	.	$8\frac{1}{2}$,,
Sides .	.	$1\frac{9}{16}$,,
,, .	.	$1\frac{1}{2}$,,
Stop .	.	$9\frac{3}{4}$,, bare

A. and H. Amati, 1592.

Length .	.	$17\frac{13}{16}$ inches full
Width .	.	$10\frac{9}{16}$,,
,, .	.	$8\frac{5}{8}$,,
Sides .	.	$1\frac{5}{8}$,,
,, .	.	$1\frac{1}{2}$,,
Stop .	.	$9\frac{3}{4}$,, bare

Stradivari, 1690 (Large).

Length .	.	$18\frac{7}{8}$ inches
Width .	.	$10\frac{3}{4}$,,
,, .	.	$8\frac{5}{8}$,, full
Sides .	.	$1\frac{11}{16}$,,
,, .	.	$1\frac{9}{16}$,,
Stop .	.	$10\frac{1}{4}$,,

VIOLAS OF SMALL SIZE.

A. and H. Amati, 1616.

Length .	.	$16\frac{1}{4}$ inches
Width .	.	$9\frac{3}{4}$,, full
,, .	.	$7\frac{3}{4}$,,
Sides .	.	$1\frac{5}{16}$,,
,, .	.	$1\frac{1}{4}$,,
Stop .	.	$8\frac{3}{4}$,,

A. Guarnerius, 1676.

Length .	.	$16\frac{3}{8}$ inches
Width .	.	$9\frac{11}{16}$,,
,, .	.	$7\frac{13}{16}$,,
Sides .	.	$1\frac{1}{2}$,,
,, .	.	$1\frac{3}{8}$,,
Stop .	.	$8\frac{11}{16}$,,

Stainer, 1660.

Length .	.	16 inches
Width .	.	$9\frac{1}{2}$,, bare
,, .	.	$7\frac{13}{16}$,,
Sides .	.	$1\frac{7}{8}$,,
,, .	.	$1\frac{13}{16}$,,
Stop .	.	$8\frac{1}{2}$,,

Stradivari, 1690.

Length .	.	$16\frac{5}{16}$ inches
Width .	.	$9\frac{9}{16}$,, full
,, .	.	$7\frac{3}{8}$,,
Sides .	.	$1\frac{9}{16}$,, bare
,, .	.	$1\frac{7}{16}$,, full
Stop .	.	$8\frac{3}{4}$,,

Stradivari, 1672.

Length .	.	$16\frac{3}{16}$ inches full
Width .	.	$9\frac{15}{16}$,,
,, .	.	$7\frac{3}{4}$,, full
Sides .	.	$1\frac{5}{16}$,,
,, .	.	$1\frac{5}{16}$,,
Stop .	.	$8\frac{1}{2}$,,

Stradivari, 1701 (The Macdonald).

Length .	.	$16\frac{3}{16}$ inches
Width .	.	$9\frac{9}{16}$,,
,, .	.	$7\frac{5}{16}$,,
Sides .	.	$1\frac{1}{2}$,,
,, .	.	$1\frac{7}{16}$,,
Stop .	.	$8\frac{5}{8}$,, bare

APPENDIX V. (TO CHAPTER IV.)

TABLE OF MEASUREMENTS.

We are only able to give the approximate dimensions of the Violoncello as made by the successive generations of the Amatis, as no example is known to us, the proportions of which have not been diminished. We believe them nevertheless to be fairly accurate.

Amati.

Length A to A	.	31 inches
Width B to B	.	$18\frac{3}{4}$,,
,, C to C	.	$14\frac{1}{2}$,,
Sides D to D	.	$4\frac{11}{16}$,,
,, E to E .	.	$4\frac{1}{2}$,, full
* Stop .	.	$16\frac{3}{4}$,,

Francesco Ruger, 1007.

Length .	.	$30\frac{5}{16}$ inches
Width .	.	$18\frac{3}{8}$,,
,,	.	$14\frac{7}{8}$,,
Sides .	.	$4\frac{5}{8}$,,
,,	.	$4\frac{1}{2}$,,
Stop .	.	$16\frac{5}{8}$,,

F. Ruger (approx.) *1670.*

Length .	.	$31\frac{1}{4}$ inches bare
Width .	.	$19\frac{1}{8}$,,
,,	.	15 ,,
Sides .	.	$5\frac{1}{8}$,,
,,	.	$4\frac{7}{8}$,,
Stop .	.	$16\frac{1}{2}$,,

F. Ruger (small form).

Length .	.	$28\frac{7}{8}$ inches
Width .	.	$17\frac{5}{8}$,, full
,,	.	$14\frac{3}{8}$,,
Sides .	.	$4\frac{7}{16}$,,
,,	.	$4\frac{5}{16}$,,
Stop .	.	$15\frac{3}{8}$,,

Andrea Guarneri (small form).

Length .	.	$29\frac{1}{4}$ inches
Width .	.	$17\frac{5}{8}$,,
,,	.	$14\frac{1}{4}$,,
Sides .	.	$4\frac{1}{2}$,,
,,	.	$4\frac{1}{2}$,,
Stop .	.	$15\frac{1}{2}$,,

J. B. Rogeri, 1700.

Length .	.	29 inches bare
Width .	.	$17\frac{1}{2}$,,
,,	.	$14\frac{5}{16}$,,
Sides .	.	$4\frac{11}{16}$,,
,,	.	$4\frac{7}{16}$,,
Stop .	.	$15\frac{3}{8}$,,

Stradivari, 1690. "The Tuscan."

Length .	.	$31\frac{3}{8}$ inches
Width .	.	$18\frac{1}{2}$,,
,,	.	$14\frac{1}{2}$,,
Sides .	.	$4\frac{3}{4}$,,
,,	.	$4\frac{1}{2}$,,
Stop .	.	$16\frac{3}{4}$,,

Stradivari (pre-*1700* form) "The Aylesford," *1696.*

Length .	.	$31\frac{1}{4}$ inches
Width .	.	$18\frac{3}{8}$,,
,,	.	$14\frac{3}{8}$,,
Sides .	.	$4\frac{3}{8}$,,
,,	.	$4\frac{1}{2}$,,
Stop .	.	$16\frac{3}{4}$,,

* The distance from top surface of bridge foot to the shoulder.

Stradivari, 1700. "The Cristiani."

Length	.	.	.	$30\frac{1}{2}$ inches bare
Width	.	.	.	$18\frac{1}{8}$ "
"	.	.	.	$14\frac{1}{8}$ "
Sides	.	.	.	$4\frac{3}{4}$ "
"	.	.	.	$4\frac{5}{8}$ "
Stop	.	.	.	$16\frac{1}{4}$ "

Stradivari, 1700. Spanish Court.

Length	.	.	.	$30\frac{1}{4}$ inches full
Width	.	.	.	18 "
"	.	.	.	14 "
Sides	.	.	.	$4\frac{1}{2}$ "
"	.	.	.	$4\frac{3}{8}$ "
Stop	.	.	.	$16\frac{1}{4}$ "

Stradivari, 1701. "The Servais."

Length	.	.	.	$31\frac{1}{8}$ inches
Width	.	.	.	$18\frac{1}{2}$ "
"	.	.	.	$14\frac{3}{8}$ "
Sides	.	.	.	5 "
"	.	.	.	$4\frac{7}{8}$ "
*Stop	.	.	.	$16\frac{3}{4}$ "

Stradivari, 1710. "The Gore-Booth."

Length	.	.	.	$29\frac{7}{8}$ inches
Width	.	.	.	$17\frac{3}{8}$ "
"	.	.	.	$13\frac{5}{8}$ "
Sides	.	.	.	$4\frac{7}{8}$ "
"	.	.	.	$4\frac{5}{8}$ "
Stop	.	.	.	$15\frac{3}{4}$ "

Stradivari, 1711. "The Duport."

Length	.	.	.	$29\frac{7}{8}$ inches
Width	.	.	.	$17\frac{7}{8}$ "
"	.	.	.	$13\frac{5}{8}$ "
Sides	.	.	.	$4\frac{5}{8}$ "
"	.	.	.	4^{1} "
Stop	.	.	.	$15\frac{3}{4}$ "

Stradivari, 1713. "ex Adam."

Length	.	.	.	$29\frac{15}{16}$ inches
Width	.	.	.	17^{1} "
"	.	.	.	$13\frac{1}{4}$ "

Sides	.	.	.	5 inches
"	.	.	.	$4\frac{3}{4}$ "
Stop	.	.	.	$15\frac{3}{4}$ "

Stradivari, 1714. "The Batta."

Length	.	.	.	$29\frac{3}{4}$ inches full
Width	.	.	.	$17\frac{3}{8}$ "
"	.	.	.	$13\frac{5}{8}$ "
Sides	.	.	.	$4\frac{13}{16}$ "
"	.	.	.	$4\frac{3}{4}$ "
Stop	.	.	.	$15\frac{3}{4}$ "

Stradivari, 1720. "The Piatti."

Length	.	.	.	$29\frac{7}{8}$ inches
Width	.	.	.	$17\frac{1}{4}$ " full
"	.	.	.	$13\frac{5}{8}$ "
Sides	.	.	.	5 "
"	.	.	.	$4\frac{7}{8}$ "
Stop	.	.	.	$15\frac{3}{4}$ "

Stradivari, 1725. "ex Gallay."

Length	.	.	.	$29\frac{7}{8}$ inches
Width	.	.	.	$17\frac{1}{2}$ "
"	.	.	.	$13\frac{1}{8}$ "
Sides	.	.	.	$4\frac{3}{4}$ "
"	.	.	.	$4\frac{9}{16}$ "
Stop	.	.	.	$15\frac{3}{4}$ "

Stradivari, 1730. Mr. Murray.

Length	.	.	.	$29\frac{1}{2}$ inches bare
Width	.	.	.	$16\frac{1}{2}$ "
"	.	.	.	$12\frac{7}{8}$ " bare
Sides	.	.	.	$4\frac{7}{8}$ "
"	.	.	.	$4\frac{5}{8}$ "
Stop	.	.	.	$15\frac{3}{4}$ "

Stradivari, period 1730. M. de Munck.

Length	.	.	.	$29\frac{1}{2}$ inches
Width	.	.	.	$16\frac{5}{8}$ "
"	.	.	.	$12\frac{15}{16}$ "
Sides	.	.	.	$4\frac{3}{4}$ "
"	.	.	.	$4\frac{5}{8}$ "
Stop	.	.	.	$15\frac{3}{4}$ "

* Servais stood the bridge at $16\frac{5}{8}$ inches.

INDEX

Supplementary Index

Names of instrument makers are in *italics*. Instruments made by Stradivari are indicated by type of instrument and date of manufacture (in italics and within parentheses) in entries for instruments and owners alike. The following abbreviations are used: *C.* for 'cello, *V.* for violin, and *Va.* for viola.

Index of Stradivari's Production
Chronologically Arranged

315

A CATALOG OF SELECTED
DOVER BOOKS
IN ALL FIELDS OF INTEREST

A CATALOG OF SELECTED DOVER
BOOKS IN ALL FIELDS OF INTEREST

DRAWINGS OF REMBRANDT, edited by Seymour Slive. Updated Lippmann, Hofstede de Groot edition, with definitive scholarly apparatus. All portraits, biblical sketches, landscapes, nudes. Oriental figures, classical studies, together with selection of work by followers. 550 illustrations. Total of 630pp. 9⅛ × 12¼.
21485-0, 21486-9 Pa., Two-vol. set $25.00

GHOST AND HORROR STORIES OF AMBROSE BIERCE, Ambrose Bierce. 24 tales vividly imagined, strangely prophetic, and decades ahead of their time in technical skill: "The Damned Thing," "An Inhabitant of Carcosa," "The Eyes of the Panther," "Moxon's Master," and 20 more. 199pp. 5⅜ × 8½. 20767-6 Pa. $3.95

ETHICAL WRITINGS OF MAIMONIDES, Maimonides. Most significant ethical works of great medieval sage, newly translated for utmost precision, readability. Laws Concerning Character Traits, Eight Chapters, more. 192pp. 5⅜ × 8½.
24522-5 Pa. $4.50

THE EXPLORATION OF THE COLORADO RIVER AND ITS CANYONS, J. W. Powell. Full text of Powell's 1,000-mile expedition down the fabled Colorado in 1869. Superb account of terrain, geology, vegetation, Indians, famine, mutiny, treacherous rapids, mighty canyons, during exploration of last unknown part of continental U.S. 400pp. 5⅜ × 8½. 20094-9 Pa. $6.95

HISTORY OF PHILOSOPHY, Julián Marías. Clearest one-volume history on the market. Every major philosopher and dozens of others, to Existentialism and later. 505pp. 5⅜ × 8½. 21739-6 Pa. $8.50

ALL ABOUT LIGHTNING, Martin A. Uman. Highly readable non-technical survey of nature and causes of lightning, thunderstorms, ball lightning, St. Elmo's Fire, much more. Illustrated. 192pp. 5⅜ × 8½. 25237-X Pa. $5.95

SAILING ALONE AROUND THE WORLD, Captain Joshua Slocum. First man to sail around the world, alone, in small boat. One of great feats of seamanship told in delightful manner. 67 illustrations. 294pp. 5⅜ × 8½. 20326-3 Pa. $4.95

LETTERS AND NOTES ON THE MANNERS, CUSTOMS AND CONDITIONS OF THE NORTH AMERICAN INDIANS, George Catlin. Classic account of life among Plains Indians: ceremonies, hunt, warfare, etc. 312 plates. 572pp. of text. 6⅛ × 9¼. 22118-0, 22119-9 Pa. Two-vol. set $15.90

ALASKA: The Harriman Expedition, 1899, John Burroughs, John Muir, et al. Informative, engrossing accounts of two-month, 9,000-mile expedition. Native peoples, wildlife, forests, geography, salmon industry, glaciers, more. Profusely illustrated. 240 black-and-white line drawings. 124 black-and-white photographs. 3 maps. Index. 576pp. 5⅜ × 8½. 25109-8 Pa. $11.95

CATALOG OF DOVER BOOKS

THE BOOK OF BEASTS: Being a Translation from a Latin Bestiary of the Twelfth Century, T. H. White. Wonderful catalog real and fanciful beasts: manticore, griffin, phoenix, amphivius, jaculus, many more. White's witty erudite commentary on scientific, historical aspects. Fascinating glimpse of medieval mind. Illustrated. 296pp. 5⅜ × 8¼. (Available in U.S. only) 24609-4 Pa. $5.95

FRANK LLOYD WRIGHT: ARCHITECTURE AND NATURE. With 160 Illustrations, Donald Hoffmann. Profusely illustrated study of influence of nature—especially prairie—on Wright's designs for Fallingwater, Robie House, Guggenheim Museum, other masterpieces. 96pp. 9¼ × 10¾. 25098-9 Pa. $7.95

FRANK LLOYD WRIGHT'S FALLINGWATER, Donald Hoffmann. Wright's famous waterfall house: planning and construction of organic idea. History of site, owners, Wright's personal involvement. Photographs of various stages of building. Preface by Edgar Kaufmann, Jr. 100 illustrations. 112pp. 9¼ × 10.
23671-4 Pa. $7.95

YEARS WITH FRANK LLOYD WRIGHT: Apprentice to Genius, Edgar Tafel. Insightful memoir by a former apprentice presents a revealing portrait of Wright the man, the inspired teacher, the greatest American architect. 372 black-and-white illustrations. Preface. Index. vi + 228pp. 8¼ × 11. 24801-1 Pa. $9.95

THE STORY OF KING ARTHUR AND HIS KNIGHTS, Howard Pyle. Enchanting version of King Arthur fable has delighted generations with imaginative narratives of exciting adventures and unforgettable illustrations by the author. 41 illustrations. xviii + 313pp. 6⅛ × 9¼. 21445-1 Pa. $6.50

THE GODS OF THE EGYPTIANS, E. A. Wallis Budge. Thorough coverage of numerous gods of ancient Egypt by foremost Egyptologist. Information on evolution of cults, rites and gods; the cult of Osiris; the Book of the Dead and its rites; the sacred animals and birds; Heaven and Hell; and more. 956pp. 6⅛ × 9¼.
22055-9, 22056-7 Pa., Two-vol. set $20.00

A THEOLOGICO-POLITICAL TREATISE, Benedict Spinoza. Also contains unfinished Political Treatise. Great classic on religious liberty, theory of government on common consent. R. Elwes translation. Total of 421pp. 5⅜ × 8½.
20249-6 Pa. $6.95

INCIDENTS OF TRAVEL IN CENTRAL AMERICA, CHIAPAS, AND YUCATAN, John L. Stephens. Almost single-handed discovery of Maya culture; exploration of ruined cities, monuments, temples; customs of Indians. 115 drawings. 892pp. 5⅜ × 8½. 22404-X, 22405-8 Pa., Two-vol. set $15.90

LOS CAPRICHOS, Francisco Goya. 80 plates of wild, grotesque monsters and caricatures. Prado manuscript included. 183pp. 6⅛ × 9⅜. 22384-1 Pa. $4.95

AUTOBIOGRAPHY: The Story of My Experiments with Truth, Mohandas K. Gandhi. Not hagiography, but Gandhi in his own words. Boyhood, legal studies, purification, the growth of the Satyagraha (nonviolent protest) movement. Critical, inspiring work of the man who freed India. 480pp. 5⅜ × 8½. (Available in U.S. only)
24593-4 Pa. $6.95

ILLUSTRATED DICTIONARY OF HISTORIC ARCHITECTURE, edited by Cyril M. Harris. Extraordinary compendium of clear, concise definitions for over 5,000 important architectural terms complemented by over 2,000 line drawings. Covers full spectrum of architecture from ancient ruins to 20th-century Modernism. Preface. 592pp. 7½ × 9⅝. 24444-X Pa. $14.95

THE NIGHT BEFORE CHRISTMAS, Clement Moore. Full text, and woodcuts from original 1848 book. Also critical, historical material. 19 illustrations. 40pp. 4⅝ × 6. 22797-9 Pa. $2.25

THE LESSON OF JAPANESE ARCHITECTURE: 165 Photographs, Jiro Harada. Memorable gallery of 165 photographs taken in the 1930's of exquisite Japanese homes of the well-to-do and historic buildings. 13 line diagrams. 192pp. 8⅜ × 11¼. 24778-3 Pa. $8.95

THE AUTOBIOGRAPHY OF CHARLES DARWIN AND SELECTED LETTERS, edited by Francis Darwin. The fascinating life of eccentric genius composed of an intimate memoir by Darwin (intended for his children); commentary by his son, Francis; hundreds of fragments from notebooks, journals, papers; and letters to and from Lyell, Hooker, Huxley, Wallace and Henslow. xi + 365pp. 5⅝ × 8. 20479-0 Pa. $6.95

WONDERS OF THE SKY: Observing Rainbows, Comets, Eclipses, the Stars and Other Phenomena, Fred Schaaf. Charming, easy-to-read poetic guide to all manner of celestial events visible to the naked eye. Mock suns, glories, Belt of Venus, more. Illustrated. 299pp. 5¼ × 8¼. 24402-4 Pa. $7.95

BURNHAM'S CELESTIAL HANDBOOK, Robert Burnham, Jr. Thorough guide to the stars beyond our solar system. Exhaustive treatment. Alphabetical by constellation: Andromeda to Cetus in Vol. 1; Chamaeleon to Orion in Vol. 2; and Pavo to Vulpecula in Vol. 3. Hundreds of illustrations. Index in Vol. 3. 2,000pp. 6⅛ × 9¼. 23567-X, 23568-8, 23673-0 Pa., Three-vol. set $38.85

STAR NAMES: Their Lore and Meaning, Richard Hinckley Allen. Fascinating history of names various cultures have given to constellations and literary and folkloristic uses that have been made of stars. Indexes to subjects. Arabic and Greek names. Biblical references. Bibliography. 563pp. 5⅜ × 8½. 21079-0 Pa. $7.95

THIRTY YEARS THAT SHOOK PHYSICS: The Story of Quantum Theory, George Gamow. Lucid, accessible introduction to influential theory of energy and matter. Careful explanations of Dirac's anti-particles, Bohr's model of the atom, much more. 12 plates. Numerous drawings. 240pp. 5⅜ × 8½. 24895-X Pa. $4.95

CHINESE DOMESTIC FURNITURE IN PHOTOGRAPHS AND MEASURED DRAWINGS, Gustav Ecke. A rare volume, now affordably priced for antique collectors, furniture buffs and art historians. Detailed review of styles ranging from early Shang to late Ming. Unabridged republication. 161 black-and-white drawings, photos. Total of 224pp. 8⅜ × 11¼. (Available in U.S. only) 25171-3 Pa. $12.95

VINCENT VAN GOGH: A Biography, Julius Meier-Graefe. Dynamic, penetrating study of artist's life, relationship with brother, Theo, painting techniques, travels, more. Readable, engrossing. 160pp. 5⅜ × 8½. (Available in U.S. only) 25253-1 Pa. $3.95

HOW TO WRITE, Gertrude Stein. Gertrude Stein claimed anyone could understand her unconventional writing—here are clues to help. Fascinating improvisations, language experiments, explanations illuminate Stein's craft and the art of writing. Total of 414pp. 4⅝ × 6⅜. 23144-5 Pa. $5.95

ADVENTURES AT SEA IN THE GREAT AGE OF SAIL: Five Firsthand Narratives, edited by Elliot Snow. Rare true accounts of exploration, whaling, shipwreck, fierce natives, trade, shipboard life, more. 33 illustrations. Introduction. 353pp. 5⅜ × 8½. 25177-2 Pa. $7.95

THE HERBAL OR GENERAL HISTORY OF PLANTS, John Gerard. Classic descriptions of about 2,850 plants—with over 2,700 illustrations—includes Latin and English names, physical descriptions, varieties, time and place of growth, more. 2,706 illustrations. xlv + 1,678pp. 8½ × 12¼. 23147-X Cloth. $75.00

DOROTHY AND THE WIZARD IN OZ, L. Frank Baum. Dorothy and the Wizard visit the center of the Earth, where people are vegetables, glass houses grow and Oz characters reappear. Classic sequel to *Wizard of Oz*. 256pp. 5⅜ × 8. 24714-7 Pa. $4.95

SONGS OF EXPERIENCE: Facsimile Reproduction with 26 Plates in Full Color, William Blake. This facsimile of Blake's original "Illuminated Book" reproduces 26 full-color plates from a rare 1826 edition. Includes "The Tyger," "London," "Holy Thursday," and other immortal poems. 26 color plates. Printed text of poems. 48pp. 5¼ × 7. 24636-1 Pa. $3.50

SONGS OF INNOCENCE, William Blake. The first and most popular of Blake's famous "Illuminated Books," in a facsimile edition reproducing all 31 brightly colored plates. Additional printed text of each poem. 64pp. 5¼ × 7. 22764-2 Pa. $3.50

PRECIOUS STONES, Max Bauer. Classic, thorough study of diamonds, rubies, emeralds, garnets, etc.: physical character, occurrence, properties, use, similar topics. 20 plates, 8 in color. 94 figures. 659pp. 6⅛ × 9¼. 21910-0, 21911-9 Pa., Two-vol. set $15.90

ENCYCLOPEDIA OF VICTORIAN NEEDLEWORK, S. F. A. Caulfeild and Blanche Saward. Full, precise descriptions of stitches, techniques for dozens of needlecrafts—most exhaustive reference of its kind. Over 800 figures. Total of 679pp. 8⅛ × 11. Two volumes. Vol. 1 22800-2 Pa. $11.95
Vol. 2 22801-0 Pa. $11.95

THE MARVELOUS LAND OF OZ, L. Frank Baum. Second Oz book, the Scarecrow and Tin Woodman are back with hero named Tip, Oz magic. 136 illustrations. 287pp. 5⅜ × 8½. 20692-0 Pa. $5.95

WILD FOWL DECOYS, Joel Barber. Basic book on the subject, by foremost authority and collector. Reveals history of decoy making and rigging, place in American culture, different kinds of decoys, how to make them, and how to use them. 140 plates. 156pp. 7⅞ × 10¾. 20011-6 Pa. $8.95

HISTORY OF LACE, Mrs. Bury Palliser. Definitive, profusely illustrated chronicle of lace from earliest times to late 19th century. Laces of Italy, Greece, England, France, Belgium, etc. Landmark of needlework scholarship. 266 illustrations. 672pp. 6⅛ × 9¼. 24742-2 Pa. $14.95

ILLUSTRATED GUIDE TO SHAKER FURNITURE, Robert Meader. All furniture and appurtenances, with much on unknown local styles. 235 photos. 146pp. 9 × 12. 22819-3 Pa. $7.95

WHALE SHIPS AND WHALING: A Pictorial Survey, George Francis Dow. Over 200 vintage engravings, drawings, photographs of barks, brigs, cutters, other vessels. Also harpoons, lances, whaling guns, many other artifacts. Comprehensive text by foremost authority. 207 black-and-white illustrations. 288pp. 6 × 9. 24808-9 Pa. $8.95

THE BERTRAMS, Anthony Trollope. Powerful portrayal of blind self-will and thwarted ambition includes one of Trollope's most heartrending love stories. 497pp. 5⅜ × 8½. 25119-5 Pa. $8.95

ADVENTURES WITH A HAND LENS, Richard Headstrom. Clearly written guide to observing and studying flowers and grasses, fish scales, moth and insect wings, egg cases, buds, feathers, seeds, leaf scars, moss, molds, ferns, common crystals, etc.—all with an ordinary, inexpensive magnifying glass. 209 exact line drawings aid in your discoveries. 220pp. 5⅜ × 8½. 23330-8 Pa. $3.95

RODIN ON ART AND ARTISTS, Auguste Rodin. Great sculptor's candid, wide-ranging comments on meaning of art; great artists; relation of sculpture to poetry, painting, music; philosophy of life, more. 76 superb black-and-white illustrations of Rodin's sculpture, drawings and prints. 119pp. 8⅜ × 11¼. 24487-3 Pa. $6.95

FIFTY CLASSIC FRENCH FILMS, 1912-1982: A Pictorial Record, Anthony Slide. Memorable stills from Grand Illusion, Beauty and the Beast, Hiroshima, Mon Amour, many more. Credits, plot synopses, reviews, etc. 160pp. 8¼ × 11. 25256-6 Pa. $11.95

THE PRINCIPLES OF PSYCHOLOGY, William James. Famous long course complete, unabridged. Stream of thought, time perception, memory, experimental methods; great work decades ahead of its time. 94 figures. 1,391pp. 5⅜ × 8½. 20381-6, 20382-4 Pa., Two-vol. set $19.90

BODIES IN A BOOKSHOP, R. T. Campbell. Challenging mystery of blackmail and murder with ingenious plot and superbly drawn characters. In the best tradition of British suspense fiction. 192pp. 5⅜ × 8½. 24720-1 Pa. $3.95

CALLAS: PORTRAIT OF A PRIMA DONNA, George Jellinek. Renowned commentator on the musical scene chronicles incredible career and life of the most controversial, fascinating, influential operatic personality of our time. 64 black-and-white photographs. 416pp. 5⅜ × 8¼. 25047-4 Pa. $7.95

GEOMETRY, RELATIVITY AND THE FOURTH DIMENSION, Rudolph Rucker. Exposition of fourth dimension, concepts of relativity as Flatland characters continue adventures. Popular, easily followed yet accurate, profound. 141 illustrations. 133pp. 5⅜ × 8½. 23400-2 Pa. $3.95

HOUSEHOLD STORIES BY THE BROTHERS GRIMM, with pictures by Walter Crane. 53 classic stories—Rumpelstiltskin, Rapunzel, Hansel and Gretel, the Fisherman and his Wife, Snow White, Tom Thumb, Sleeping Beauty, Cinderella, and so much more—lavishly illustrated with original 19th century drawings. 114 illustrations. x + 269pp. 5⅜ × 8½. 21080-4 Pa. $4.50

SUNDIALS, Albert Waugh. Far and away the best, most thorough coverage of ideas, mathematics concerned, types, construction, adjusting anywhere. Over 100 illustrations. 230pp. 5⅜ × 8½. 22947-5 Pa. $4.50

PICTURE HISTORY OF THE NORMANDIE: With 190 Illustrations, Frank O. Braynard. Full story of legendary French ocean liner: Art Deco interiors, design innovations, furnishings, celebrities, maiden voyage, tragic fire, much more. Extensive text. 144pp. 8⅜ × 11¾. 25257-4 Pa. $9.95

THE FIRST AMERICAN COOKBOOK: A Facsimile of "American Cookery," 1796, Amelia Simmons. Facsimile of the first American-written cookbook published in the United States contains authentic recipes for colonial favorites—pumpkin pudding, winter squash pudding, spruce beer, Indian slapjacks, and more. Introductory Essay and Glossary of colonial cooking terms. 80pp. 5⅜ × 8½. 24710-4 Pa. $3.50

101 PUZZLES IN THOUGHT AND LOGIC, C. R. Wylie, Jr. Solve murders and robberies, find out which fishermen are liars, how a blind man could possibly identify a color—purely by your own reasoning! 107pp. 5⅜ × 8½. 20367-0 Pa. $2.50

THE BOOK OF WORLD-FAMOUS MUSIC—CLASSICAL, POPULAR AND FOLK, James J. Fuld. Revised and enlarged republication of landmark work in musico-bibliography. Full information about nearly 1,000 songs and compositions including first lines of music and lyrics. New supplement. Index. 800pp. 5⅜ × 8¼. 24857-7 Pa. $14.95

ANTHROPOLOGY AND MODERN LIFE, Franz Boas. Great anthropologist's classic treatise on race and culture. Introduction by Ruth Bunzel. Only inexpensive paperback edition. 255pp. 5⅜ × 8½. 25245-0 Pa. $5.95

THE TALE OF PETER RABBIT, Beatrix Potter. The inimitable Peter's terrifying adventure in Mr. McGregor's garden, with all 27 wonderful, full-color Potter illustrations. 55pp. 4¼ × 5½. (Available in U.S. only) 22827-4 Pa. $1.75

THREE PROPHETIC SCIENCE FICTION NOVELS, H. G. Wells. *When the Sleeper Wakes, A Story of the Days to Come* and *The Time Machine* (full version). 335pp. 5⅜ × 8½. (Available in U.S. only) 20605-X Pa. $5.95

APICIUS COOKERY AND DINING IN IMPERIAL ROME, edited and translated by Joseph Dommers Vehling. Oldest known cookbook in existence offers readers a clear picture of what foods Romans ate, how they prepared them, etc. 49 illustrations. 301pp. 6⅛ × 9¼. 23563-7 Pa. $6.50

SHAKESPEARE LEXICON AND QUOTATION DICTIONARY, Alexander Schmidt. Full definitions, locations, shades of meaning of every word in plays and poems. More than 50,000 exact quotations. 1,485pp. 6½ × 9¼. 22726-X, 22727-8 Pa., Two-vol. set $27.90

THE WORLD'S GREAT SPEECHES, edited by Lewis Copeland and Lawrence W. Lamm. Vast collection of 278 speeches from Greeks to 1970. Powerful and effective models; unique look at history. 842pp. 5⅜ × 8½. 20468-5 Pa. $11.95

THE BLUE FAIRY BOOK, Andrew Lang. The first, most famous collection, with many familiar tales: Little Red Riding Hood, Aladdin and the Wonderful Lamp, Puss in Boots, Sleeping Beauty, Hansel and Gretel, Rumpelstiltskin; 37 in all. 138 illustrations. 390pp. 5⅜ × 8½. 21437-0 Pa. $5.95

THE STORY OF THE CHAMPIONS OF THE ROUND TABLE, Howard Pyle. Sir Launcelot, Sir Tristram and Sir Percival in spirited adventures of love and triumph retold in Pyle's inimitable style. 50 drawings, 31 full-page. xviii + 329pp. 6½ × 9¼. 21883-X Pa. $6.95

AUDUBON AND HIS JOURNALS, Maria Audubon. Unmatched two-volume portrait of the great artist, naturalist and author contains his journals, an excellent biography by his granddaughter, expert annotations by the noted ornithologist, Dr. Elliott Coues, and 37 superb illustrations. Total of 1,200pp. 5⅜ × 8.

Vol. I 25143-8 Pa. $8.95
Vol. II 25144-6 Pa. $8.95

GREAT DINOSAUR HUNTERS AND THEIR DISCOVERIES, Edwin H. Colbert. Fascinating, lavishly illustrated chronicle of dinosaur research, 1820's to 1960. Achievements of Cope, Marsh, Brown, Buckland, Mantell, Huxley, many others. 384pp. 5¼ × 8¼. 24701-5 Pa. $6.95

THE TASTEMAKERS, Russell Lynes. Informal, illustrated social history of American taste 1850's–1950's. First popularized categories Highbrow, Lowbrow, Middlebrow. 129 illustrations. New (1979) afterword. 384pp. 6 × 9.

23993-4 Pa. $6.95

DOUBLE CROSS PURPOSES, Ronald A. Knox. A treasure hunt in the Scottish Highlands, an old map, unidentified corpse, surprise discoveries keep reader guessing in this cleverly intricate tale of financial skullduggery. 2 black-and-white maps. 320pp. 5⅜ × 8½. (Available in U.S. only) 25032-6 Pa. $5.95

AUTHENTIC VICTORIAN DECORATION AND ORNAMENTATION IN FULL COLOR: 46 Plates from "Studies in Design," Christopher Dresser. Superb full-color lithographs reproduced from rare original portfolio of a major Victorian designer. 48pp. 9¼ × 12¼. 25083-0 Pa. $7.95

PRIMITIVE ART, Franz Boas. Remains the best text ever prepared on subject, thoroughly discussing Indian, African, Asian, Australian, and, especially, Northern American primitive art. Over 950 illustrations show ceramics, masks, totem poles, weapons, textiles, paintings, much more. 376pp. 5⅜ × 8. 20025-6 Pa. $6.95

SIDELIGHTS ON RELATIVITY, Albert Einstein. Unabridged republication of two lectures delivered by the great physicist in 1920–21. *Ether and Relativity* and *Geometry and Experience*. Elegant ideas in non-mathematical form, accessible to intelligent layman. vi + 56pp. 5⅜ × 8½. 24511-X Pa. $2.95

THE WIT AND HUMOR OF OSCAR WILDE, edited by Alvin Redman. More than 1,000 ripostes, paradoxes, wisecracks: Work is the curse of the drinking classes, I can resist everything except temptation, etc. 258pp. 5⅜ × 8½. 20602-5 Pa. $4.50

ADVENTURES WITH A MICROSCOPE, Richard Headstrom. 59 adventures with clothing fibers, protozoa, ferns and lichens, roots and leaves, much more. 142 illustrations. 232pp. 5⅜ × 8½. 23471-1 Pa. $3.95

PLANTS OF THE BIBLE, Harold N. Moldenke and Alma L. Moldenke. Standard reference to all 230 plants mentioned in Scriptures. Latin name, biblical reference, uses, modern identity, much more. Unsurpassed encyclopedic resource for scholars, botanists, nature lovers, students of Bible. Bibliography. Indexes. 123 black-and-white illustrations. 384pp. 6 × 9. 25069-5 Pa. $8.95

FAMOUS AMERICAN WOMEN: A Biographical Dictionary from Colonial Times to the Present, Robert McHenry, ed. From Pocahontas to Rosa Parks, 1,035 distinguished American women documented in separate biographical entries. Accurate, up-to-date data, numerous categories, spans 400 years. Indices. 493pp. 6½ × 9¼. 24523-3 Pa. $9.95

THE FABULOUS INTERIORS OF THE GREAT OCEAN LINERS IN HISTORIC PHOTOGRAPHS, William H. Miller, Jr. Some 200 superb photographs capture exquisite interiors of world's great "floating palaces"—1890's to 1980's: *Titanic, Ile de France, Queen Elizabeth, United States, Europa,* more. Approx. 200 black-and-white photographs. Captions. Text. Introduction. 160pp. 8⅞ × 11¾. 24756-2 Pa. $9.95

THE GREAT LUXURY LINERS, 1927–1954: A Photographic Record, William H. Miller, Jr. Nostalgic tribute to heyday of ocean liners. 186 photos of Ile de France, Normandie, Leviathan, Queen Elizabeth, United States, many others. Interior and exterior views. Introduction. Captions. 160pp. 9 × 12. 24056-8 Pa. $9.95

A NATURAL HISTORY OF THE DUCKS, John Charles Phillips. Great landmark of ornithology offers complete detailed coverage of nearly 200 species and subspecies of ducks: gadwall, sheldrake, merganser, pintail, many more. 74 full-color plates, 102 black-and-white. Bibliography. Total of 1,920pp. 8⅝ × 11¼. 25141-1, 25142-X Cloth. Two-vol. set $100.00

THE SEAWEED HANDBOOK: An Illustrated Guide to Seaweeds from North Carolina to Canada, Thomas F. Lee. Concise reference covers 78 species. Scientific and common names, habitat, distribution, more. Finding keys for easy identification. 224pp. 5⅜ × 8½. 25215-9 Pa. $5.95

THE TEN BOOKS OF ARCHITECTURE: The 1755 Leoni Edition, Leon Battista Alberti. Rare classic helped introduce the glories of ancient architecture to the Renaissance. 68 black-and-white plates. 336pp. 8⅜ × 11¼. 25239-6 Pa. $14.95

MISS MACKENZIE, Anthony Trollope. Minor masterpieces by Victorian master unmasks many truths about life in 19th-century England. First inexpensive edition in years. 392pp. 5⅜ × 8½. 25201-9 Pa. $7.95

THE RIME OF THE ANCIENT MARINER, Gustave Doré, Samuel Taylor Coleridge. Dramatic engravings considered by many to be his greatest work. The terrifying space of the open sea, the storms and whirlpools of an unknown ocean, the ice of Antarctica, more—all rendered in a powerful, chilling manner. Full text. 38 plates. 77pp. 9¼ × 12. 22305-1 Pa. $4.95

THE EXPEDITIONS OF ZEBULON MONTGOMERY PIKE, Zebulon Montgomery Pike. Fascinating first-hand accounts (1805–6) of exploration of Mississippi River, Indian wars, capture by Spanish dragoons, much more. 1,088pp. 5⅜ × 8½. 25254-X, 25255-8 Pa. Two-vol. set $23.90

A CONCISE HISTORY OF PHOTOGRAPHY: Third Revised Edition, Helmut Gernsheim. Best one-volume history—camera obscura, photochemistry, daguerreotypes, evolution of cameras, film, more. Also artistic aspects—landscape, portraits, fine art, etc. 281 black-and-white photographs. 26 in color. 176pp. 8⅜ × 11¼. 25128-4 Pa. $12.95

THE DORÉ BIBLE ILLUSTRATIONS, Gustave Doré. 241 detailed plates from the Bible: the Creation scenes, Adam and Eve, Flood, Babylon, battle sequences, life of Jesus, etc. Each plate is accompanied by the verses from the King James version of the Bible. 241pp. 9 × 12. 23004-X Pa. $8.95

HUGGER-MUGGER IN THE LOUVRE, Elliot Paul. Second Homer Evans mystery-comedy. Theft at the Louvre involves sleuth in hilarious, madcap caper. "A knockout."—Books. 336pp. 5⅜ × 8½. 25185-3 Pa. $5.95

FLATLAND, E. A. Abbott. Intriguing and enormously popular science-fiction classic explores the complexities of trying to survive as a two-dimensional being in a three-dimensional world. Amusingly illustrated by the author. 16 illustrations. 103pp. 5⅜ × 8½. 20001-9 Pa. $2.25

THE HISTORY OF THE LEWIS AND CLARK EXPEDITION, Meriwether Lewis and William Clark, edited by Elliott Coues. Classic edition of Lewis and Clark's day-by-day journals that later became the basis for U.S. claims to Oregon and the West. Accurate and invaluable geographical, botanical, biological, meteorological and anthropological material. Total of 1,508pp. 5⅜ × 8½.
21268-8, 21269-6, 21270-X Pa. Three-vol. set $25.50

LANGUAGE, TRUTH AND LOGIC, Alfred J. Ayer. Famous, clear introduction to Vienna, Cambridge schools of Logical Positivism. Role of philosophy, elimination of metaphysics, nature of analysis, etc. 160pp. 5⅜ × 8½. (Available in U.S. and Canada only) 20010-8 Pa. $2.95

MATHEMATICS FOR THE NONMATHEMATICIAN, Morris Kline. Detailed, college-level treatment of mathematics in cultural and historical context, with numerous exercises. For liberal arts students. Preface. Recommended Reading Lists. Tables. Index. Numerous black-and-white figures. xvi + 641pp. 5⅜ × 8½.
24823-2 Pa. $11.95

28 SCIENCE FICTION STORIES, H. G. Wells. Novels, *Star Begotten* and *Men Like Gods,* plus 26 short stories: "Empire of the Ants," "A Story of the Stone Age," "The Stolen Bacillus," "In the Abyss," etc. 915pp. 5⅜ × 8½. (Available in U.S. only)
20265-8 Cloth. $10.95

HANDBOOK OF PICTORIAL SYMBOLS, Rudolph Modley. 3,250 signs and symbols, many systems in full; official or heavy commercial use. Arranged by subject. Most in Pictorial Archive series. 143pp. 8⅛ × 11. 23357-X Pa. $5.95

INCIDENTS OF TRAVEL IN YUCATAN, John L. Stephens. Classic (1843) exploration of jungles of Yucatan, looking for evidences of Maya civilization. Travel adventures, Mexican and Indian culture, etc. Total of 669pp. 5⅜ × 8½.
20926-1, 20927-X Pa., Two-vol. set $9.90

DEGAS: An Intimate Portrait, Ambroise Vollard. Charming, anecdotal memoir by famous art dealer of one of the greatest 19th-century French painters. 14 black-and-white illustrations. Introduction by Harold L. Van Doren. 96pp. 5⅜ × 8½.
25131-4 Pa. $3.95

PERSONAL NARRATIVE OF A PILGRIMAGE TO ALMANDINAH AND MECCAH, Richard Burton. Great travel classic by remarkably colorful personality. Burton, disguised as a Moroccan, visited sacred shrines of Islam, narrowly escaping death. 47 illustrations. 959pp. 5⅜ × 8½.   21217-3, 21218-1 Pa., Two-vol. set $19.90

PHRASE AND WORD ORIGINS, A. H. Holt. Entertaining, reliable, modern study of more than 1,200 colorful words, phrases, origins and histories. Much unexpected information. 254pp. 5⅜ × 8½.   20758-7 Pa. $4.95

THE RED THUMB MARK, R. Austin Freeman. In this first Dr. Thorndyke case, the great scientific detective draws fascinating conclusions from the nature of a single fingerprint. Exciting story, authentic science. 320pp. 5⅜ × 8½. (Available in U.S. only)   25210-8 Pa. $5.95

AN EGYPTIAN HIEROGLYPHIC DICTIONARY, E. A. Wallis Budge. Monumental work containing about 25,000 words or terms that occur in texts ranging from 3000 B.C. to 600 A.D. Each entry consists of a transliteration of the word, the word in hieroglyphs, and the meaning in English. 1,314pp. 6⅜ × 10.
23615-3, 23616-1 Pa., Two-vol. set $27.90

THE COMPLEAT STRATEGYST: Being a Primer on the Theory of Games of Strategy, J. D. Williams. Highly entertaining classic describes, with many illustrated examples, how to select best strategies in conflict situations. Prefaces. Appendices. xvi + 268pp. 5⅜ × 8½.   25101-2 Pa. $5.95

THE ROAD TO OZ, L. Frank Baum. Dorothy meets the Shaggy Man, little Button-Bright and the Rainbow's beautiful daughter in this delightful trip to the magical Land of Oz. 272pp. 5⅜ × 8.   25208-6 Pa. $4.95

POINT AND LINE TO PLANE, Wassily Kandinsky. Seminal exposition of role of point, line, other elements in non-objective painting. Essential to understanding 20th-century art. 127 illustrations. 192pp. 6½ × 9¼.   23808-3 Pa. $4.50

LADY ANNA, Anthony Trollope. Moving chronicle of Countess Lovel's bitter struggle to win for herself and daughter Anna their rightful rank and fortune—perhaps at cost of sanity itself. 384pp. 5⅜ × 8½.   24669-8 Pa. $6.95

EGYPTIAN MAGIC, E. A. Wallis Budge. Sums up all that is known about magic in Ancient Egypt: the role of magic in controlling the gods, powerful amulets that warded off evil spirits, scarabs of immortality, use of wax images, formulas and spells, the secret name, much more. 253pp. 5⅜ × 8½.   22681-6 Pa. $4.00

THE DANCE OF SIVA, Ananda Coomaraswamy. Preeminent authority unfolds the vast metaphysic of India: the revelation of her art, conception of the universe, social organization, etc. 27 reproductions of art masterpieces. 192pp. 5⅜ × 8½.
24817-8 Pa. $5.95

CHRISTMAS CUSTOMS AND TRADITIONS, Clement A. Miles. Origin, evolution, significance of religious, secular practices. Caroling, gifts, yule logs, much more. Full, scholarly yet fascinating; non-sectarian. 400pp. 5⅜ × 8½.
23354-5 Pa. $6.50

THE HUMAN FIGURE IN MOTION, Eadweard Muybridge. More than 4,500 stopped-action photos, in action series, showing undraped men, women, children jumping, lying down, throwing, sitting, wrestling, carrying, etc. 390pp. 7⅞ × 10⅝.
20204-6 Cloth. $21.95

THE MAN WHO WAS THURSDAY, Gilbert Keith Chesterton. Witty, fast-paced novel about a club of anarchists in turn-of-the-century London. Brilliant social, religious, philosophical speculations. 128pp. 5⅜ × 8½.
25121-7 Pa. $3.95

A CEZANNE SKETCHBOOK: Figures, Portraits, Landscapes and Still Lifes, Paul Cezanne. Great artist experiments with tonal effects, light, mass, other qualities in over 100 drawings. A revealing view of developing master painter, precursor of Cubism. 102 black-and-white illustrations. 144pp. 8¾ × 6⅜.
24790-2 Pa. $5.95

AN ENCYCLOPEDIA OF BATTLES: Accounts of Over 1,560 Battles from 1479 B.C. to the Present, David Eggenberger. Presents essential details of every major battle in recorded history, from the first battle of Megiddo in 1479 B.C. to Grenada in 1984. List of Battle Maps. New Appendix covering the years 1967–1984. Index. 99 illustrations. 544pp. 6½ × 9¼.
24913-1 Pa. $14.95

AN ETYMOLOGICAL DICTIONARY OF MODERN ENGLISH, Ernest Weekley. Richest, fullest work, by foremost British lexicographer. Detailed word histories. Inexhaustible. Total of 856pp. 6½ × 9¼.
21873-2, 21874-0 Pa., Two-vol. set $17.00

WEBSTER'S AMERICAN MILITARY BIOGRAPHIES, edited by Robert McHenry. Over 1,000 figures who shaped 3 centuries of American military history. Detailed biographies of Nathan Hale, Douglas MacArthur, Mary Hallaren, others. Chronologies of engagements, more. Introduction. Addenda. 1,033 entries in alphabetical order. xi + 548pp. 6½ × 9¼. (Available in U.S. only)
24758-9 Pa. $11.95

LIFE IN ANCIENT EGYPT, Adolf Erman. Detailed older account, with much not in more recent books: domestic life, religion, magic, medicine, commerce, and whatever else needed for complete picture. Many illustrations. 597pp. 5⅜ × 8½.
22632-8 Pa. $8.50

HISTORIC COSTUME IN PICTURES, Braun & Schneider. Over 1,450 costumed figures shown, covering a wide variety of peoples: kings, emperors, nobles, priests, servants, soldiers, scholars, townsfolk, peasants, merchants, courtiers, cavaliers, and more. 256pp. 8⅜ × 11¼.
23150-X Pa. $7.95

THE NOTEBOOKS OF LEONARDO DA VINCI, edited by J. P. Richter. Extracts from manuscripts reveal great genius; on painting, sculpture, anatomy, sciences, geography, etc. Both Italian and English. 186 ms. pages reproduced, plus 500 additional drawings, including studies for *Last Supper*, *Sforza* monument, etc. 860pp. 7⅞ × 10¾. (Available in U.S. only) 22572-0, 22573-9 Pa., Two-vol. set $25.90

THE ART NOUVEAU STYLE BOOK OF ALPHONSE MUCHA: All 72 Plates from "Documents Decoratifs" in Original Color, Alphonse Mucha. Rare copyright-free design portfolio by high priest of Art Nouveau. Jewelry, wallpaper, stained glass, furniture, figure studies, plant and animal motifs, etc. Only complete one-volume edition. 80pp. 9⅜ × 12¼.   24044-4 Pa. $8.95

ANIMALS: 1,419 COPYRIGHT-FREE ILLUSTRATIONS OF MAMMALS, BIRDS, FISH, INSECTS, ETC., edited by Jim Harter. Clear wood engravings present, in extremely lifelike poses, over 1,000 species of animals. One of the most extensive pictorial sourcebooks of its kind. Captions. Index. 284pp. 9 × 12.
23766-4 Pa. $9.95

OBELISTS FLY HIGH, C. Daly King. Masterpiece of American detective fiction, long out of print, involves murder on a 1935 transcontinental flight—"a very thrilling story"—NY Times. Unabridged and unaltered republication of the edition published by William Collins Sons & Co. Ltd., London, 1935. 288pp. 5⅜ × 8½. (Available in U.S. only)   25036-9 Pa. $4.95

VICTORIAN AND EDWARDIAN FASHION: A Photographic Survey, Alison Gernsheim. First fashion history completely illustrated by contemporary photographs. Full text plus 235 photos, 1840–1914, in which many celebrities appear. 240pp. 6½ × 9¼.   24205-6 Pa. $6.00

THE ART OF THE FRENCH ILLUSTRATED BOOK, 1700–1914, Gordon N. Ray. Over 630 superb book illustrations by Fragonard, Delacroix, Daumier, Doré, Grandville, Manet, Mucha, Steinlen, Toulouse-Lautrec and many others. Preface. Introduction. 633 halftones. Indices of artists, authors & titles, binders and provenances. Appendices. Bibliography. 608pp. 8⅜ × 11¼.   25086-5 Pa. $24.95

THE WONDERFUL WIZARD OF OZ, L. Frank Baum. Facsimile in full color of America's finest children's classic. 143 illustrations by W. W. Denslow. 267pp. 5⅜ × 8½.   20691-2 Pa. $5.95

FRONTIERS OF MODERN PHYSICS: New Perspectives on Cosmology, Relativity, Black Holes and Extraterrestrial Intelligence, Tony Rothman, et al. For the intelligent layman. Subjects include: cosmological models of the universe; black holes; the neutrino; the search for extraterrestrial intelligence. Introduction. 46 black-and-white illustrations. 192pp. 5⅜ × 8½.   24587-X Pa. $6.95

THE FRIENDLY STARS, Martha Evans Martin & Donald Howard Menzel. Classic text marshalls the stars together in an engaging, non-technical survey, presenting them as sources of beauty in night sky. 23 illustrations. Foreword. 2 star charts. Index. 147pp. 5⅜ × 8½.   21099-5 Pa. $3.50

FADS AND FALLACIES IN THE NAME OF SCIENCE, Martin Gardner. Fair, witty appraisal of cranks, quacks, and quackeries of science and pseudoscience: hollow earth, Velikovsky, orgone energy, Dianetics, flying saucers, Bridey Murphy, food and medical fads, etc. Revised, expanded In the Name of Science. "A very able and even-tempered presentation."—The New Yorker. 363pp. 5⅜ × 8.
20394-8 Pa. $6.50

ANCIENT EGYPT: ITS CULTURE AND HISTORY, J. E Manchip White. From pre-dynastics through Ptolemies: society, history, political structure, religion, daily life, literature, cultural heritage. 48 plates. 217pp. 5⅜ × 8½.   22548-8 Pa. $4.95

SIR HARRY HOTSPUR OF HUMBLETHWAITE, Anthony Trollope. Incisive, unconventional psychological study of a conflict between a wealthy baronet, his idealistic daughter, and their scapegrace cousin. The 1870 novel in its first inexpensive edition in years. 250pp. 5⅜ × 8½.			24953-0 Pa. $5.95

LASERS AND HOLOGRAPHY, Winston E. Kock. Sound introduction to burgeoning field, expanded (1981) for second edition. Wave patterns, coherence, lasers, diffraction, zone plates, properties of holograms, recent advances. 84 illustrations. 160pp. 5⅜ × 8¼. (Except in United Kingdom)		24041-X Pa. $3.50

INTRODUCTION TO ARTIFICIAL INTELLIGENCE: SECOND, EN-LARGED EDITION, Philip C. Jackson, Jr. Comprehensive survey of artificial intelligence—the study of how machines (computers) can be made to act intelli-gently. Includes introductory and advanced material. Extensive notes updating the main text. 132 black-and-white illustrations. 512pp. 5⅜ × 8½.		24864-X Pa. $8.95

HISTORY OF INDIAN AND INDONESIAN ART, Ananda K. Coomaraswamy. Over 400 illustrations illuminate classic study of Indian art from earliest Harappa finds to early 20th century. Provides philosophical, religious and social insights. 304pp. 6⅝ × 9⅜.			25005-9 Pa. $8.95

THE GOLEM, Gustav Meyrink. Most famous supernatural novel in modern European literature, set in Ghetto of Old Prague around 1890. Compelling story of mystical experiences, strange transformations, profound terror. 13 black-and-white illustrations. 224pp. 5⅜ × 8½. (Available in U.S. only)		25025-3 Pa. $5.95

ARMADALE, Wilkie Collins. Third great mystery novel by the author of *The Woman in White* and *The Moonstone*. Original magazine version with 40 illustrations. 597pp. 5⅜ × 8½.			23429-0 Pa. $9.95

PICTORIAL ENCYCLOPEDIA OF HISTORIC ARCHITECTURAL PLANS, DETAILS AND ELEMENTS: With 1,880 Line Drawings of Arches, Domes, Doorways, Facades, Gables, Windows, etc., John Theodore Haneman. Sourcebook of inspiration for architects, designers, others. Bibliography. Captions. 141pp. 9 × 12.			24605-1 Pa. $6.95

BENCHLEY LOST AND FOUND, Robert Benchley. Finest humor from early 30's, about pet peeves, child psychologists, post office and others. Mostly unavailable elsewhere. 73 illustrations by Peter Arno and others. 183pp. 5⅜ × 8½.
			22410-4 Pa. $3.95

ERTÉ GRAPHICS, Erté. Collection of striking color graphics: *Seasons, Alphabet, Numerals, Aces* and *Precious Stones*. 50 plates, including 4 on covers. 48pp. 9⅜ × 12¼.			23580-7 Pa. $6.95

THE JOURNAL OF HENRY D. THOREAU, edited by Bradford Torrey, F. H. Allen. Complete reprinting of 14 volumes, 1837–61, over two million words; the sourcebooks for *Walden*, etc. Definitive. All original sketches, plus 75 photographs. 1,804pp. 8½ × 12¼.		20312-3, 20313-1 Cloth., Two-vol. set $80.00

CASTLES: THEIR CONSTRUCTION AND HISTORY, Sidney Toy. Traces castle development from ancient roots. Nearly 200 photographs and drawings illustrate moats, keeps, baileys, many other features. Caernarvon, Dover Castles, Hadrian's Wall, Tower of London, dozens more. 256pp. 5⅜ × 8¼.
			24898-4 Pa. $5.95

CATALOG OF DOVER BOOKS

AMERICAN CLIPPER SHIPS: 1833–1858, Octavius T. Howe & Frederick C. Matthews. Fully-illustrated, encyclopedic review of 352 clipper ships from the period of America's greatest maritime supremacy. Introduction. 109 halftones. 5 black-and-white line illustrations. Index. Total of 928pp. 5⅜ × 8½.
25115-2, 25116-0 Pa., Two-vol. set $17.90

TOWARDS A NEW ARCHITECTURE, Le Corbusier. Pioneering manifesto by great architect, near legendary founder of "International School." Technical and aesthetic theories, views on industry, economics, relation of form to function, "mass-production spirit," much more. Profusely illustrated. Unabridged translation of 13th French edition. Introduction by Frederick Etchells. 320pp. 6⅛ × 9¼. (Available in U.S. only) 25023-7 Pa. $8.95

THE BOOK OF KELLS, edited by Blanche Cirker. Inexpensive collection of 32 full-color, full-page plates from the greatest illuminated manuscript of the Middle Ages, painstakingly reproduced from rare facsimile edition. Publisher's Note. Captions. 32pp. 9⅜ × 12¼. 24345-1 Pa. $4.95

BEST SCIENCE FICTION STORIES OF H. G. WELLS, H. G. Wells. Full novel *The Invisible Man*, plus 17 short stories: "The Crystal Egg," "Aepyornis Island," "The Strange Orchid," etc. 303pp. 5⅜ × 8½. (Available in U.S. only)
21531-8 Pa. $4.95

AMERICAN SAILING SHIPS: Their Plans and History, Charles G. Davis. Photos, construction details of schooners, frigates, clippers, other sailcraft of 18th to early 20th centuries—plus entertaining discourse on design, rigging, nautical lore, much more. 137 black-and-white illustrations. 240pp. 6⅛ × 9¼
24658-2 Pa. $5.95

ENTERTAINING MATHEMATICAL PUZZLES, Martin Gardner. Selection of author's favorite conundrums involving arithmetic, money, speed, etc., with lively commentary. Complete solutions. 112pp. 5⅜ × 8½. 25211-6 Pa. $2.95

THE WILL TO BELIEVE, HUMAN IMMORTALITY, William James. Two books bound together. Effect of irrational on logical, and arguments for human immortality. 402pp. 5⅜ × 8½. 20291-7 Pa. $7.50

THE HAUNTED MONASTERY and THE CHINESE MAZE MURDERS, Robert Van Gulik. 2 full novels by Van Gulik continue adventures of Judge Dee and his companions. An evil Taoist monastery, seemingly supernatural events; overgrown topiary maze that hides strange crimes. Set in 7th-century China. 27 illustrations. 328pp. 5⅜ × 8½. 23502-5 Pa. $5.95

CELEBRATED CASES OF JUDGE DEE (DEE GOONG AN), translated by Robert Van Gulik. Authentic 18th-century Chinese detective novel; Dee and associates solve three interlocked cases. Led to Van Gulik's own stories with same characters. Extensive introduction. 9 illustrations. 237pp. 5⅜ × 8½.
23337-5 Pa. $4.95

Prices subject to change without notice.
Available at your book dealer or write for free catalog to Dept. GI, Dover Publications, Inc., 31 East 2nd St., Mineola, N.Y. 11501. Dover publishes more than 175 books each year on science, elementary and advanced mathematics, biology, music, art, literary history, social sciences and other areas.